Driving

Dad Home

Driving
Dad Home

a memoir

John
Halter

NODIN PRESS

Acknowledgements:

Thanks to John Kerr for column space in his *Riverview Times*; to Shannon Pennefeather of Borealis Books for a first attempt at publication; to Kathy Oakley for constant encouragement; to Mark and Sue Halter for making Dad's final years comfortable; to Jim Searls and Mike O'Rourke for early reading and comment; to Susan Halter Jones for a treasure-trove of forgotten correspondence; to Norton Stillman of Nodin Press; to John Toren for making me look like a real writer; and to Jan, for enduring my many years of work on this project: I'm afraid the well's not dry.

ISBN: 978-1-947237-55-1

Library of Congress Control Number 2023944915

Published by
Nodin Press, LLC
210 Edge Place
Minneapolis, MN 55418
www.nodinpress.com

Printed in U.S.A.

To Sam and Nick; may the circle be unbroken.

Contents

Driving
Dad Home

DAY ONE

1

HI DAD, IT'S ME AGAIN...

"Ah, hello – "

"Hi Dad, it's me again ..."

"*Who?*"

"John. Your son John? In Saint Paul? *Big* John?"

"Oh, *John*! Yes, okay, *Big Bad John!*"

"Right. So, I'm calling to remind you about tomorrow, Dad ... same as last night. Do you remember me calling you last night?"

"You called last night? The hell you say."

"I did, Dad. I called to remind you about our trip—the car trip we'll be taking later this week."

"Car trip? I don't know anything about any car trip. What are you talking about?"

"C'mon now, Dad, think. I've been calling you every day for the last week to talk about this."

"Not a clue."

"Hmm ... well ... "

"Is that all you wanted? The news is about to start."

"You're watching the news? So you're done with dinner? Or have you not started yet?"

"Hell yes, I'm done with dinner! It's 6 o'clock for Christ sakes! These goddamn aides start dinner at four-thirty and want you finished by five. Who the hell eats that early? Bunch of *bullshit* if you ask me."

"Did Eunice eat dinner with you?"

"No."

"Is she—"

"*Godammit*, Eunice hasn't gotten out of bed in two weeks! I thought you knew that."

"I did. I mean, I do. I just thought—"

"She could die any minute, if that's what you're wondering. *Godammit to hell!*"

"Okay Dad, sorry …"

"Is that it? Are you done?"

"No, ah … Say, was there any leftover birthday cake?"

"Birthday cake?"

"Last night you told me the aides baked you a birthday cake. A nice lemon cake with white frosting and only one big candle instead of ninety-six little ones."

"I told you that? More bullshit. And I'd sure like to know who the hell's paying for all these aides to be messing up the kitchen day after day. It sure as hell better not be me!"

"Easy now, Dad. You're still being nice to the aides, I hope. No more incidents?"

"Well, Jesus Christ, I try to be nice to them, but my god... There's a little Mexican gal here right now—Luna, Lulu—I can't remember all their names. But you oughta see the *boozums* on this one. Boy oh boy, if I wasn't married!"

"Okay, calm down, Valentino. Now, about tomorrow morning—"

"Godammit, the news is starting."

"Wait, Dad, now listen. I called to remind you I'll be there first thing tomorrow morning. And in a few days I expect to be on the road, just the two of us—"

"You're coming here?"

"Yes, Dad, like I told you last night, like we've been telling you for the past two weeks, all of us—Kath, Mark, Betsey, and me—it's time for you to come home."

"I don't know what the hell you're talking about."

"Dad, I'm flying out in the morning to drive you home."

"This *is* my home."

"Dad, we've been over this a hundred times. You can't live there anymore."

"What about Eunice?"

"Eunice is going to stay behind, in hospice care, remember? She's too sick to travel."

"I'm sorry, but I'm not going anywhere without Eunice."

"Dad..."

"You're wasting your time if you're coming out here. I'm not going anywhere without Eunice, and that's that!"

"Dad..."

"Dad, you still there?"

Godammit, Dad.

DAY TWO

2

THE WARM PLACE

The airport shuttle swings in off 91st Avenue and pulls a sharp one-eighty outside the entrance gate of a trailer-park retirement community. "Casa del Calor," the driver shouts, with a bit of Chicago accent: "Cay-sa," he pronounces it, and "Cay-lor." Caysa de Caylor: the warm place. I'd guess he's at least fifteen years older than me and wearing aviator sunglasses and a shirt with shoulder epaulets, as if he's piloting an Airbus and not the poorly air-conditioned passenger van in which I've been sweating for the past forty-five minutes. I'm thinking this is a retirement job, something to keep him busy until… until what? My father has never quite understood people who take retirement jobs, wondering why anyone in their seventies or even eighties would choose to spend their remaining years flipping hamburgers at Burger King or greeting shoppers at Walmart, all for four or five bucks an hour. "If they knew this is what they were going to be doing for the rest of their lives," he argues, "why the *hell* would they quit their regular jobs in the first place?" He suspects they're bored, something he could never be accused of, not here in Phoenix, in the Valley of the Sun.

The driver jumps out to hurry around and throw open the double doors on my side of the van. Bent at the waist, I squeeze past the few remaining passengers and exit backwards through the opening, my large frame clumsy in the cramped quarters. "Watch your step, buddy," the driver cautions, "there you go," and I feel his hand lightly on the small of my back. I repress an urge to bat it away; does his helping hand imply that I somehow belong here? That I'm *old?* Instead, I force a smile and start toward the rear of the van for my bag. He's way out ahead of me, flinging open the doors to display the remaining luggage.

"That one," I tell him, and hand him a couple bucks, folded so he can't see the denomination. I'm sure he's ferried bigger tight-wads than me around exurban Phoenix, but he doesn't even look at what I've given him as he slams the doors shut and hurries back up to his cockpit. A moment later his blue airship accelerates into the slipstream of the morning traffic. I stretch and take a look around.

In all likelihood, this will be the last of perhaps a dozen trips I've made over the years to this retirement community. My parents began coming to Arizona in the 1970s when both were still working, looking for a place to retire to. My father had always entertained ideas of moving to Montana, to some sort of hobby farm in the foothills of the Rockies where he might keep a horse and tend a large garden. He imagined himself

Mom, Dad, and Tuffy at Casa del Calor, 1980

with a beard and bib overalls, vowing to burn every "goddamn necktie" he owned. He'd spent most of his working life as a salesman of heavy construction equipment, a profession he'd never really enjoyed but at which he was successful. No one believed the hobby farm was ever more than a pipe dream, especially my mother, who had vastly different ideas. She insisted they put Montana at the bottom of their list. During the years they spent searching they tried Florida (too crowded), California (too expensive), and the Texas gulf coast (too desolate), before finally settling on Peoria, a suburb northwest of Phoenix, where they found a situation that suited their disparate individual requirements.

I first visited in the spring of 1976, when I was home on leave after a tour of military duty overseas. My brother Jim and I were headed west on a road trip to California, an adventure which would eventually take us to the Mexican Baja. We stopped off to spend the night with Mom and Dad—an opportunity to check out their latest winter getaway. At the time, they were only renting, still sifting the sand, so to speak, of this southwest Mecca. Back then, as I recall, the landscape west of 91st Avenue, where I'm now standing, was filled with citrus groves and sheep ranches stretching all the way to the White Tank Mountains, the craggy peaks of which are faintly visible through the morning haze. Now the entire valley has been developed into gated retirement communities, with some of the older developments showing signs of age. Sun City and Sun City West lie a few miles further up Grand Avenue, but my parents considered those places a step above their price range. When they finally decided to purchase in 1979, they settled here, in Peoria. At the time, it was one of the fastest growing cities in America.

I caught the red-eye flight from Minneapolis and have been awake since 3 a.m. My caffeine-induced buzz only heightens the anxiety I've been feeling for the past few weeks. The mission I'm on is to drive my ninety-six-year-old father to a memory-care facility in La Crosse, Wisconsin, where, in all likelihood, he'll spend the remainder of his life, and it's full of roadblocks. My siblings and I have being trying for weeks to convince Dad that this is the only option he has left. He insists we're wrong and has informed us in no uncertain terms that he's not leaving. In our final phone conversation last night I tried to remind him I'd be here this morning, and that if everything went according to plan he could expect to be on the road in a couple of days. He hung up on me.

So, I'm a little on edge. And warm; the jeans and long-sleeved shirt I chose this morning in a much chillier Minnesota feel like wet wool on my skin—even more so in the shade of the palm trees lining the entrance. It's just mid-morning, but the temperature has already climbed to 85. "Dry heat," as my father liked to remind me during the regular Sunday-night phone conversations we've shared for the past twenty-five years. The weather was always our first topic of conversation.

"It's hot, *hell yes*," he would insist. "But you don't sweat in this heat, or at least not like you do on a hot day in Minnesota."

Dry heat or not, I'm sweating, and before I do anything else I drop my bag and begin rummaging through it for one of the short-sleeved shirts I've packed. The traffic whizzes by on 91st Avenue, and if anyone is concerned about the large guy with pale skin standing half-naked along the road, it's their problem, not mine. At fifty-seven, I've learned it's vitally important to dress appropriately for the job at hand. An old river foreman once advised me to "get comfortable" as I prepared to strike an arc on an explosive fuel hold. He must have thought I looked nervous. So now I grab a well-worn, loose-fitting Aloha shirt from the bag and slip it on, my confidence building with the fastening of every button. Feeling much more comfortable, I hoist the bag and approach the security gate, wondering what it's going to take to get through. What with Dad's abrupt hang-up last night I have neither key nor code.

Suddenly a car swings in off 91st Avenue and the security gate begins to slide sideways, its drive chain rattling over the sprocket. The silver-haired matron behind the wheel acknowledges me with a pleasant smile and seems not at all concerned that I am about to gain entrance on her dime. It dawns on me that with my gray hair and comfortable waist-line, I'm probably no more a threat to her than any of the hundreds of other senior citizens who call this place home. Indeed, when she lowers her window to ask if I need a lift, I reply that I've been flying all night and the walk will do me good. "I'm here to see my father, Russ Halter," I inform her. One of her eyebrows lifts just enough to make me wonder if she's thinking, *Well, it's about time!* But then she nods sympathetically. "Tell your dad 'Hello ... and Eunice, too," she adds, perhaps a bit hesitantly. When the gate is fully open, she idles through, allowing me ample time to follow on foot.

Palm trees and cactus plants line the manicured streets and boulevards, the smooth pavement neatly bordered with whitewashed curbstones. Signage is posted conspicuously and in abundance; nothing is left to chance. I've been here often enough to know my way around. Natural grass seems to be a luxury that only a few can afford; the lawns of most homes are composed of crushed rock or flagstone, with indigenous plants like mesquite and cactus supplying the desired greenery. Most of the homes are single or double-wide trailers, permanently installed and held captive by attached screen porches and metal carports. There's nothing grandiose or opulent about any of it, just a plain and well-kept retirement community built with the Greatest Generation in mind, nearly all of the residents "snowbirds" from the Midwest. Until recently, my father has been very happy here.

Lately, though, there's been an influx of newcomers, and the younger retirees are making changes around the park. Some of the aging trailers have been replaced by attractive bungalows with pitched roofs and vinyl siding. My father complains that he has nothing in common with these "newcomers," that they're unsociable and rude, preferring to spend their afternoons drinking beer around the pool and playing loud music. Worse, he knows his aging double-wide is rapidly deteriorating in value and he'll never be able to sell it for what he has in it. But he's always insisted his real estate issues are nothing any of us have to worry about, should the day ever come that he has to vacate. Unfortunately, that day *has* come and it *is* going to be a problem we'll have to deal with.

Smiling seniors cruise past on bicycles or in golf carts; others amble by in measured strides. Exercise in the Valley of the Sun is best completed before noon. For many years Dad was a fixture on these morning streets aboard the English three-speed bike I'd given him one September back in Minnesota. It was a women's model I'd found at a garage sale and it seemed perfectly suited to his needs and ability. Three times a day he'd make two leisurely trips around the perimeter of the park, always in the company of his faithful dachshund "Tuffy" riding lookout in a basket between the handlebars. An unfortunate spill from the bike one winter sent him sprawling across the asphalt, scraping his knees, elbows, and confidence. Tuffy survived without incident, but the bike went up for sale at the next community flea market. It would be a couple years before Dad regained the confidence to ride again, this time behind the handlebars of a three-wheeler he borrowed from a widowed neighbor. He complained that the stabilized bike made him feel like an old woman but he kept riding it nonetheless. The neighbors were once again pleased to see Tuffy's flapping ears and wet snout during their morning walks.

I circumnavigate the green expanse of the "pitch and putt" course, a venue enjoyed by nearly everyone in the park. Dad gave it a try in his first few winters here, buying a second-hand set of clubs and joining the men's league play. But, in his own words, he'd "started too late" in life to be any good at golf. Eventually, he would rediscover horseshoes as his sport of choice. He'd grown up "throwing shoe" in South Dakota, and found that the hadn't lost his touch. In our Sunday night conversations he would often boast of the "two bits" or even the buck he'd taken off a competitor in an afternoon tournament. Two bits was a notable haul in his Depression-era sense of economics.

Beyond the pitch and putt is the park's Rec Center, with

its adjacent outdoor swimming pool. The pool had been one of my mother's favorite places to socialize during the brief time she spent here, before cancer took her in 1984. My dad, however, was never one to waste an afternoon lying idly in the sun. But in the past few years he seems to have developed a special aversion to it, something to do with the pool itself. He's heard rumors that a few of the older residents were swimming with disposable diapers beneath their bathing suits, an absolute crime in his opinion. *"Jesus Christ,"* he cursed over the phone one Sunday night. "Can you even imagine it? Be the same as swimming in a goddamn septic tank." Worse, in his estimation, were the grandchildren who showed up for a week's stay with their grandparents. Some of the more irresponsible grandmas had been seen dunking *bare naked* infants in the pool!

The Rec Center, however, is a different story. When my mother was still alive the two of them were in the middle of every social gathering in the park. The pot-luck dinners, the Tuesday night Bridge Club, the Saturday night dances, the talent shows, the flea markets, the fund-raisers: if something was happening at the Rec Center, my mother had either organized it or had volunteered to work it, and Dad came included in the package. Even after she died, he remained a part of it. It took a year or two, but eventually he resumed the social schedule Mom had initiated. One winter he sent me a photo from the park's recent talent show in which he and a couple of his buddies had taken first prize. There he was, dressed up in one of my mother's formal evening gowns, wearing makeup and her blonde chemo wig, shamelessly lip-syncing with his partners to an old Andrews Sisters number. From the expression on his face you could see he was enjoying himself. And it was good to see him enjoying life again.

Things look pretty quiet now around the Rec Center.

As I head deeper into the surrounding neighborhood I begin to notice samples of Dad's handiwork everywhere. Upon retirement, he took up wood carving and found a niche whittling birds engaged in various activities. I spot a mother quail hurrying her cowed covey across a graveled lawn, and a few houses on, I see a mother robin poised over a nest of hungry fledglings. His customers loved the humor and whimsy of his creations and he made a nice name for himself, along with a little beer-and-cigarette money, at weekend flea markets around Peoria.

I arrive at last at his place, number 95, on a sun-baked corner of the park. It's a 1970s-vintage, double-wide trailer, nicely-maintained but showing signs of age.

The unexpected heat has sapped my stamina, and I duck into the shade of Dad's carport and drop my bag next to the back door. It's cool here and quiet, though I can hear a symphony of air conditioning units humming in the distance. The carport is empty because Dad's car, a 2007 Chrysler minivan, is parked at the other end of town. A year ago he failed his driver's test, and a few weeks later he'd been caught by the park manager sneaking off the premises behind the wheel of his car to get a haircut. The manager called my sister Kathy and warned her he'd call the police if he caught Dad driving again. "I hate to do it," he told her, "but I have to assure the safety of our other residents."

It was then that we realized our stubborn and independent-minded father might require a little maintenance.

It's 10:45. I'm scheduled to meet with Roseanne, a social worker Kathy's been working with to facilitate the move, at 11:30. I drop into a nearby chair a spend a few minutes trying to imagine how all this is going to play out.

3

THE BIRDS

The obstacle here is Eunice, my father's wife. She's bedridden and near death, but no one seems to know how imminent that may be—a week, a month, a *year*? In truth, she's been killing herself for the past twenty years, a slow suicide brought on by nicotine and alcohol abuse. Everyone seems to understand this except my father, who simply refuses to believe it. It's become the biggest source of conflict in our relationship. A year ago, when he turned ninety-five, I had flown out to celebrate his birthday and, unfortunately, in the course of my visit, the discord over his wife's drinking reached a climax.

I hadn't planned on making the trip; in the past few years Dad had burned some bridges, not only in his dwindling network of friends, but also within his family. Two years earlier he had sold the small house in northern Minnesota where he and Eunice spent their summers, to move full-time to the Arizona trailer park where he had wintered since the 1970s. My siblings and I tried to convince him it made more sense to sell the Arizona place and spend his remaining years in Minnesota, specifically the Twin Cities, where he might be closer to his children, grandchildren, and great-grandchildren. His health was beginning to fail, but worse, Eunice's alcohol addiction had become so toxic that she was endangering not only her life but also his. My eldest sister, Kathy—we call her Kath—had looked into a number of assisted-living apartments in the Twin Cities where the two of them might live comfortably and independently. My father seemed interested in the idea at first, but in the end he said no, citing Eunice's special needs. In addition to her heavy drinking, Eunice also had a two-pack-a-day cigarette habit and refused to live anywhere she couldn't smoke. He wouldn't listen to reason, and later that year he and Eunice moved away for good.

But living in Arizona year-round proved to be more difficult than he'd imagined. He made it through the first winter without any real change in his routine, but when spring arrived all of his neighbors and friends migrated back to their northern homes, leaving the trailer park a much lonelier place than he'd ever known. Gone were the weekly bridge tournaments, the Saturday night dances, the horseshoe matches, even the daily parade of neighbors strolling along the manicured streets. He learned that summers in the Valley of the Sun were brutally hot, a place where undertaking any sort of outdoor activity carried a lethal risk. Now, with only his alcoholic wife for company, the double-wide trailer they inhabited began to feel more like a prison cell than a home. The phone calls to his children in the Midwest turned into bitch sessions, yet we tried to refrain from reminding him that his problems were of his own doing; it only made him angrier. He eventually came to accept that he'd made a serious mistake. But at the same time he did nothing to correct it. Before long his own health issues became more pronounced. His diabetes numbers began ticking up and his heart developed arrhythmia. But what bothered him most was a growing sense of abandonment.

"*Jesus Christ!*" he cursed over the phone one Sunday evening. "Why doesn't anyone come to visit anymore?" I could think of any number of reasons, not the least of which was Eunice, whom I'd come to regard as the true source of his misery. But his plea struck a note of pity in me, and one night in mid-April I flew out to spend a couple days with him in celebration of his ninety-fifth birthday.

The visit began well enough. From years of experience I had learned how to conduct myself in Eunice's presence, to smile benignly at her coarse language, to look away when her behavior became embarrassing, to grit my teeth when she became all but unbearable. I arrived late one evening and spent the night in a nearby hotel, making it over to the trailer park the next morning after breakfast. Upon my arrival I greeted Eunice as cordially as I could and then proposed a plan for the day: I'd take Dad out for a drive in the afternoon, just the two of us, and take the two of them out for dinner later. Eunice eyed me suspiciously. I promised her that the place we'd go for dinner would be nice, and then, without waiting for her approval, I loaded Dad into my rented car. We headed north with no real destination in mind, my intention being simply to stay away from Eunice as much as possible during my visit. Dad didn't seem to notice.

We wandered through the valley and eventually made our way to Lake Pleasant, a reservoir some twenty miles north of Phoenix. Once we were out of the car, I asked Dad if he was still capable of walking any sort of distance, and before he could reply I started him down the dock of a huge lakeside marina. A breeze cooled by the open water carried the fresh aroma of the lake. We admired boats in their slips, watched schools of fish hovering in the shadows beneath the docks, and even took a moment to ogle the young bikini-clad women bouncing around the harbor on jet skis.

"Boy oh boy," Dad exclaimed. "I need to get out more often!"

As a reward for his strenuous afternoon I treated him to a slice of mudslide pie at a floating restaurant on the premises. The waitress stuck a couple of candles in his piece and joined me in singing "Happy Birthday." On the ride home he claimed it had been a long time since he'd enjoyed a piece of pie as much as that one, or a day as much as the one we'd just spent together at Lake Pleasant.

I wish the rest of my visit had gone as well.

As promised, we went out for dinner that evening. After getting cleaned up at the hotel I swung by the trailer park to pick them up. I found Eunice on the front porch smoking a final cigarette before getting into my car. She had dressed for the occasion but her eyes had the glassy quality I'd come to associate with her drinking, along with a smile that seemed to slide sideways across her face. She sat in the rear seat behind my father and barely spoke on the twenty-minute ride, occasionally sipping from the Yeti cup of "ice water" she'd brought along. But once inside the restaurant, she began to take notice of everything, even as we were being escorted to our table:

"Oh my, Russ, look at the boobs on that one!" she shouted to my father. "*Cleavage!*"

Everyone within earshot turned to look, and Dad and I both winced as I brusquely hurried Eunice into our booth. I pushed a menu in her face and tried to keep her busy with questions about the various entrees. Of course she had opinions on just about everything, most of them beginning with "shit" and ending with "shit." In an effort to restore peace I granted her the privilege of one drink but realized my mistake at once. She was loud and obnoxious throughout the entire meal, and I began to see more clearly why my father's social circle had dwindled, and also why the two of them rarely went out for dinner any more. Eunice hardly touched her food and got overly demanding about the way it was boxed up to take home. She got even ornerier when I refused her a second drink. She glowered at my father, hoping he'd intervene, but I reminded her that the dinner was my treat. It was a very long evening.

The next morning, before departing for the airport, I stopped in to say goodbye. I found the two of them in their living room recliners in front of the TV, the volume turned blaringly high. Dad had become hard of hearing yet stubbornly refused to use a hearing aid. I pulled a chair up closely beside him and turned the TV down so we could talk. After last night, I had the uneasy feeling that this might be my last trip to Arizona and quite likely my last opportunity to converse with him in person.

"So, what have you been doing this morning?" I asked cheerfully.

He smiled pleasantly. "Oh, I do what I do most mornings around here; I have my coffee and read the paper and then I go out to feed the birds."

Up to this point Eunice, sitting beside Dad in her matching recliner, had remained mostly silent. When I had turned the volume down on the TV she registered a small complaint—an audible grunt delivered beneath glowering bushy eyebrows and gray hair pulled so severely tight it looked as if her skin might tear. Then she began to pout, her jowls drooping like a basset hound. Whatever hint of beauty or elegance she may have possessed twenty-five years ago, when my father first met her, was now long gone. She was seventy-two, some twenty-three years younger than my father, but a lifetime of drinking and smoking had taken its toll. I could only imagine what mornings-after must have been like for her.

But now, something my father said had made her especially grumpy.

"THOSE AREN'T BIRDS!" she suddenly barked.

My father regarded her with an arched eyebrow. "I beg your pardon," he said politely. "I'm pretty sure they were birds. I don't think I'm imagining this."

Eunice set her jaw. "THOSE ARE *PIGEONS!*" she croaked. "A GOT-DAMN PIGEON IS NOT A BIRD!"

My father blinked a couple of times, then smiled wryly. "Well, I'm pretty sure a pigeon is a bird. If it's not a bird, what the hell is it?"

"IT"S NOT A BIRD!" she repeated. "IT"S A FILTHY, DISGUSTING RAT WITH WINGS. IT'S A –"

And that's when I lost my temper. I had endured her long enough.

"Eunice!" I said sharply. "*Shut up!*"

And surprisingly, she did, her mouth clamping shut like a snapping turtle's, her eyes narrowing to slits behind her glasses. She glared at me. But I was only beginning.

Breathing deeply to control my anger I explained to her that this might possibly be the last time I'd ever get to visit with my father in person, and that I'd like to remember it as a pleasant moment, not one interrupted by her drunken observations on nature.

Eunice's eyebrows lifted. "I am not drunk," she said quietly, almost to herself.

"Fine," I said. "But I'd like to spend these last few minutes alone with Dad. So if you don't mind, could you please go do something else for awhile?"

"I am not drunk," she repeated, this time more forcefully.

I pursed my lips. "Eunice, *please*," I said. I was not about to let this progress any further. But she was insistent. "I AM NOT DRUNK!"

I felt the resentment of twenty years boiling up as I struggled to control myself. But it was no use. "*God damn it, Eunice,*" I shouted, "*get the hell out of here!*" And I rose to my feet, standing over her with my fists clenched at my sides. My sudden outburst succeeded in frightening her, and she fumbled up out of the recliner and shuffled off to the kitchen. My father sat in his chair staring up at me with wide terrified eyes, speechless. Once Eunice was gone I sat down again to resume our conversation, but I'd let my emotions get the best of me. My hands trembled, my voice quavered.

"I'm sorry," I said, and I took Dad's hands in mine to prove it. But he just stared past me at the TV, his face blank.

I looked up again to find Eunice slumped in the kitchen doorway, her bony hands clutching the cup of ice water she kept perpetually on the windowsill above the sink. I had sampled it upon our return from the restaurant: straight brandy poured over ice.

Fortified with a fresh dose of liquid courage, Eunice once again fixed me with her hot anger and refused to look away. "I am not drunk," she insisted, almost like a mission statement.

"Well, you're not drunk *yet,*" I replied. "But you're getting there. Now stop staring at me!" I let go of Dad's hands and motioned to the door. "Why don't you take your *ice water* out on the porch for awhile so Dad and I can talk. Would that be okay? You can sit out there and drink and smoke and feed the goddamn rats and pigeons until I leave, and then I'll never bother you again. I promise. Okay?"

"I am not drunk," she mumbled.

My god, the woman was as stubborn as my father.

"*Eunice* ... " I said, and I rose again from my chair.

She started for the door, her body scuttling sideways like a crab, her angry eyes never leaving mine. At the door she made a harsh face at my father, then opened the door and slammed it shut behind her. Dad stared after her with the same look of terror on his face.

"Oh boy, I'm never going to hear the end of this," he said.

"Could it be any worse than it is now?" I asked.

"I've never seen her so pissed off."

"Why should we have to sit here and listen to her BS about pigeons?"

"She can't help it," he said sadly.

"Oh, come on Dad, *really?*"

☙

I*n the past year* things have only gotten worse, and my father's weekly phone calls have turned into running commentaries on Eunice's misadventures. Her drinking has gotten out of control, so much so that she's begun passing out. In the past, when she passed out in her recliner, Dad could easily throw an afghan over her and let her sleep it off. But one night he heard a thud in the kitchen and went in to find her on the floor, as lifeless as a dishrag. He tried lifting her, realized he couldn't, and called a neighbor, a spry eighty-five year old. But the two of them couldn't lift her either, and they had to stop trying when the neighbor wrenched his back.

Defying Eunice's strict orders that he was to never call an ambulance (what would the neighbors think?), Dad went ahead and called one anyway. In the hospital Eunice underwent a thorough exam for the first time in years. The doctors discovered a cracked pelvis, acute pancreatitis, and a cancerous lung. But Eunice being Eunice, she refused any treatment or therapy and demanded to be returned home, to my father's care—a ninety-five-year-old man barely capable of opening a can of soup for dinner. In our phone conversations he feigned ignorance of everything and claimed they were both doing fine. He plainly didn't want any of us meddling in his life.

Later that year, in July, it was his turn to fall. Going out one morning to fetch the paper, he took a nose-dive in the driveway and lay on the concrete for forty-five minutes before someone finally happened by. He suffered a cracked rib, internal bleeding, a concussion, and was incoherent during much of his month-long confinement in the hospital. Then it was Eunice's turn again, back to the hospital for a lobectomy of her cancerous lung. The doctors insisted she needed to quit smoking—and drinking—before it was too late. Again, she refused therapy, and once safely back home she discovered the liquor store made deliveries, including cigarettes, even the Virginia Slims 100s she preferred. What could be easier? Her liver began to shut down and now she could barely get out of bed.

With the added stress of Eunice's incapacitation, my father began to lose his grip on reality. He started seeing things, hallucinating, like imagining that his long-deceased brothers had shown up for lunch. A social worker from the hospital stopped by to check on them and immediately phoned Kath with her appraisal: the situation required immediate attention, maybe even an intervention. Kath flew down to investigate and was shocked at what she found. All signs of Eunice's formerly fastidious housekeeping had vanished. A thin, jaundiced Eunice, her belly swollen with liver failure, lay in bed between dirty gray sheets. The pervading stench was overwhelming, the filth unimaginable. In the kitchen Kath discovered a refrigerator filled with rotting leftovers. Hidden in a cupboard she unearthed a cardboard box full of empty vodka and brandy bottles. Garbage cans overflowing, stale bread on the sideboard, mold-covered plates in the dishwasher. On the bathroom floor, as well as in the bathtub and on the vanity top, she found a dozen or more Tupperware bowls filled with Eunice's

soiled underwear soaking in fetid water. It was all too much; Kath
began cleaning that afternoon, starting with the worst of it and
gagging until she nearly threw up.

Sadly, Dad's condition wasn't much better. Kath guessed he
was down at least fifteen pounds and looked completely disheveled, his glasses broken, his shirt splattered with a week's worth of
spilled food, and his mind a muddled fog. In what may have been
the biggest understatement of his life, he told her, "We're in a bit
of a mess here."

Mess indeed. That's when Kath heard about Roseanne, a semi-
retired social worker living on the other side of the trailer park.
Roseanne agreed to help, and she was a godsend in navigating the
Arizona social services network. She was also instrumental in finding the short-term, round-the-clock nursing care that Dad and Eunice required. Kath stayed the rest of the week—long enough to
satisfy herself that the aides understood the severity of the situation.
She was thrilled at the kindness and capability they showed to both
Dad and Eunice, and when she finally flew home it was with the
hope that the arrangements she and Roseanne had instituted would
last at least until Eunice's death, which seemed imminent.

Unfortunately, those arrangements didn't work out. Not
three days after returning home Kath got an urgent call from
the health care agency stating they could no longer assign workers to my father's care. In the past few days he'd grown irascible
and unruly. It had gotten so bad that he'd taken a swing at one
of the aides and connected, landing a violent blow to her chest.
The agency couldn't be liable for that kind of abuse; they were
pulling out.

Kath begged them to hold off until she had time to confer
with her siblings about a plan of action. That night the four of
us—my sisters Kathy and Betsey, my brother Mark and I—got
on the phone to talk things out. We argued, we fought, but after much deliberation we finally agreed that Dad's and Eunice's
needs had diverged to the point that they required different so-
lutions. Our father needed to come home. His increasing de-

mentia and the threat of violence that came with it had become unmanageable; he would need to be confined to a memory-care unit, preferably one near us. But Eunice had clearly become too incapacitated—too near death—to make the move with him. Through Roseanne, Kath was able to arrange hospice care for Eunice, allowing her the dignity of staying in her own home until the end. And my brother Mark would secure a room in a facility near his home in La Crosse, Wisconsin, where Dad would be relatively close to all his children and grandchildren, and also to Mark's farm, a place reminiscent of Dad's childhood and one he'd always enjoyed visiting. It seemed that things were falling into place.

But getting Dad moved from Arizona to Wisconsin would be complicated. With him it's always complicated. With anyone else it might be as simple as escorting him on a three-hour flight back home, sending his belongings on ahead in a moving van, having it all assembled and ready for him upon his arrival. But not our dad. He hasn't flown since commercial airliners had propellers and, as far as anyone remembers, that was only once, back in 1959. At age ninety-six, in precarious mental and physical health, flying was out of the question.

The original plan called for Mark and me to fly down together, load Dad's belongings into a U-Haul, and then drive the eighteen-hundred miles to his new residence in La Crosse. We'd make a leisurely trip of it, taking turns behind the wheel, maybe even letting the old man drive a mile or two on a less-traveled stretch of road—one last trick behind the wheel of his own car. But we had to act quickly. I adjusted my work schedule and freed up an entire week. I cashed-in some frequent flier miles and bought a cheap one-way ticket. I walked the dog, kissed my wife and caught the red-eye to Sky Harbor, Phoenix. I never did tell Mark of my departure because I knew he was busy with the launching of a new business and might have trouble breaking away. But that's only partially true. He wouldn't learn of my change in plans until a day or two later, when it was too late. The fact is, I wanted to be alone with Dad on this final journey of his life. As the old saying goes, *It all looked good on paper.*

Now here I am standing at the back door of his trailer wondering how I'm going to convince him it's time to leave. I check the time again: 11:00. Another half-hour before Roseanne, the social worker, arrives. I hope she's got some ideas.

4

SANCTUARY

At Kath's insistence I've been calling Roseanne in the days leading up to my arrival, mostly to get acquainted but also to go over our game plan. Roseanne informed me she's been stopping by on a daily basis to talk to Dad about the impending move to La Crosse. She thinks our idea of moving him to La Crosse is a good one and as such, she's been showing him photographs of Mark's farm, reminding him how he used to enjoy visiting there in the past. In my final phone conversation with Roseanne last night she outlined a tentative scenario for today: At 11:30 she'll stop by in Dad's minivan to pick us up for lunch at a nearby restaurant. While eating, she'd like to steer the conversation to his impending move to Wisconsin, to reinforce the idea that he'll be better off there than he is here. Coming from the two of us, she reasoned, it should begin to make better sense than just her telling him, because in truth, she's still having a hard time convincing him on her own.

"He can be so awfully stubborn," she said. To which I could only laugh; she has no idea. God knows I've spent the past forty years dealing firsthand with his stubbornness, our disagreements at times becoming so heated—so *divisive*—that we often said things we didn't mean. He'd been a wonderful father for the first dozen or so years of my life, but then events and issues of the larger world began to make me see him in a different light. It was bad timing; I came of age in the 1960s when the Vietnam War, college protests, race riots, and corrupt politicians came together as one to drive a wedge through the core of middle class American life, my own included.

It didn't help that had I inherited some of my father's stubbornness and to a lesser degree (I hope), his temper. If there was an opening salvo in our long battle of wills it probably occurred during my sophomore year in high school. The previous summer we had moved from our two-story stucco house in South Minneapolis to a modern ranch-style home in an upscale neighborhood of Saint Louis Park, a respectable suburb west of Minneapolis.

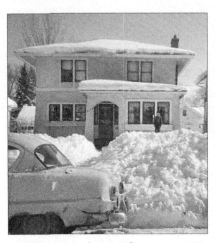

4135 Pleasant Avenue S, winter 1962

Dad claimed he made the move out of a fear that our neighborhood was going to hell. He would never say it, but I know he felt our house lay too close to the imaginary border defined by Nicollet Avenue, across which the African-American population was beginning to encroach. (And "African-American" was definitely not a term either he or my mother ever used.) He also felt the streets in our neighborhood had become an undisciplined playground for the seemingly endless supply of children conceived and brought into the world by by our predominately Catholic neighbors. Our own Catholic family of five—Kathy, Mark, Betsey, me and Jim—was considered small by comparison. My mother once counted some seventy kids living on our block alone, the number fluctuating as older boys went off to Vietnam, or when one of the neighborhood mothers announced yet another pregnancy. Lawns and landscaping took a beating under the constant pressure of kids playing yard games like Kick the Can, Ditch or Pom Pom Pullaway. I'm afraid I was one of the main culprits, organizing basketball games on our backyard garage court, touch football games waged between the cars parked along Pleasant Avenue, and Hotbox baseball games played on the sidewalks along the boulevard. In summer, a huge throng of us would assemble each morning for the half-mile hike to Lake

Harriet where we would swim and horse around all day, our parents' only edict that we be home in time for supper. In winter we played organized sports at Incarnation School, went sliding down King's Hill and skated on any of three frozen lakes within walking distance. I thought of our Pleasant Avenue home as the center of the world and couldn't imagine living anywhere else.

When my father announced one night in the summer of 1970 that we were moving, I was devastated. How could he do this to me? He claimed he'd always dreamed of a big green lawn on a quiet street, and also a larger garden plot than the one he tended on Pleasant Avenue. And my mother, then starting her second act in life as a newly-minted interior decorator with Gabberts Furniture, was thrilled by the possibilities the Saint Louis Park house presented. The new home was a realization of their dreams. By then my two oldest siblings, Kathy and Mark, had married and moved on, leaving only Betsey, Jim, and me to occupy the new home. We each got our own bedrooms, a luxury none of us had known in our old house. Mine was a knotty-pine paneled space in the finished basement. We had finally achieved the suburbs, the realization of the American Dream. The only problem with the new house was me: I hated everything about it.

For the remainder of that summer I made long bike rides back and forth to the old neighborhood, hung out with my old friends, and was invited to stay for dinner which often meant staying overnight, which is exactly what I wanted. But I was fighting a losing battle. Winter came and because I was still too young to drive, my visits to the old neighborhood petered out and eventually came to an end. In protest, I quit going to church.

Sunday Mass had always been mandatory in our Catholic upbringing and, as such, was part of a ritual. For reasons I'll explain later our mother never attended services but instead stayed home to prepare the enormous breakfast that awaited us upon our return, the reward, it would seem, for the fasting we were required to do as part of church doctrine. When I quit going, things got a little tense. One Sunday morning I waited until I heard the returning footsteps of my church-going siblings before I emerged from my basement lair. I picture myself as my father must have seen me then, unwashed and disheveled, my hair nearing my shoulders and my face in full bloom with the severe acne I suffered in my early teens. As I slumped to my place across the breakfast table from him, he studied me quietly, methodically chewing a piece of bacon, fried crisp the way he liked it. Up until then he had kept in check his growing resentment of my skipping church, but now he had seen enough.

"Jesus Christ," he muttered. "Go back downstairs and wash your goddamned face before you come up here again! You look like a Philadelphia whore."

"*Russ!*" my mother shouted from the stove, where she stood frying eggs. *Russ* or *Oh, Russ* was her way of rebuking anything inappropriate he said or did.

I stared defiantly across the table at him and understood at once the complexities of the situation. No one in our family had ever dared challenge his authority. My two sisters at times may have used tears to get their points across, but I wasn't about to show one drop of weakness now. A quick check of both Betsey and Jim, their faces glued to their plates, assured me I was alone in my defiance, and I realized I was on thin ice. At the ripe old age of fifteen I decided I'd had enough of his bullshit and I was going to prove it to him. I cocked my head to one side and gave him an inquisitive look.

"How would you know what a Philadelphia whore looks like?" I asked. It seemed like a legitimate question.

He grew as angry as I'd ever seen him, his big catcher's mitt of a hand slamming the table with such force the silverware jumped and the juice glasses slopped their pulpy contents. I could feel Jim's and Betsey's eyes staring at me with real concern, fearful of what might happen next. I'm sure it was as close to hitting me as he would ever come, which to his credit, he never did. But he was definitely on the verge of it that morning as he roared, "*You get the hell out of here!*"

And I did, sliding quietly out of my seat and returning to the basement where, for the next half-hour or so, I stood before the bathroom mirror squeezing pimples to diffuse my anger. How could a father say such a thing to a son? And why would I ever want to grow up to become someone like him?

It would get worse. I recall an incident a few years later when the two of us were in front of the TV watching the evening news. Mom was in the kitchen getting dinner ready when the opening story on the local channel detailed a violent war protest that afternoon on the campus of the University of Minnesota. My high school lay less than a mile from the disturbance, and during a commercial break I told Dad about the whiff of tear gas I'd gotten and how it made my eyes water. My comment seemed to trigger something deep inside him.

"Shit," he said, his eyes flashing angrily. He gestured at the TV. "Look at these filthy assholes. Your generation would like nothing better than to invite the communists in and take over this country. And you wouldn't do a goddamn thing to stop them."

I could see he was truly upset, that his perception of the social decay in the country he had fought so hard to protect had filled him with disgust. In retrospect I guess I can't fault him for that, but the fact that he seemed to be blaming it on me, his own son, offended me. From the time I was twelve years old until then, when I was seventeen, I had watched the Vietnam War play out on our TV screen every night, a grim and regular feature of my teenage life. Later that same year, on my eighteenth birthday, I would be required to register for the draft, and the war might still be raging when I graduated the following spring. I remember the feeling of hopelessness I experienced in those days—that you were as good as dead if you went to Vietnam, or a chickenshit if you tried to avoid it. What had I done to deserve any of it? But more importantly, why was my own father accusing me of being a communist? When had he become such a patriotic hero? His accusation infuriated me and I wasn't about to let it pass.

Before the commercial break was over I turned to him with

a defiant voice. "Okay," I said, "exactly how many Germans did you personally kill in World War II?"

It was a cheap shot and I knew it. From his stories of the war I knew he'd done all his fighting from the bridge of a ship. But sure enough, my question enraged him. He angrily reminded me of the particular role he had played in the killing of many Germans, and Japs, too for that matter. And he reinforced the fact that it all might just as easily have gone the other way had he not been so lucky, at which point I wouldn't be sitting here on my sorry ass living under *his* roof eating the food *he* provided. Just then, thankfully, Mom called that dinner was ready and he got up and stormed out. I didn't immediately follow, aware that once more I had succeeded in pushing all his buttons. I seemed capable of doing that more and more in those days. I wasn't happy about it but I felt like the time had come for me stand up for myself, to start defending my own ideals. The battle lines were drawn.

For the next forty years we would argue about everything. Our disagreements were wide-ranging and diverse, anything from the Vietnam War and his right-leaning views on politics, to his dogmatic beliefs in the Catholic Church, to his narrow-minded opinions on social justice and civil rights. I can see now that our differences were largely a result of our upbringing. His childhood was one of rural isolation, while mine took place in a neighborhood teeming with different cultures and ethnicities. Ironically, I would later join the service, and even when I was overseas his letters would usually include a subtle barb about something I had written in an earlier letter, something he didn't quite agree with or refused to accept. Later still, when I married and started my own family, he was never reluctant to point out something he thought I was doing wrong in raising my children, the conversation usually beginning with, "It's none of my damn business, but ..."

When he and my mother retired and moved up north, and later to their winter place in Arizona, the telephone became our regular battleground. Our Sunday night conversations grew even more heated with the safety of miles between us. We'd argue about abortion, Catholic doctrines, mixed-race marriages, Black protest marches, Ford versus Chevy, his taste in women, Tiger Woods's taste in women, Vikings football, under-cooked bacon, and even the problem of his trailer park neighbors wearing disposable diapers in the swimming pool; you name it, we argued about it. Sometimes our discussions would become so intense that he would abruptly hang up—end of conversation. When we reconnected the following Sunday he would act like nothing had ever happened, and we would start over with a clean slate. Other times, especially in the past few years, when I sensed the conversation going sour I would play the role of "dutiful son" and switch to something more to his liking, something he enjoyed talking about, like his childhood on the farm, for example, or an incident from the war. He could go on and on until I would cut him off with a friendly reminder that it was late, that I had to be to work in the morning, feed my family, blah blah blah. Even more recently, in the past year or so, as his memory began to slip, I'd let him go on about anything he felt like talking about, some of it so sadly incoherent that I dreaded thinking about what it would eventually lead to, which is exactly the reason I'm here now.

It's still fifteen minutes before Roseanne is due to arrive. I get up from the chair and walk down to the end of the carport, to the open door of the small utility shed that has been my father's sanctuary for as long as he's lived here. Peeking inside, I'm surprised to find some things I hadn't expected, things that weren't here a year ago. Then I remember Kath telling me that Roseanne had already starting moving a few of the larger pieces of furniture that I'm to take back. Suddenly it makes sense: on the left there's a single-sized box spring and mattress standing upright against the wall, as well as a headboard and metal frame and also a bag of sheets and linens. At the rear of the shed there's a small bureau and mirror which, to me, seem a bit excessive given that all of this needs to fit in the small U-Haul trailer I've yet to rent. Who made the decision to include these? Poking out behind the bureau I see the front tire of the three-wheeled bike I fixed a year ago when I was here for Dad's birthday. On our afternoon ride to Lake Pleasant he let me know he'd quit riding the bike because the gears wouldn't shift anymore. Later, I spent an hour working on the bike's derailleur before finally pronouncing it fit for full duty. But judging from the dust on the fender, it hasn't moved since. The bike, I'm sorry to say, will not be going.

Turning to the other side of the shed I'm suddenly startled by the sight of the empty workbench. It's completely bare, stripped clean, with only its paint-splattered surface offering any evidence of past activity. This workbench was once the source of everything both practical and artistic my father attempted in this last chapter of his life, most notably the wood carving. I smile when I remember how he got started. My mother's brother, Uncle Rich, had taken up woodcarving while serving overseas during the Korean War. He was quite good at it and his work had always been on display in my grandmother's kitchen—brightly colored little figurines of cartoon characters taken from the funny pages, along with a few creations from Uncle Rich's own imagination. Years later, when I, too, was stationed overseas, I remembered Uncle Rich's handiwork and decided to try my own hand at carving. One of my first attempts was a rendition of a crusty seadog I dubbed The Old Salt, the name burned into the pedestal on which I'd mounted it. Upon returning home, I gave it to Dad for Father's Day and he was duly impressed. At Christmas a few years later, after he and Mom had retired to Arizona, he presented me with a sample of his own work, a carving he'd just completed, his own first attempt. When I opened the small package I was surprised to find an exact replica of the "Old Salt" figure I'd given him.

"Hey!" I said cheerfully. "Nice job. But you couldn't think of something different than the same thing I carved for you?"

I was only chiding him, or so I thought, because my comment apparently hurt. He quickly countered, "Well, screw you then, buster, I'll give it to somebody else." He tried to snatch it away from me but I wouldn't let him. It's sitting here now, on a shelf above the desk where I'm writing this. But he took the hint and tried his hand at a number of different subjects before settling on the caricature birds that became his specialty, all of them created in this small workshop.

The emptiness is a bit unnerving, not to mention heartbreaking. Gone from the middle of the bench is the heavy band-

saw on which he "rough-cut" basswood blanks into the general outlines of the birds he would later whittle into shape. I can see the holes where the saw was bolted to the bench. Gone from an upper shelf is the inventory of those same basswood blanks, carefully arranged by size and shape, the exact dimensions written along their bases in the black script of my father's neat hand for easy identification. Also missing are the tied bundles of branches and tree limbs brought back from Minneso-

The woodcarver

ta—the props on which he mounted his finished work On the wall along the back of the bench is the empty face of the pegboard where the rows of chisels and knives were arranged, each in its appointed place outlined in black magic marker. Now only the outlines remain. Here too hung other tools, the hammers and mallets; the screwdrivers and wrenches; the pliers, the punches, the probes. All gone. The narrow shelf below the window once held his paintbrushes and the scores of pint-size cans of enamels with which he tried to match the natural patterns of the feathers. "The painting is the hardest part of the whole goddamn process," he used to complain. "It separates the amateurs from the pros." This same shelf also held thinners and solvents and exotic finishing oils, along with a small library of books, patterns, and woodcarver magazines. And I remember a small green tackle box in which he kept the receipts and invoices that he so meticulously drew up. A faded photo of Pope Pius XII once hung on the same wall—a photo that had made its way to Arizona from the wall of our garage in South Minneapolis—to stand watch over him as he worked. Now it was gone. Why have thou forsaken your faithful servant, Pope Pius?

Beneath the bench I see a sagging, dust-covered shelf that once held the battered toolboxes, wooden crates and galvanized pails containing all those items pertaining to household repairs—the spare fan belts, the assortment of light bulbs, the coffee cans of nuts and bolts, the glass jars of screws and nails, the copper plumbing fittings, the spare electrical parts. It's as empty now as a looted grocery store shelf. Where did it all go? Even his *radio*, for godsakes, the ugly brown clock radio with its missing "snooze" button, its clock face splattered with spider shit and its dial eternally tuned to a "Music of Your Life" station. The hours, the days and weeks he sat out here every afternoon for the past thirty years whittling birds, humming along to the music, whiling his life away. It's all gone. Every bit of it.

Gone. As he'll soon be.

The emptiness of this hallowed space overwhelms me with the finality of what it is I'm about to do. Now I'm filled with doubt, bordering on guilt. I mean, here it is, our long decades of disagreement finally reaching its denouement, with me, the son with whom he's always been at odds, as the facilitator. God knows we've had our disagreements over the years, some of them painful though usually reconcilable in the end. But this ... this is permanent.

He's to be confined in a memory-care unit for the rest of his life.

Am I really up to this?

It's suddenly warm in the shed and I step back out into the cooler air of the carport. I hear voices in the street and turn to see a couple of neighbors striding past, the woman slowing as she notices someone in the far shadows of the carport. She raises her hand to wave—the man also turning now to look— but then realizes I'm not the person she expected to see. There's a hesitation, a moment of awkwardness, before they resume their conversation and continue on. I turn and quietly close the door to the shed. I suddenly feel like I don't belong here, like I'm not worthy of the responsibility befallen me. I wander back to the plastic chair and sit down again. Ten more minutes until Roseanne arrives. Hmm ...

Yes, Roseanne is coming. Goddammit, I *do* belong here. My father's life here has reached its logical conclusion, and now changes need to be made. Somehow I have to convince him of that, sell him on the idea. Now I'm to be the salesman, selling my father on an idea he's been running from for the past ten years. It's not going to be easy, but I volunteered to do it.

The time has come to make my opening pitch.

5

Miss America

I rap a couple of times on the back door of the trailer before entering. I'm not sure who's on duty this morning and I don't want to surprise anyone by arriving unannounced. The names change constantly and the aides work eight-hour shifts, 24/7. In light of my father's recent outburst, I'm not even certain the same aide will work more than one shift, so I enter cautiously, ready for anything.

I quietly close the door behind me. It's calm and cool inside. There's an A/C vent directly overhead and I take a moment to soak up the refreshing air. To my left, in the kitchen, a middle-aged Black woman is humming to herself as she cuts up raw chicken at the counter. She suddenly notices me and is momentarily startled but recovers quickly; she must have been expecting me. She offers me a bright smile as she wipes her hands on her apron.

"You must be John," she says warmly. "Roseanne told me you were coming. Oh my! Don't you look just like your daddy!"

I've heard this same observation repeatedly over the course of my life, but because of our other differences it was a long time before I came to accept it. But it's true; I do look like him, except in the past few years, when he's shown advanced signs of aging.

Dad loves to chat, and in spite of his limited formal education he's well-read and knowledgeable. A few years ago he advised me to stop sending him books for Christmas, claiming he'd reached a point in his life where he could finish a book and then, because of his failing memory, go back to the beginning and start over again. He also considers himself an unabashed charmer of women. He's flirted with every waitress he's ever encountered, which, when I was young, I found embarrassing. In high school I was reluctant to bring girlfriends around, afraid of what he might say or do. By then other things about him were also beginning to annoy me.

The aide, who informs me her name is Jocelyn, asks me if I'd like something cool to drink. I tell her I would, thank you, and she removes a can of lemonade from the refrigerator. I finish the can in a few gulps, wipe my mouth on my arm, and place the empty can on the countertop. I don't see my father anywhere.

"Is he around here somewhere?"

"Oh yes!" she replies. "He's out on the front porch helping me get dinner ready. I try to keep him busy all day."

I give her a questioning look. *Helping you with dinner? He can barely boil water.* He's probably out there looking at photos in food magazines. I thank her for the lemonade and go to find Dad.

I drop my bag in an out-of-the-way corner and head through the living room. I'm suddenly stopped short by the sight of the open door to Eunice's bedroom. She's in there; I can tell by the sound of her labored breathing. I step quietly into the doorway. The blinds are drawn but in the cool darkness I notice a bedpan on the nightstand and an ominous-looking plastic bucket on the floor. The air smells of death laced with Pine-sol. Eunice is unconscious, her jaundiced head looking small and shrunken on the pillow.

Proceeding through the living room I pause at the front door. This is the moment of truth, the moment my father has been avoiding his entire adult life—the beginning of the end. Looking around, I don't see much to indicate he's been getting ready to leave. In spite of the beds and linens out in the shed, everything in here looks exactly the way it did a year ago—all the furniture in the same location; the TV trays standing open beside the matching recliners, a TV guide lying open on one; the lime-colored shag carpeting worn flat at the foot of Dad's recliner, the section in front of Eunice's looking recently vacuumed. I take a deep breath and open the door to the porch.

My father is sitting at the far side of the metal patio table, his back to the wall. His large brown hands lie folded in his lap and his chin rests quietly on his chest. He's asleep. (So this is how he stays busy. Sure.) He's wearing his signature outfit of the past twenty years: khaki pants with white walking shoes, a long-sleeved shirt fixed at the collar with a turquoise bolo tie, and a brown cardigan sweater buttoned to midpoint. His head is tipped forward enough to expose some thinning in his otherwise neatly combed, snow-white hair. For most of his life his skin has been permanently tan, olive-colored perhaps, a gift of his French ancestry. But now, except for the patch of pink in his bald spot, his skin is pale, chalk-like. A radio on the table (the workbench radio!) is droning with a melancholy instrumental from the 1940s. The morning newspaper is folded open to the sports page with an empty coffee cup sitting beside it. A half-dozen opened birthday cards lay next to the radio and I notice mine on top. I walk over and put a hand on his shoulder, give it a little squeeze. His chin rises from his chest.

"Well," he says, looking up, his eyes widening with confusion behind his glasses.

"Hi Dad, it's me—John."

"Well!" he says again, this time with more authority. "What are you doing here?"

"I'm checking up on you," I reply. "The lady in the kitchen tells me you're out here peeling potatoes and husking sweet corn."

"There's a lady in the kitchen?"

"Yup. And it looks like she's making something with chicken in it."

He smiles and shakes his head. "Chicken? I don't know what the hell you're talking about."

"That's okay," I reply. "How was your birthday?"

"It's your birthday?"

"No Dad, it was *your* birthday. Four days ago. Did you get any cards?"

"Nope. Not a one."

"I sent you one. Didn't you get it?"

"You sent me a card? The hell you say." He looks away and shakes his head as if he's insulted.

I pull up a chair and sit down, facing him. "What a beautiful morning!"

"It's a little chilly," he replies. "Tell me again why you're here."

"Don't you remember me calling you last night?" I ask.

"You called me last night?"

Okay. So this is how it's going to be. I better slow this down. "I sure did," I tell him. "I've been calling you a lot lately, Dad. We all have—Kath, Mark, Betsey."

"Betsey called me?"

"Yes, she did. You're about the only thing we talk about anymore."

"The hell …"

"Yup. We've been talking about how nice it would be if you lived closer to us."

"Closer to *you?*"

"Wouldn't that be nice, moving back home?"

His forehead furrows. "I *am* home. This is my home."

"But we think you should come back and live closer to us now."

He regards me skeptically. "What about Eunice?"

"Eunice is going to stay here until she's better. She's too sick to travel right now."

Now his eyes narrow and he forcefully shakes his head side to side. "No," he says.

"But Dad, this what we've been talking about for a couple weeks now—"

"You don't seem to be listening to me, buster," he blurts. "I'm not going anywhere. I'm sorry, but you came all this way for nothing."

So. It took less than a minute, but it seems I've already blown it. We sit staring at each other for a moment, his eyes as menacing as they were when I was fifteen, back when he called all the shots. This isn't going to work, I realize. I'll have to come up with something different.

"Hey!" I say cheerfully, "I heard you have a new friend. Is her name… Roseanne?"

"Roseanne, yes!" he says, and suddenly his irritation vanishes. It seems he can't say enough about her. "Roseanne is one of the nicest people I've ever met. Not bad looking, either. Not beautiful, a little broad in the beam, but who the hell cares? She's married, but goddamnit if she wasn't, I'd be half-tempted to marry her myself!"

"Eunice might have something to say about that," I remind him.

He laughs heartily. "Oh Christ, I forgot—I already have a wife!"

His laughter is encouraging but I'm still troubled about how I'm going to return to the subject at hand. For now, I decide it's best to keep him upbeat.

"Hey Dad, do you remember a year ago when I was here for your birthday? When we drove up to Lake Pleasant for the day? Just the two of us?"

The mention of the lake jogs his memory. "Why yes, I do remember. You bullshitted that security guard into letting us down to the marina."

This is also encouraging. I had forgotten about the security guard, but he hasn't. "And then what did we do?" I ask.

"Well, let's see ..." He has to stop and think about it, but then he erupts. "We had about the biggest goddamn piece of chocolate pie I've ever eaten in my life!" he says. "Hell yes I remember!"

Yes, yes, *yes!*

"Great!" I tell him. "How would you like to do something like that again? Just the two of us, you and me taking another road trip, maybe this time a little bit longer?"

His mouth droops. "A road trip? What the hell are you talking about?"

But before I can answer we're interrupted by a car pulling up in front of the porch. It's a silver minivan, Dad's Chrysler I realize, and then I see that Roseanne is driving it. She's right on time for our scheduled lunch date. At last. She bounds up the porch stairs and strides forcefully across the green Astroturf, a handsome, energetic woman who greets my father with a peck on the lips and me with a strong handshake. Dad breaks into his best Bert Parks imitation, crooning the same tune he sang every time I dared bring a girlfriend home: "There she is, Miss A-*merrrr*-i-ca …"

Roseanne, still pumping my hand, remarks, "Wow, you really *do* look like your father!"

I purse my lips. "Thank you."

She pulls up a chair on Dad's side of the table and begins explaining to him, in a sing-song voice, how I have come to take him home. "Oh Russ, what a *won*derful trip it will be," she says, "with the desert starting to *bloom*, the trees beginning to *bud*, the snow *melting* in the mountains!" But Dad's not listening. He seems more transfixed by the sound of her voice than the words pouring forth, and in the next moment he takes both her arms in his clumsy paws. He gazes into face her with an expression of pure bliss, his hands reaching for her waist, her sides, her … breasts! To my utter embarrassment, my father is groping this brave woman.

But Roseanne has dealt with this before. "You behave yourself, young man!" she scolds, and she pins Dad's arms to his sides.

"Isn't she beautiful?" he moans. "Won't you marry me, Roseanne?"

⁊

ON OUR WAY to the restaurant the minivan behaves erratically. I was afraid of this. Kath had warned me about it when she was here a few weeks ago. And then just last night Roseanne reminded me again: "Your father's car," she said. "You'll need to drive it to decide for yourself if you think it's up to pulling a trailer all the way back to Wisconsin. I drove it this past week, I think it may need some work."

The transmission begins down-shifting with a metallic bang every time I slow to a stop. When Kath was here it got so bad she took it to a garage to have it checked; the repair estimate came in at $6,000. I didn't believe her then but I do now.

Arriving at the restaurant, Roseanne escorts Dad inside while I pop the hood of the car to have a look around. It's got less than fifty thousand miles on it and looks like it just rolled off the show-room floor. Goddamn Chrysler transmissions. I once tried to per-suade Dad that he should consider buying a Honda or Toyota, but he looked at me as if he'd just swallowed rat poison. "A *Jap* car! Not in a million years, buster!" Now it looks like I'll have to get this piece of shit fixed before I dare start our 1,800-mile odyssey.

Over lunch, while Dad paws Roseanne beneath the table, I unfold the mechanic's estimate Kath had given me and start poring over the itemized discrepancies. I'm dubious. For years my father complained that Phoenix-area mechanics were crooks, every one of them predisposed to pad the bills of "snowbirds," the retired pensioners from the Midwest. Whether this is true or not, the expense of having round-the-clock care for both he and Eunice is eating a hole in his retirement savings, and the price tag of the memory-care home he'll be moving to won't help. I need to be prudent. After lunch I drop both he and Roseanne at the trailer park and head for the repair garage.

The service manager, Juan, leans on the counter as he studies my edited version of the estimate. I've crossed off all the hose and belt replacements, the engine tuneup, the lube job and oil change.

"I'm not looking for a complete overhaul of the vehicle," I inform him. "I just need one more trip out of it, one more eighteen-hundred-mile jaunt to deliver my father to the Promised Land."

Juan glances up at me with a mournful expression and ex-plains that Arizona heat is very hard on things like rubber hoses and belts, and that I'm making a "yuge" mistake by not replacing them. "How many miles to Wees-consin?" he asks.

"Enough that there's still ice on the lakes," I reply. I may be stretching the truth a bit, but no more than he is. "I'm sure the hoses will be fine," I say. "My only concern is the transmission. When can you start on it?"

He again studies the estimate, shaking his head. "Not today, I'm afraid." He runs down a litany of reasons for the delay, telling me it will take awhile to order the parts, that one of his mechanics is out sick, another on vacation. Maybe, just maybe, he can get to it by the weekend.

"*The weekend?*" I say. "Really? You don't look that busy to me." I motion beyond him into the window of his service bay, which at the moment appears to be empty. He glances over his shoulder and smiles forlornly, shakes his head. And says nothing.

But I'm not giving up. "Help me here, Juan," I begin. "My father is ninety-six and in poor health. He can no longer fly and the more we delay the worse it's going to get. This Arizona heat, it's also hard on old people, just like the hoses, yes? We need to get started as soon as possible, so I'd really appreciate it if you could get to it today."

I stare hard, trying to convince him I'm not going to fall for any bullshit.

He makes a clucking noise with his tongue and then sighs. "Hokay," he says finally. "I'll see what I can do. Leave the car and I will try to get the parts ordered tonight. No promises, hokay? I will call you later." He picks up the service phone and begins pushing buttons.

I take a cab back to Dad's, grab my bag, then walk to a hotel just around the corner from the trailer park. After a nap and a shower, I head back to have dinner with Roseanne and the public health nurse assigned to Dad's case, to tie up a few loose ends.

The walk from the hotel takes me down Ninety-first Avenue along a sidewalk skirting the length of the adobe wall protecting the trailer park. Dad used to walk his dog along this sidewalk every night after dinner. He'd be damned if he was going to walk his dog *inside* the park where the rules required residents to pick up after their pets. "It's dogshit, for Christ sake!" he insisted. "I've never picked up dogshit in my life and I'll god-damned if I'm going to start now."

One night as Tuffy sniffed beneath the bushes, Dad spotted something of interest lying near the wall and went in for a closer look. What he picked up, he discovered, was a roll of money held together with a rubber band. He quickly shoved it in his pocket and hurried Tuffy along with his business, then headed straight home. At the kitchen table he unrolled the treasure and discovered it was exactly six-hundred bucks, in six, one hundred-dollar bills. He couldn't believe it. He called me that night to share the news.

"Where do you think it came from?" he asked.

"Hmm…" I replied. "Could be a drug deal. You might have stumbled into a drop zone."

"Jesus Christ! You think so?"

"How else would you explain it? I wouldn't go walking out there for awhile until you're sure. Or … you could just put it back."

"Oh, I don't think I'd better do that! What if they saw me?"

"Well, then maybe you should call the police," I said. "Turn it over to them."

"No, I don't think so. Finders keepers."

"Right," I said. "Finders keepers. Well then, just to be on the safe side, maybe you should start walking Tuffy *inside* the park. Until the coast is clear. And you know what that means …"

There was a long pause as Dad considered the options. When he didn't respond, I said, "You'll need to get some plastic bags."

"Jesus Christ …" he muttered.

The found money would bother him for a long time, making him suspicious of every Hispanic male he ever saw walking along the sidewalk or even doing day-labor inside the park. Eventually, he spent the money, cashing the C-notes one at a time, usually at stores located a long way from Casa del Calor.

Now, on this warm evening in April, I return to Dad's trailer to find him in the shade of the carport, sound asleep in the plastic chair beside the back door. Just like this morning, I put my hand on his shoulder to wake him, and once again he's surprised to see me.

"What are you doing here?" he asks.

"I've come to join you for supper," I say cheerfully. "Shall we see if it's ready?"

"You came all this way to have supper with me?" I help him out of the chair and we head inside.

In the kitchen we're greeted by Jocelyn, who is just then putting dinner in the oven—chicken and rice casserole, green beans and mashed potatoes, gravy on the stovetop. And there's fruit salad for dessert.

"Your daddy loves his fruit salad!" she says, which she proves by opening the refrigerator door to reveal the two dozen or more additional Styrofoam cups of fruit salad she's prepared for our trip home. Jocelyn informs me that the night nurse is having car trouble and will be a little late. Do I mind? I don't.

She departs and I'm suddenly alone with Dad. With time to kill, I challenge him to a hand of cribbage, a game at which he once excelled. He's reluctant to play but I insist, bribing him with a bowl of Spanish peanuts and a glass of lemonade. At first the scoring confuses him but suddenly a dam breaks somewhere in his mind and he's slapping the cards down and laughing as he pegs his points. With a little creative pegging on my part, he beats me in the first game and then excuses himself to go check on Eunice. His diligence amazes me; I'd completely forgotten she was still alive.

While he's in the bedroom Roseanne arrives and then the public health nurse. The three of us sit at the dining room table signing release forms and going over the case files I'm to present to the staff at the memory care facility in La Crosse. By the time my father joins us the nurse is filling his medication dispenser—an enormous plastic case on which the days of week are marked by bold initials. To me it looks more like a tackle box, and I ask if Dad really needs all this stuff.

"Oh yes," she replies and begins giving me a brief explanation of each one. My father takes a chair between us, quietly listening, saying nothing. Then he begins caressing the nurse's arm as he glances over at me.

"Hasn't she got a beautiful smile?" he says.

"We're going to miss you, Russ," the nurse replies.

My father looks confused. "Are you going somewhere?"

"No, of course not, silly. *You* are. Your son is taking you back to Minnesota."

I scowl. My father turns to me with a look of panic.

"You're taking me to Minnesota?"

"No Dad, not Minnesota. Wisconsin. It's what we've been talking about for a while now, remember? You're actually going to live close to Mark, near his farm in La Crosse. He's found a nice---"

But before I can finish he lashes out at me with cold anger. "I'm not going *anywhere* with you, buster. You can kiss my ass!"

"Russ!" shouts Roseanne from across the table. "We don't talk like that anymore!"

"*Bullshit!*" he snaps. And he fixes me with a look of utter contempt.

The nurse digs through her paraphernalia and produces a small kit which she begins opening on the table. "Russ, shall we show your son how we take our blood-sugar reading? Do you remember?"

And with this his mood swings wildly in another direction, like he's suddenly a little boy learning to tie his shoes. Diabetes is the most recent of his afflictions, one more thing to deal with. But he's quite proud of this new achievement, the way he's learned to prick his finger and dab blood on a test strip, something the nurse has been teaching him in preparation for the trip home. While he busies himself with the test she begins a long dissertation on his general health and her concerns about the trip we're undertaking. She wishes we were flying but understands that doing so is out of the question with him. She advises me to take it easy, to stop frequently so that he can stretch his legs and walk around. She could prescribe sleep medication, she says, but would rather not, what with all the other medication he's taking. I'm free to give him an over-the-counter sedative if his insomnia becomes a problem.

"Do you think it will become a problem?" I ask. I hadn't even considered this.

"Very possibly. It's common among the elderly. Also, sundown syndrome."

"*Sundown syndrome?*"

Roseanne and the nurse take turns explaining a condition brought on by anxiety, a lack of sleep, or any one of numerous other issues, usually manifesting itself at sundown and sometimes lasting well into the night. I've never heard of it and am suddenly concerned about this new complication.

Roseanne squeezes my arm. "You'll be fine," she assures me. "He trusts you."

He does? Dad sits before us like he's watching a tennis match, his eyes following our comments back and forth across the table. Suddenly he says, "You're talking about me, aren't you?" and seems flattered by the attention. He glances in my direction. "What are they saying about me?"

I smile. "They're both saying how they wish they'd known you in your dancing days."

"God *damn!*" he says, and the excitement in his voice causes it to jump an octave. He's so excited he begins waving his hands above his head as if he's ready to dance right now.

Instead, Roseanne and the nurse depart, and Dad and I get ready for dinner.

6

EUNICE

The chicken and rice casserole prepared by Jocelyn before she departed is wonderful and I help myself to seconds. There's plenty, especially considering there's only the two of us; the night nurse has yet to arrive. Dad finishes what's on his plate, no more no less; his eating habits are nowhere near what they used to be. After the war he discovered the pleasure of ice cream for dessert and it became a lifelong obsession. Sixty years of ice cream, as well as buttered popcorn, chocolate fudge, and large helpings of my mother's good cooking, had ballooned him up into the heavyweight division, and he was never able to take the weight off until the last few years. Now, at ninety-six, he's frail and greatly reduced in stature.

The night nurse calls to inform me she's still having car trouble but says her brother is coming to pick her up. I assure her it's no problem, that in fact I'm happy to have the time alone with my father. When I inform Dad of the situation he gets a worried look on face and goes at once into the bedroom to check on Eunice. He's so devoted to her but in reality it never should have come to this. He never should have married her in the first place.

When his first wife, my mother, died in October of 1984, he was stunned. She was nearly ten years his junior and he never imagined she would be the first to go. His grief was understandable; they had recently retired to a lake home in northern Minnesota where they were living the life they had worked so hard to attain, one filled with grandchildren and gardening, flea-marketing and fishing, happy-hour sunsets shared with friends on a deck overlooking the lake. After her death Dad went through a painful year of mourning during which he made some questionable decisions. For one, he put the lake home up for sale, claiming he could no longer live in a place so imbued with memories of his dead wife. He put it on the market, then departed early for Arizona, retreating to his second home at Casa del Calor, where he felt safe. He would never admit it, but I'm fairly certain he was running away from us, his children, who in the aftermath of their mother's death developed a growing concern about his welfare. He was a proud and stubborn man who didn't appreciate anyone, let alone his children, meddling in his affairs. Nevertheless, the following spring he returned to Minnesota, finalized the sale of the lake home, and then rented a cabin on a different lake where he spent the summer. He joined a horseshoe league, kept a small garden, and took lunch at the local senior citizen hall. This would become his pattern for the next few years. He never did learn to cook.

He set aside one week every summer for "visiting." He packed a suitcase and drove to the Twin Cities to spend a night or two with either Kath or me and our respective families. During the same trip he would make the rounds of our old neighborhood in South Minneapolis, stopping in to call on former friends, sometimes even venturing into the hospitals or nursing homes where some of them had landed.

He also made longer trips to visit Mark's family in La Crosse. Mark's farm sat amidst the scenic coulees and bluffs of Wisconsin's "driftless area" where he raised beef cattle and alfalfa. Dad liked nothing better than to spend a morning in the barn helping his son feed the herd, inhaling the sweet memories of his youth. Climbing behind the wheel of a tractor gave him a thrill he hadn't known in decades. Mark once even suggested he consider moving there permanently, at least during the summer months when he could stay in the spare bedroom Mark had fixed up especially for that purpose. But Dad declined with the excuse he "didn't want to burden anyone." One summer he rode the Amtrak all the way to central Michigan to visit my sister Betsey and her family. It was quite an adventure, he later claimed, especially in Chicago where he had to change trains and mingle with the masses. Still, it was better than flying, with its threat of sky-jacking, engine failure, or pilot error.

Every fall, before his return to Arizona, he would make one last trip to the Twin Cities to treat everyone to a farewell Sunday brunch. For him, this amounted to Thanksgiving, Christmas, New Year's and Easter, as well as any weddings or funerals that might occur over the coming winter, all rolled into one. (His fear of flying became his standard excuse for missing most of his siblings' funerals and virtually all of his grandchildren's weddings). At his insistence, the brunch venue was always upscale—The St Paul Grille or Kozlak's Royal Oak—and in spite of his frugality, it pleased him to pick up the tab. At one such fall gathering he let it be known that he'd been "stepping out" over the summer with a "gal" he'd met up north. We were overjoyed. "Stepping out," he assured us, was just another way of saying he was dating, and should not be confused with "shacking up," which he wasn't ready for. No doubt the loneliness of bachelorhood had become a burden, but it's also true he couldn't cook, his culinary expertise beginning and ending with heating a can of tomato soup in a saucepan. His admission that he was stepping out was encouraging; then in his early seventies, he still had a lot of his life in front of him.

His chances increased tenfold when he returned again to Peoria. It's not hard to imagine my father as a hot commodity in the Arizona retirement scene; a handsome widower of moderate means, a pleasant conversationalist, a good dancer, an accomplished bridge player. That he was living in an area teeming with available widows only improved his chances. His letters began arriving with photos of himself joining the hunt, most of them taken on a dance floor filled with other active seniors. When he and his partner mugged for the camera, the smile on Dad's face was never quite as convincing as that of his date's. If he seemed a bit reluctant I suspect it was because he was being as selective as he could afford to be, not falling for the first pretty face that came along. So I was a bit surprised when he called one Sunday night to inform me he'd been spending a lot of time with someone he'd recently met, a woman named Ava.

"Ava," I said. "Sounds exotic. Is she attractive?"

He hesitated. "Well, she's got a lot of wrinkles," he finally admitted. "And when you see her first thing in the morning before she puts her makeup on, well … shit, *you* wouldn't call her attractive."

"You've seen her first thing in the morning? Are you two shacking up?"

"God damn you!" he said laughing. And it was good to hear him laugh.

That spring he brought Ava back to Minnesota, not so much to show her off, I suspect, as to gauge our opinion of her. Their first stop was St. Paul and the Mississippi River towboat company where I was employed as port engineer. Ava and I hit it off immediately, her interest and curiosity about the river filling her with a million questions:

"What's the name of that bridge?" she asked. The three of us were standing out on the open deck of the floating wharfbarge where I kept shop, directly beneath the soaring arches of a Saint Paul landmark.

"It's called the High Bridge," I replied, to which she nodded approvingly, her eyes fixed aloft. She was spry and energetic, her khaki-colored clothing apropos for a day of urban exploration, right down to the pair of Nike cross-trainers on her feet. Something above us gave her pause.

"The High Bridge," she mused. "Has anyone ever jumped from up there?" Her intuition caught me off-guard; how could she have known that?

"More often than you'd think," I said. "It's not a pleasant sight."

She gave me a sympathetic look and we moved on to other subjects. She inquired about the depth of the channel, the strength of the current, the species of fish in the water. She noticed the purple martin nests in the eaves of the shop rafters, and the emergence of buds in the cottonwoods along the riverbank. "Messy trees," she remarked in passing, "always shedding something or other."

Inside the shop, she admired the quality of the welding beads on a steel rudder I was then constructing, something no one else had ever noticed. My affection for her swelled. When she asked about the model and horsepower of a diesel engine awaiting parts in an overhaul stand, I looked at her in wonder. "What do you know about diesel engines?"

Ava's eyebrows arched. "Not much," she replied. "But my late husband would have nothing but John Deeres on our farm. He claimed they were bulletproof."

Bulletproof? My God, if she'd suddenly asked for a wrench, I'd have handed her one!

Before they departed, I pulled my father aside and expressed my approval over his new lady friend Ava. "She could be the one!" I whispered conspiratorially.

"The one for what?" he replied with a deadpan expression. He didn't seem to share in my enthusiasm.

"Why, marriage of course. Isn't that what this is all about?"

"Shit," he said with a pensive look, shaking his head as he turned away.

Now what? I thought.

Imagine my disappointment when over the course of the following year he let his relationship with Ava fade and eventually die. His excuse? She was forever trying to get him on a regimen of exercise and vitamins, encouraging him to lose weight, and to be mindful of what he ate. Worse, she insisted on paying her half of the bill wherever they went, something his chauvinistic ideals would never tolerate. He got cold feet when she began including him in future plans for excursions to Ireland, Greece, and the Orient. Travel expenses were of no concern; she was quite wealthy. And I think that's what finally scared him off for good; he would be no one's *kept* man.

In the end she wound up marrying another widower from the park, a "sucker" as my father described him, a man who later accompanied his new bride on an around-the-world honeymoon cruise, much to Dad's chagrin. I didn't hesitate to tell him I thought he had blown it and that now he was acting like a jealous teenager. To which he replied, "You can kiss my ass, buster; it's none of your goddamn business." And I suppose it wasn't.

Nevertheless, he continued dating, sending more photos from Arizona and, back home in Minnesota, showing up every now and then with his latest "lady friend." Some of them seemed pleasant enough, but none of them, in my opinion, would ever hold a candle to Ava. I remained disappointed that he'd dumped her, and I paid scant attention to those that followed.

In the fall of 1990, when we gathered for his annual farewell brunch, he brought along a woman he'd recently met, this one from northern Minnesota. Her name was Eunice and she was slim and petite with a ponytail that hung to her waist and black brooding eyebrows. Everything about her appeared color-coordinated and tasteful, right down to her fingernail polish and lipstick. Her most striking feature was her youth, for she appeared to be at least twenty-five years younger than our father.

During the meal, Eunice sat erectly beside Dad picking at her food, smiling occasionally but not offering much in the way of conversation. Her voice had the deep, phlegmatic raspiness of a smoker, later proved by the sequined cigarette case she pulled from her purse and kept open beside her plate. She reached for it at regular intervals to extract a Virginia Slim, which she held elegantly in her lacquered fingers while lighting. The little sock which held her disposable lighter was sequined to match the cigarette case, and I realized that this was a woman who took her smoking seriously. And it made me wonder what other vices she might enjoy.

At the end of brunch Dad surprised everyone when he announced that Eunice would be accompanying him to Arizona that winter, to which we all more or less mumbled our approval. We barely knew her.

Later, Kath did a little investigating and discovered that Eunice was indeed some twenty-three years younger than Dad, and also divorced, with two grown children. In a phone call to Dad not long after his arrival in Arizona, I questioned him about Eunice and what his plans for her might be. I wanted to know about her divorce and how that set with the tenets of the Catholic Church, which he'd always seemed determined to live by. He got defensive and claimed that none of us, especially me, had liked Eunice from the start. Which was true. But before I could utter a word in my defense, he angrily shouted "Tough shit!" and hung up.

That same winter, I found out later, he wrote a few checks to the Archdiocese of Phoenix and succeeded in getting Eunice's first marriage annulled. Apparently money can buy you sanctity. A year later they were married.

It didn't take long to discover that Eunice's smoking was the least of her problems. Returning to Minnesota that summer, the newlyweds got off to a rocky start. Where in years past Dad had always managed to find seasonal lodging in a pleasant lakeside setting, for this particular summer he decided to take the frugal route. He boasted of the great deal he got on an old farmhouse located in the middle of nowhere, a place so bleak I couldn't imagine a worse scenario in which to begin a marriage. The sway-backed house stood upon a windswept lot within sight and sound of a busy interstate highway. No neighbors within a mile, no town closer than ten, no lake or water visible in any direction as far as the eye could see.

On a weekend outing with my family to visit a friend's lake cabin farther north, we stopped off at Dad's to pay homage. We all sat in the living room for awhile listening to Eunice's complaints about the dump my father had rented. Dad sat in a threadbare recliner listening passively, or maybe not at all; by then his hearing had grown decidedly weaker. I on the other hand endured her rant for as long as I could, then grabbed my two young sons and escaped outdoors for a walk around the premises. Back behind the garage we came across a rusted drum filled with empty bottles—all of them brandy. It appeared someone had a drinking problem. For the longest time he skirted the issue of her drinking, focusing instead on the wonderful meals she cooked, or how elegantly she dressed, or how gracefully she seemed to glide across a dance floor. But little by little he began to acknowledge her shortcomings, remarking in passing that she'd never read a book in her life, refused to play cards, and wasn't much of a conversationalist. Gradually, the issue of her drinking emerged as the problem behind everything. She could be loud and embarrassing. She would fall unexpectedly. She'd spend half the day on the front porch in her robe smoking cigarettes and sipping from her ubiquitous tumbler. He confessed that her behavior was taking a toll on the quality of his life: they were going out less frequently and the large circle of friends he once enjoyed seemed to be slowly diminishing.

"She's a drunk," he finally admitted one night over the phone.

"Then why did you marry her?" I asked.

He paused, and when he finally responded I could hear the defeat in his voice. "I felt sorry for her," he said. "I found out her first husband used to beat her." And after another pause he added, "I guess I don't blame him."

Not that he would ever resort to such a thing. Above everything else he was a gentleman, and gentlemen don't hit women. For twenty years he hid her alcoholism behind a curtain of domestic serenity, fooling himself into thinking he was some sort of aging Lothario with a young wife, the two of them making smooth music as they glided across the dance floor. And what with their seasonal escapes back and forth between residences, he could hide her alcoholism between different sets of friends, leaving just as folks might begin to catch on, allowing them the opportunity to lose track of (and in some cases, interest in) Eunice's problem.

But he wasn't fooling me. As her drinking grew worse he became so despondent I urged him to do something about it. He insisted he'd been trying.

"I quit smoking," he said. That was true enough. He'd smoked for over sixty years and he quit overnight, certain that she would follow suit. But she didn't.

Then he quit drinking, something that had never been a

problem for him and was certainly of no consequence once he finally decided to quit for good. But as with the smoking, it had no effect on Eunice's drinking. He stood by and watched as she'd drink herself into a stupor, pass out, and at times injure herself.

"*Why does someone have to drink like that?*" he wailed one night over the phone.

"Because you allow her to!" I replied, as frustrated as he was. "You're as much at fault here as she is. You're co-dependent!" This made no sense to him and he would abruptly hang up, only to call again sometime later to inform me Eunice had passed out and fallen again, at which point our conversation about his welfare would begin anew. I finally suggested it was time he got a divorce, that she was, in effect, committing slow suicide and taking him down with her. I even went so far as to contact a lawyer I knew who offered to counsel him *pro bono* over the phone, to explain how it all worked. But he wouldn't bite. Divorce was a mortal sin in the Catholic Church, but worse:

"What would the neighbors think if I left her now?' he cried. "How would it look if I left her when she needs me more than ever?"

He could frustrate me to tears. It felt like Eunice was dragging me down with the two of them. "*Then stop calling me!*" I shouted in frustration one night, and this time it was me who hung up on him. But the following Sunday the phone would ring and all would be right with the world. He would rhapsodize about the wonderful roast Eunice had made for dinner, or how no one on earth could make apple crumble the way she did, or how hard she worked in keeping the house clean, and most of all how she had to put up with someone as grouchy and stubborn as he was. And then, "Did you happen to catch the Vikings game this afternoon? You did? Oh boy, wasn't that something?" And so the cycle would begin again, back to square one.

಄

DAD AND I PLAY one more game of cribbage before the night nurse arrives. It's Luna, his favorite, and he barely notices when I say goodnight and head back to the hotel. It's been a long day and I fall immediately to sleep. But I awaken a few hours later, my mind a jumble of what tomorrow might bring. Will Dad's car be ready in time? Am I being careless? Should I have had the old hoses and belts replaced? What if the car breaks down in the middle of nowhere and Dad wanders off into the desert while I'm trying to flag down help? What about the U-Haul trailer? How long will it take to find one and get it hooked up? What if it's the wrong size and I can't fit all his belongings in it? What if he doesn't even recognize me in the morning, takes a swing at me, and accuses me of attempting to kidnap him?

7

Bullshit

By now you've probably noticed that my father is fond of profanity. There is ample evidence that his propensity for coarse language began at a young age. Swearing, he always claimed, was but one of the many questionable habits he picked up in his childhood on the farm. Another two were storytelling (with a tendency to embellish) and gossiping—sometimes to the point of character assassination. All three habits fell under the general heading of "Bullshit." Bullshitting, he claimed, was the family affliction. "We were *born* bullshitters," was how he put it. He'd get no argument from me. Some of the most cherished memories of my own childhood are the ones in which he's in the company of his older brothers and sisters, especially when the storytelling began. Sitting at a picnic table say, in the shade of a South Dakota farmhouse, it wouldn't take much to get them started—the mention of a hapless neighbor perhaps, or the misadventures of a long-departed dog. Pretty soon events from a generation ago would emerge. The underlying tragedy of their situation—the motherless household, their father's abject moodiness, the privations and austerity of life on a Depression-era farm—seemed to heighten rather than diminish the humanity and humor of the stories. One story would lead to another, and before long these vivid, "uncensored" narratives made me feel as much a part of the family history—not to mention the history of Moody County, South Dakota—as if I'd lived it myself.

Like the rest of his family, my father was naturally soft-spoken and at times reserved. He had a tenor's voice, mild and without much carry. When we were kids, he liked to sit near stronger singers in church, like Mr. Klanchnik, the father of a friend of mine, whose deep baritone would carry over the weaker voices of those nearby. "My god, that sonofabitch has a beautiful voice!" Dad would remark on the car ride home, no doubt wishing he had a voice as strong. But he made do with what he had. He might begin a story meekly enough, but once he got warmed up—once he got a few anecdotes into a story he really enjoyed telling—his personality rose to the surface. He had an innate ability to capture a listener's ear with a smooth delivery, and also an inflection in his speech pattern that held the promise of something worth listening to.

Whether or not he was aware of it, he created tension with a rising pitch, added excitement with a sudden hitch or gasp, and showed anger or disgust with a strategically placed expletive. Oh, how he could swear. And his expletives were always delivered democratically, with little regard for the listener's age or sensitivities. By comparison, my mother's side of the family, reserved Scandinavians mostly, spoke in gentle, civil tones; I can't remember a single coarse word coming from the lot of them. And while it's possible these same Scandinavians might have smiled awkwardly at my father's salty language, I can't remember any of them ever shying away or even telling him "enough!" Like everyone else, they loved a good story, and my father could indeed tell a good story.

I grew up listening to his stories, some of them told so often they became family lore. Unlike most of the other fathers in the South Minneapolis neighborhood where I grew up, nearly all of whom were veterans of WWII, my father was never reluctant in sharing the stories of his wartime experiences. To be honest, I think he needed to tell them—a form of therapy, perhaps. I've often wondered if his undeniable luck in having survived some of the harrowing experiences he described didn't instill in him a sense of wonder, a feeling of euphoria, because he had lived long enough to tell of them.

One my earliest recollections of his storytelling takes place in an upstairs bedroom of our house on Pleasant Avenue. All five of us—Kathy, Mark, Betsey, Jimmy and me—are sprawled in our pajamas across my sisters' twin beds. It's dark, with only a gray twilight visible through the windows, and a thin shaft of light leaking above the closed hallway door. My father sits astride the same wooden chair he used for his various projects, its surface splattered with a landscape of colors and textures, the seat cracked from use as a step-ladder or sawhorse. He is then in his early forties, the thickening around his middle still in its early stages. His wavy hair is nearly black but flecks of gray are beginning to show at the temples. The "farmer's tan" he's had since childhood seems even darker here in the diminished light. Dressed simply in frayed khakis and a wrinkled tee shirt, he's propped open one of the windows an inch or so to vent the smoke from his cigarette, its tip glowing as he pauses to take a drag. The ashes are tapped without hesitation into the palm of a thick hand, to be deposited later, along with the butts, in the toilet down the hall.

He's telling us about the day his ship, the USS *Leedstown*, was torpedoed by a German U-boat during the invasion of North Africa. It's perhaps his favorite story, and one I will hear over and over in the course of his long life. But on this particular night it's new and thus terrifying. It's my first introduction to terms like "Goddamn Nazis" and "chickenshit Vichy French." At the height of the story he has abandoned the sinking ship and is swimming with all his might in an attempt to get clear of the foundering hull. There is oil on the water and men screaming, with waves and fire making the swimming difficult. When he feels as if he has swum halfway to France, he turns to check his progress and discovers to his horror that he's gotten nowhere. In fact, he's being drawn backwards in the suction created by the sinking ship and is just moments from being swept back inside it *through* the torpedo hole.

At this point, as he describes his frantic attempts to reach a rope-ladder hanging from the side of the ship, his voice takes on a noticeably higher pitch.

"*Sonofabitch!*" he cries, "I was barely able to grab it!" But to my relief, he does manage to grab the ladder and climb back aboard. He proceeds to abandon the ship again, this time from the other, safer, side, and eventually makes it to shore, where he's rescued from the raging surf by peasant girls using long reeds as lifelines—another story in itself.

Afterwards, the room is quiet; we're all in a meditative mood, especially me. It's more than my six-year-old imagination can absorb. I sit in the darkness trying to imagine how much different my *own* life would have been had things turned out differently. At length, one of my siblings turns on a light and Dad gets up to leave, grabbing the chair with one hand, the other still cupping the cigarette butts. As he heads for the door my boiling consternation spills over in an anguished plea:

"Wait!" I cry. "What if there hadn't been a rope? What if you'd gotten sucked back inside the ship?"

He turns to me with a distracted, almost impatient look on his face. (There's a bowl of ice cream waiting downstairs). But finally he replies, "Damned if I know. You kids go to sleep now."

Which is how he ended most of his stories—*You kids go to sleep now.* As if that were even remotely possible.

చ

HIS SWEARING WAS such a regular part of his vocabulary that when I was young, I gave it no more consideration than say, the clothes he wore or the way he combed his hair. He used the word "shit" in any conversation where the question of authenticity or intention came into play, such as, "*Shit*, you really think so?" or "*Shit*, you'd be a fool to try something as stupid as that." He often laughed when using the word, even more so when he embellished it and turned it into "bullshit" or "horseshit," both of which he used with great frequency. "Damn" and "goddamn" were a couple of others he used a lot, and also "son of a bitch" which, in his rendering, came out as one word—*sonofabitch*. But, again, these were so commonplace and so much a part of his regular vernacular that they were of no real consequence to me. The F-Bomb, on the other hand, meant business and was held in reserve for those special occasions when something he had done, or tried to do, had gone terribly awry.

On weekends, he seemed to be perpetually engaged in some sort of home improvement project—plastering or painting, building a fence, adding a bedroom closet, or remodeling a basement rec room. He couldn't sit still. He even had enough confidence in his mechanical ability to overhaul or replace the engines in the many second-hand cars he bought for my mother. As handy as he was, he could be careless sometimes. Take electricity, for example. The fuse box in our old house was located in the peak of the attic, all but unreachable. As such, he rarely took the time or effort to kill the power before beginning an electrical project. Invariably, a few jolts of stray voltage would knock him on his ass and the F-Bombs would fly, the air turning blue in whatever room he happened to be working. If there were children present, as there often were, Mom would suddenly appear from nowhere shouting "*Russ!*" as she shepherded us out of earshot.

He could turn off the profanity when he had to, but those occasions were rare, usually occurring in the presence of strangers or clients whose sensibilities he had not yet gauged. But he could turn it on again just as quickly once he'd gained someone's confidence and wanted to leave an impression or finalize a deal. He could be clever this way. He had a salesman's knack for sizing people up and noting their qualities, both good and bad. He was a skilled listener and kept track of everything he heard or saw—the attention people paid to their lawns and landscaping, the weight gain (or loss) of every housewife in the neighborhood, the make and model of the cars their husbands drove, the natural athletes amongst the children playing in the street, the breed of the dogs that ran through our yard, the way people in church dressed, the noises their children made during the service, the fiery rhetoric of a priest's homily or the lack thereof.

In church, he always expected to be reproached for his weekly sins and seemed disappointed if a particular priest's homily didn't quite fit the bill. He might accuse someone of being a "bullshit artist" if he thought he was being conned, or he might remark on someone's physical abnormality if he thought it could get a laugh. He nicknamed one of my sister's early boyfriends "Zits." And he labeled any neighbor he didn't quite agree with an "old fart." As I recall, there were quite a few "old farts" in our neighborhood. He wasn't shy about sharing his observations, either, but I never thought of them or his judgments as being especially cruel or even mean-spirited. The comments were just another part of his nature, and over time I came to think of them as the "family curse" he knew he'd inherited, which was perhaps part of his subconscious.

Toward the end of his life he became completely unfiltered and began swearing more than ever. Not that it particularly bothered anyone, but we began to wonder if he was even aware of it. Mark and I decided to conduct a test. One weekend when Dad was in his early nineties, I drove him from his home up in northern Minnesota to Mark's farm in Wisconsin, the same place I'm planning to deliver him now. He loved being around the cattle and the open fields, and on this particular visit Mark allowed him to drive the tractor, something he'd learned to do as a child. But it had been decades since he'd been behind the wheel of one, and on this afternoon he nearly unseated himself by driving beneath the low limbs of a tree. By the grace of God he didn't get knocked to the ground, a fall that might well have been fatal.

"Sonofabitch!" he shouted excitedly as we helped him down off the seat.

"Sonofabitch!" Mark and I shouted in unison, as per our plan. Every time Dad uttered a swear word we would chime in together with the same expletive. After about fifteen minutes of this he grew confused.

"Say, what the hell's the matter with you two?" he cried. And when we explained what we were doing, he just shook his head. "You two are out of your goddamned minds," he muttered. And our suspicions were confirmed.

I doubt he ever once considered himself profane.

8

The Farm

He was born Francis Russell Halter on April 11, 1916, on a farm in the southeast corner of South Dakota, some three miles west of the town of Egan, in Moody County. The bullshit began at birth: he grew up believing his name was Russell Francis and it wasn't until he joined the Navy in 1936 that he learned his name had been inverted. No one had ever bothered to inform him of this, much less explain why it happened—not even his father, George, who only told him then because he thought the discrepancy might create problems with Navy record-keeping. The revelation infuriated my father. He *hated* the name Francis, thought it feminine, and refused to use it. I remember that once, when a letter came to our house addressed to a "Frank Halter," Dad stared at it disdainfully before muttering, "What stupid son of a bitch sent this?" He was never going to be a Frank. For his entire adult life he referred to himself as F.R. in his professional career and Russell Halter—Russ—to his family and friends. He didn't completely dismiss his legal name, however. He thought enough of "Francis" to pass it on to me as my middle name which, in my adolescence, caused me some degree of embarrassment. But not enough to stop me from doing the same with my second son, Nicholas Francis, who in fact loves it.

His father's negligence in communicating essential information to his children was but one of the shortcomings my dad saw in him. There were plenty of others, none of which he ever tried to conceal or omit from the stories he told of his childhood on the farm. He could go on and on about George's moodiness, his questionable decision-making, his miserly way with a buck, but in the end we were always led to believe that it was George's woeful lack of communication that irked my father most. Oddly enough, even after an especially harsh assessment of his father's character, Dad would often apologize for being too judgmental about him, and then go on to list any number of excuses for his father's behavior, finally insisting that he himself was no better. But he never once apologized for the simple fact that he didn't like him.

I never met my grandfather George. He was the eldest son of eleven children born to immigrants Louis Halter and Louisa Doerr Halter, French and German respectively, who settled on a farm in Marshall County, Iowa, in the 1870s. My father has little memory of his paternal grandparents except that each came to visit, one at a time, after his mother died. He remembered Grandfather Louis, a full-blooded Frenchman, as "quite a nice man," and Grandmother Louisa for a decidedly different reason. When her daughter-in-law died, Grandmother Louisa came from Iowa to stay with the family and help them over the terrible loss of their mother. She was a small, stout woman with a thick accent who apparently liked the taste of her own cooking. One morning in the kitchen my father, still an infant, watched as she combined eggs, potatoes, and bacon in a large skillet atop the wood-burning stove. While watching it simmer, Grandma Louisa took a sampling from the skillet, tasted it, and remarked, "Gosh dot's goot!" It was the only memory my father had of her, and for the rest of his life he would utter the same expression every time he sampled something especially tasty.

In 1901, Louis and Louisa's eldest son George married Anna O'Leary, a pretty schoolteacher and the daughter of Irish immigrants. In 1906 George and Anna, along with their first three children, followed an uncle who had moved there ten years earlier, to Moody County, South Dakota, where he took up farming. He worked hard. On the quarter-section of land he purchased near an intersection of roads called "Lone Tree" by the locals, George built by hand the huge barn that, one hundred years later, still stands on the property. Said to be good with animals, he farmed with horses, preferring them to the tractors he eventually felt obliged to acquire. He understood horses; machinery, not so much. All of the labor he performed would be called "back-breaking" by today's standards.

Anna bore him eight children, of which my father was seventh. When Anna contracted tuberculosis in 1919, George sent her to a sanatorium in Arizona where it was believed the drier air would heal her lungs. Unfortunately it didn't, and Anna died a year later. She was forty-six. There would be more deaths. In the span of three years, from 1918 to 1921, the family lost their mother Anna, their youngest sibling Ruth (to the Spanish Flu epidemic of 1918) and then finally, and tragically, Leo, the eldest boy, to a burst appendix.

His mother's passing created a large hole in my father's young life. Barely four years old at the time, he was left with scant remembrance of her and had to rely on descriptions and memories from neighbors and older siblings. For the rest of his life he hung onto every old photograph and scrap of paper he could find relevant to his mother's life: her State of Iowa teacher's certificate, her marriage certificate, even the unfinished letter she wrote to the family while confined in the sanatorium. When he was eighty-three years old my father wrote a remembrance of his childhood on the farm. In one passage he remarks that artifacts associated with his mother gave him "some semblance of closeness to her – something I couldn't experience as a child, as she was out of my life at three years old. [Her death] left me with the greatest void in life that was ever left to a human being—and that void is still there to this day."

Every time we've been together watching a televised sports event and a jubilant athlete suddenly shouted or mouthed "Hi, Mom!" I would hear him groan. He never got over the sadness he experienced in being denied a mother's love.

Until he started school, little Russell was left largely to his own amusements around the family farm. Awakening every morning to an empty house, he would come downstairs to eat the cold bowl of oatmeal left for him on the table by older sister

Adeline who had long since departed for school. Breakfast over, he was free to roam around the barnyard for the rest of the day, chasing after the dog, visiting the hen house, waiting for his older brothers and sisters to return from school or the fields. One morning a stray black cat frightened him so badly he "crapped his pants," much to the chagrin of his father, who later "cleaned him up as best he could with corncobs" and then of course put the same pants back on him. "You can well imagine," my father wrote, "that everyone stayed up-wind of me for some time."

Because of the situation at home he was allowed to start school a year early and admits that he was "an undeveloped shrimp, both in mind and body, all through my school years." Nevertheless, school offered a welcome respite from the loneliness and boredom he experienced at home. Grades one through eight were all convened in a one-room school house called "Shady Lawn," located a mile east of the Halter farm. His ten or twelve fellow students (depending on the particular year) were the children from the large farm families in the surrounding township, often no more than three or four families in all. The teachers—and he remembered every one—served at the discretion of the school

Francis Halter (left); Egan, South Dakota, 1921

board, which was made up of the same farmers whose children were enrolled. Tenures rarely lasted more than one or two years as teachers got married and started families of their own. One of my father's favorite teachers was a Miss Stombaugh, who instilled in him the lifelong pleasure of reading. In his memoir, he describes the sensuousness with which she taught:

"Miss Stombaugh was "an all-American girl, nice-looking, [with a] good figure and a very pleasing personality ... At the beginning of the afternoon session, she would read about fifteen minutes to all the classes, from *Uncle Tom's Cabin,* or *Anne of Green Gables.* [She] would stand in front of the [room] with the book in her right hand, and gently massage her stomach with her left hand. You could hear a pin drop when she read. We were all so interested that she promised to read again, just before closing, if we all studied hard. And I think we all did."

Another teacher who left an indelible impression on the curious mind of the shrimpy first grader was a Miss Johnson. One morning Miss Johnson came down the row of desks, pausing here and there to check the progress of each student's work. Bending over at a nearby desk, Miss Johnson's considerable posterior loomed large and inviting before young Russell's eyes. Unable to control himself, as he describes it, "[I] reached over and poked her on the rump with my finger. I didn't know it would have such a reaction, but she spontaneously expelled a huge amount of gas, and it surely startled me as well." (This was another story he loved to tell, and in each of his retellings the velocity and volume of the gas grew stronger and larger.)

In the fourth grade he was singled out for his oral reading ability. It was the first time in his life he'd ever been told he could do something better than anyone else. Apparently, compliments around George's household were in short supply. In subsequent years the Halter boys—he and older brothers Bill and Ernie— became champions of the local spelling bees, easily bettering the competition. One year Bill made it all the way to the state finals.

Lunchtime at school invariably meant the jar of creamed potatoes prepared by Adeline to take to school. "Hot lunch" came by virtue of the stove in the back of the school, atop which the jars were placed for heating an hour before lunchtime. One winter when he was in the sixth grade, my father was accused of nearly burning down the schoolhouse when he used the stove's hot poker to a burn a hole in the exposed wooden rafters. Apparently, he'd

George (l) at Lone Tree with Leo, age 10

become somewhat of a troublemaker. He claimed that the teacher, a Miss Hjort, had lost control of the classroom and admits that he was part of the problem. It all came to a head one day when a fellow student, Mildred Gregg, accused him of swearing at the teacher. Word of his malfeasance got back to his father:

"The big showdown," Dad wrote, "came just before Christmas when all the parents were required to meet at the school with students and teacher. The meeting came to order and my dad was the first to jump up. I was slinking further and further down into my desk" when George shouted, "'Did my Russell ever swear at you?'" And to his utter astonishment Miss Hjort replied, "Why no, he never did." Thus my father was saved for another day, and his proclivity for cursing went unchecked. But the unfortunate Miss Hjort was dismissed over Christmas break and replaced with a firebrand who rode herd on the unruly boys, my father included.

George never remarried after Anna's death and instead placed the burden of running his household squarely on the shoulders of his eldest daughter, Adeline, then twelve years old. My father would all but cry when telling stories about Adeline and her lost childhood on the farm. George allowed her to continue her education up to the eighth grade, but after that he pulled her out of school permanently and installed her full-time in the role of housekeeper, a position she would fill for the next sixteen years.

Cooking (all of it done on a wood-burning stove) became her main concern, but she was also responsible for the laundry (done by hand); mending clothing (also by hand); cleaning house (four bedrooms, six males); butchering calves, hogs, and chickens; organizing and preparing the enormous spreads for threshing crews and hired help; raising chickens for the small egg revenue they produced; and going to town once a week with her miserly father to buy groceries and other sundries. As George was preoccupied by the outside appearance of his farm and its adjacent buildings, it was up to Adeline to furnish the interior of the large house. With the small inheritance she received from her mother's estate, along with the meager profits of her egg business, she bought the only furniture the house would ever know. She used this same source of income to treat the family to Christmas presents and also to buy the school supplies her younger siblings who were still in school needed.

Adeline was smart and savvy enough to affiliate herself with a local women's club where she gleaned the knowledge necessary to survive her plight. As indentured and hopeless as her life may have seemed, she did in fact attract the attention of a few suitors, one of whom saw in her the makings of a future farmwife. But in my father's recollection, Adeline spurned the awkward attempts of the young man, hiding in her bedroom every time he showed his sunburned face around the premises. My father believed Adeline had decided early-on that she would not replace one life of farm slavery with another. She never did marry. In 1938, then the last remaining child at home, she landed a job in town as an assistant cook at the hospital. Two years later she escaped South Dakota for good, heading to Los Angeles, where she found work as a live-in nurse to the ailing wife of R.C. Baker, the wealthy business partner in Howard Hughes's oil well ventures. In addition to her salary, Adeline was paid in company stock options, and after Mr. Baker's wife died, she became his personal secretary. By the time Adeline died in 2004 at age ninety-eight, she had amassed a small fortune. My father helped spread her ashes on the Pacific Ocean, off the coast of her home on Balboa Island, grieving the sister he'd loved like a mother.

He believed his older brother Leo's death might have been avoided given a timely diagnosis and treatment. Apparently George thought his eldest son's ailment was nothing more than laziness on the particular morning he complained of a stomach ache. He waited too long to send for a doctor, who unfortunately misdiagnosed the problem. By then it was too late; the burst appendix took nineteen-year-old Leo painfully, if not quickly.

Dad's few memories of Leo are touching. He was a young man of means, having "worked out" on neighboring farms where he was paid in livestock. When their mother died in 1920, Leo moved back home to help out, arriving in his own Model T Ford and with enough disposable income to ease the family's strained conditions. Sleeping arrangements were tight, the family members divided by two into the house's four upstairs bedrooms. For some reason, my father was chosen to sleep in the same bed as his father, an arrangement he would endure until his senior year of high school. Leo must have sensed his infant brother's despondency at having to share a bed with their gloomy father, so every once in awhile he offered young Russell a nickel to sleep in his bed, claiming his little feet helped keep the bed warm on cold winter nights. Once, while helping the older boys clean the barn, five-year-old Russell accidentally flung a shovelful of manure into Leo's face; to which Leo responded by chasing him all over the barnyard, making sure he never caught him. My father was too young to fully grasp the severity of Leo's death, at least until the funeral, when a cousin lifted him up to look in the coffin. There lay his beloved big brother, his wavy black hair combed and shining, his Sunday suit pressed, his eyes closed for eternity.

Leo's death only further widened the abyss created when their mother died. Apparently Leo had been never been afraid to stand up to George, especially when it came to questioning his authority in matters of the farm. After all, Leo had contributed twelve of his own cattle to the family herd and had also donated his Model T for the family good, the first car they owned. But now, with Leo's passing, George was free to rule the roost unchallenged. For the remainder of his time living at home, my father remembered evening dinner gatherings as morose affairs in which no one dared talk about anything.

One of the most telling examples of George's tyranny came the September morning in 1929 when Russell joined his older brothers Bill and Ernie in the barnyard to await instructions from their father. It was the first day of the new school year and all three boys were excited about their prospects. Bill, entering eleventh grade, had made it to the finals of the statewide spelling bee the year before and entertained hopes of winning it all this year. He was a good student and loved going to school. For Ernie, the coming school year would mean leaving the antiquity of the one-room schoolhouse at Shady Lawn School for the excitement of the big consolidated high school in Egan. In the case of my father, who was then about to begin eighth grade at Shady Lawn, the beginning of school once again marked the end of the loneliness and drudgery he'd first experienced when his mother died. All three boys couldn't be more excited.

They waited until George emerged from the barn to join them beside the John Deere tractor sitting in the middle of of the farmyard. For the first few moments no one spoke and the situation grew tense. As my father remembered:

"You could see that the deep silence was bothering the old codger, but it didn't last long. Out of the clear blue" he ordered Bill aboard the tractor with instructions to begin plowing the lower forty. He told Ernie to head to the barn where he would join him later for some nondescript chore. And then (to my father's utter relief) he released Russell to return to school for at least one more year of education.

"Can you possibly understand how something like this could happen?" my father exclaimed, incredulous. "Why wasn't it discussed weeks in advance, so that a young man on the verge of adulthood might begin making plans for his own future?" George's "total disregard for education" was but one more thing that infuriated my father. Then again, my father would be the only one of George's sons allowed to complete all four years of high school. But not without difficulties. In Dad's sophomore year the ag teacher, Mr. Halvorson, assigned the farm boys a project in animal husbandry. Each student was to procure a sow and keep records of its growth and eating habits over the course of a year, incorporating the practices taught in class. By then my father had become so defeated by George's silence and miserliness that he didn't even bother asking him for the required hog, knowing full well it would be useless. Instead, he fabricated a lie about his imaginary sow and produced a backlog of fake data he hoped the teacher would accept as legitimate. Imagine his horror and shame when Mr. Halvorson loaded up the school bus with his ag students one day and began driving to each boy's farm to see the results of their animal husbandry firsthand. What would my father say when the bus reached his farm? How could he possibly explain the false documentation without exposing himself as a liar and cheat? His prayers were answered when the weather turned winter-like and the teacher cancelled the last remaining inspection tour—the one to my father's farm. He was "one hundred percent sure that [Mr. Halvorson] knew I didn't have a project and was saving me from embarrassment."

By his own admission, Dad wasn't a popular high school student. He had three close friends—Luverne Jorgensen, George Becker, and Warren Kern—with whom he would escape during lunch hour to hang out at Irv Stombach's filling station for a "half-hour gab-fest." He later claimed he was "stupid" in subjects like chemistry and math, had no musical ability, and was never an athlete, although he did enjoy attending Egan Bluebird basketball games when his farm schedule allowed. English class, taught by Miss Ruth Petersen, was his favorite. Here's a small sampling of his poetic ability:

> *We look about, and in the halls,*
> *We see exhibits on the walls.*
> *It makes us think of the toilsome day*
> *We strived our best to receive an "A."*

Okay, he was no Keats, but his interest in letters did inspire him in his junior year to sign up for a recently added class called "Typewriting," for which the school had purchased ten new Woodstock typewriters. He picked it up easily and received the coveted "A" for his ability to type 60 words per minute, a skill that would serve him well later when he joined the Navy. When he graduated from high school in the spring of 1933 he had just turned seventeen, perhaps the youngest graduate in his class. He would spend the next four summers in harness to his father on the family farm, the last of his male siblings so enslaved.

My father insists he was fortunate to have grown up on a farm, especially because of the animals. For many years he got to ride a pony to school; he got to watch calves and shoats and chicks being born; got to hunt rabbits and pheasants and the occasional fox. He got to run barefoot all summer and knew the special thrill of receiving new shoes in the fall. In winter, he learned to skate on a frozen slough using double-bladed skates clamped to his shoes, and he got to slide down snow-covered pasture hills on sleds fashioned from discarded lumber. Because it was the Depression, everyone in his small world was in the same state of poverty and there was no such thing as "class separation." Everyone was poor, and no one seemed to notice.

Rural electrification brought light into the house after sunset, which created time to read the daily Sioux Falls *Argus Leader* from front to back, including box scores of baseball games from

around the country. The arrival of the radio in the 1920s proved
to be "the greatest thing that [ever] happened" in his home life.
Tuning in to WNAX Yankton, or KSOO Sioux Falls, brought
music, weather, and market reports, as well as entertainment—
shows like *Amos and Andy, The Air Adventures of Jimmie Allen,* and
The National Barn Dance on Saturday night. Dancing, in general,
was a popular diversion in those days, and somehow the Halter
boys were able to finagle their moody father into hosting winter
dances in the big living room of their farmhouse. A three-piece
combo supplied the music, with square dancing proving to be
the most popular. Around midnight the 32-volt battery bank (the
source of power before rural electrification) would begin to lose its
charge and the sweating couples broke for a meal while the gaso-
line-powered light plant was cranked up to recharge the batteries.

The home dances proved to be so successful that my father
and a pal named Russell Gregg saw a business opportunity. They
rented the second-story space above the Flandreau Pool Hall and
organized a Saturday night dance party. Farm kids from around
the county showed up, and after paying off the band at the end of
the night the two Russells realized a $4.00 profit each, enough for
my father to buy the same pair of white oxfords and shiny slacks
he would wear to dances around the county for the next few years.
In spite of the shyness he displayed in his younger days, he was
beginning by then to break out of his shell, with a keen interest in
the opposite sex. He began to consider life beyond the immediate
boundaries of his father's farm.

It's no surprise that by the time he had reached age twenty,
all of my father's siblings except his sister Adeline had long since
departed. By then, Adeline was working days in the Flandreau
hospital and, presumably, only returning home to sleep and to
prepare dinner for her father and brother. My dad must have
taken a cold hard look around the premises and considered his
prospects.

The year was 1936—the height of the Depression. Older
brothers Bill and Harold had escaped to farms of their own, re-

spectively as owner and hired man. Ernie had headed west with a buddy to seek his fortune in Washington State. By some sort of miracle, his sister Grace had cajoled their father into paying her way through college, later beginning a career as a school-teacher before finally marrying a farmer, my uncle Lester Jorgensen. And Adeline would be gone soon, too, breaking free of her father's imposed servitude and fleeing to California. My father, then three years out of high school and living the life of a bachelor farmer with only his taciturn father for company, must have looked around the deserted farmhouse and realized it was time for him to go, too. Why he chose to enlist in the Navy is not immediately clear. His friend from high school, Luverne "Jingles" Jorgensen, had enlisted three years earlier and while home on leave might have impressed my father with his newfound wealth by jingling the spare change in his pants pockets. And it's also possible that he was simply following the Egan Class of 1933's motto to "Sail On." Whatever the reason, the decision could not have come easily. He suffered homesickness to the extent that on those rare occasions when he did find himself away from home (seven nights in nearly 21 years), he "couldn't eat without gagging on the food."

But leave he did. As he would later explain in the memoir of his childhood:

"It was on October 24, 1936, that I finished milking four cows, took off my ragged work shirt, tore it up and said to myself, 'My life on the farm is over.'"

DAY THREE

9

U-Haul

I'm up early the next morning, awakened by the sound of car doors slamming in the parking lot below my hotel window, the harbinger of a busy day. I make coffee and fill a few pages in my journal, but by 7 a.m. I'm on the phone with Juan at the repair shop. Good news: he was able to start on the transmission over second shift last night and expects to have it completed by noon today, maybe sooner. He says he'll send a driver around to the hotel to pick me up when it's ready. I've always been a firm believer in omens, especially when good news early in the day sets the tone for what follows. And right now I'm buoyed by my prospects.

When I begin calling around to the local U-Haul franchises about renting a trailer, the news is not so good. I'm told I first have to purchase and install an adequate hitch to fit Dad's mini-van, all of which has to be scheduled in advance. Since when? It used to be you'd go down to a local service station where a guy in greasy overalls would bolt a temporary hitch to your bumper, hook up the trailer, and away you went. Now I'm directed to a national service center where a snooty operator informs me there's a twenty-four waiting period before the hitch can be installed.

"Twenty-four hours?" I say. "You've got to be kidding me."

"Sir, this call is being monitored for accuracy."

"But I need it today."

"That's out of the question. Would you like to make an appointment for tomorrow?"

"An appointment? What is this, a fucking dentist's office?"

"Sir, please."

So, with no other option, I make an appointment to have the hitch installed tomorrow, Thursday. I write down the address and phone number of the franchise where the work will be done, and immediately call the facility to get the manager on the line. I explain my situation and ask if there's any way he can get me in today. He doesn't say yes, but he does offer a ray of hope:

"Bring it in after lunch and I'll see what I can do."

My earlier feelings about the day are holding true. It's important to retain a positive attitude.

At eleven, Juan himself arrives with my father's car, and the mere sight of the minivan in the hotel breezeway fills me with confidence. I go ahead and check out of my room, convinced I'll be on the road by the end of the day. I throw my bag on the rear seat and climb in behind the wheel. As we pull out onto the freeway Juan gives me an impatient look. "Test drive, no?" he says. "Stoomp on it!" and I oblige. The transmission shifts smoothly through all six gears, decelerates without a hitch, starts and stops as it should at a half-dozen intersections, then glides quietly into the parking lot of Juan's repair shop. He gives the dashboard a couple of pats and turns to me with a questioning smile. "She ees good, no?"

I nod approvingly. "She is *muy bien,* mi amigo. Gracias."

Juan lifts an eyebrow. In perfect English he says, "You're welcome. And good luck. I hope for your father's sake the hoses and belts hold."

I do, too.

Back at Casa del Calor I pull the van into the carport where I find my father dozing in his auxiliary napping chair beside the steps. At the sound of the car door closing his eyes flutter open and are immediately filled with confusion.

"That looks like *my* car," he says.

"It *is* your car," I reply.

Without missing a beat, he says, "Who the hell said you could drive it?"

"I had to drive it home from the garage," I tell him. "The transmission needed some work."

"There's *nothing* wrong with the transmission!" he says angrily, and he begins walking around the car as if he's looking for any other damage I may have caused. Then he gives me an even angrier look and says, "Just what in the *hell* do you think you're doing?"

I smile and grab him by the shoulders, gently pushing and pulling him in a teasing manner. "Right now I'm looking for something to eat," I say. "Do you think the two of us could sneak inside and make ourselves a sandwich?"

This throws him off balance and he glances uncertainly at the door, then back at me, his co-conspirator. My question has diffused his anger. "Well, I don't know …" he says, "I suppose we could try."

But inside, our lunch is already on the table and Roseanne and the nursing aide, a different woman than yesterday, are in the bedroom packing boxes. The aide comes out to help Dad get settled with his lunch and I take her place in the bedroom. Roseanne shows me a box she has filled with Dad's personal papers—bank statements, letters, military records and the like. Another box is filled with old photo albums and framed pictures, things she's sure Dad will want in his new setting. There are other things on the dresser and in the top dresser drawer for which I'll have to evaluate and make a decision. Most of it is the junk he's accumulated in ninety-six years of living—old wristwatches, tie-clips, cigarette lighters, fingernail clippers, foreign coins, rosaries, medals, plastic combs, pocket knives, rings, etc. Roseanne shows me the overnight bag she's packed with underwear and socks, a few shirts, slacks, and the sweaters he likes to wear, and also a warm jacket. The rest of his wardrobe is up to me.

The walk-in closet is full of clothing he hasn't worn in years, most of it too big for his shrunken frame. I rifle through the hangers wondering what he'll need in a chillier climate, the rest of it to be donated to Goodwill. Most of it can be given away, I decide, but I make a mental note to pick up a couple of the wardrobe cartons I know they sell at most U-Haul franchises. When Roseanne and I emerge from the closet we discover my father standing in the bedroom doorway staring at his possessions strewn about the floor. There's a look of panic on his face.

"What the *hell* is going on in here?"

Roseanne sweeps him up in her arms and turns him toward the living room where she settles him into his recliner. But he's not so easily pacified this time: there's something terrible going on in his bedroom and he wants answers. He flails at Roseanne's arms as he cranes his head past her body for an unobstructed look.

"Goddammit, somebody better tell me just what the *hell* is going on here, and I mean *right now!*" He is furious.

Roseanne's voice is calm. "Russ," she says soothingly, "John is getting ready to take you home."

A bitter look clouds his face. "Goddamnit, I *am* home!" And to emphasize his point, he takes a back-handed swing at Roseanne, which she manages to dodge.

"That's not a very nice thing to do to your favorite girlfriend," she says, unruffled. I can tell she's been in these situations before, and I'm glad she's here. She pins my father's arms to the chair but he won't be controlled; he continues cursing and struggling to get free. Roseanne looks up and asks me to retrieve the small red shoebox from one of the packed boxes in the bedroom. It's full of photos, she explains, my father's favorites, and when I hand her the coverless box she pulls a few photos from the middle of the collection and kneels down beside him.

"Russ, whose little girl is this?" she asks, and she holds one of the photos before his face. In a heartbeat he is suddenly calm, like a screaming child into whose mouth a lollipop has been shoved. He takes the photo from her fingers and holds it up to the light, examining it like a rare document.

"Oh gosh, that's Marisa," he says sadly, now completely subdued. "Poor little Marisa." Marisa is my sister Betsey's eldest daughter who died of leukemia a few years ago.

"That's right," says Roseanne. And she then shows him another. "How about this one? Whose house is this?"

"Why, that's our house in Saint Louis Park!" he says, brightening. "Where did you get these?"

I sneak past and slip out the back door, thinking I should stay out of sight for awhile until he forgets I'm even here. In fact, maybe it's time I headed to the U-Haul store. I quietly get into his car, put the gearshift in neutral, then get out and push it down the short incline to the street before starting it. Safely around the corner I take a moment to stop and think. Dad's mood swings have thrown me off course, or at least given me pause. He's so much different from a year ago when I was here. We'd spent the day together talking, laughing, telling old stories, interacting with strangers. Not once did he lose his train of thought or have to be distracted or placated. And for sure he never lost his temper. It was on the basis of that trip that I'd been so encouraged to undertake this one. But now... What am I going to do if he has one of these outbursts while I'm driving? And what's he going to be like at night in a strange motel room, without Roseanne or one of the nurse's aides to comfort him? Maybe I've oversimplified the complexity of what I'm about to do, and in so-doing set myself up for something tragic.

What if in his agitation on the trip home he were to suddenly die?

☙

THERE ARE TWO customers ahead of me at the U-Haul franchise and only one technician working in the service bay. The manager promises he can get me in but says it might be three or three-thirty before he can get the hitch installed. I take a seat in the customer lounge and strike up a conversation with an affable older gentleman who informs me he's from Alaska but won't be returning there right away. First he has to deliver the "nice little Honda" he found for his granddaughter back in Minnesota. That's his pickup in the service bay getting the tow-hitch installed, he says, and he points through the window.

"You're headed to Minnesota?" I ask.

"Yessir," he says. "My daughter lives there."

I tell him about my impending trip with my father. "Could you recommend a good route?"

It turns out he's made the trip a million times, and when I retrieve my atlas from the car he outlines the best, most scenic way to go, including motels, restaurants, and service stations.

"It's pretty straightforward," he says, "just make sure you catch I-25 north out of Albuquerque." He insists it's the least boring route, one sure to keep my father's mind occupied. Such an insightful gentleman, and in a U-Haul waiting room, no less. Another good omen.

Things continue to go my way and the wait for the hitch isn't as long as the manager expected. It's barely three by the time the job is finished and I start back. Dad's minivan is now equipped with a Class 2 hitch, pulling a five foot by eight foot single axle trailer displaying colorful leaping dolphins along both flanks and a Florida license plate behind. The temperature is ninety-six, same as Dad's age. The freeway is beginning to fill with the afternoon rush hour, but not too badly; out here in Arizona they build their expressways wide and straight. Any thoughts I may have had about postponing our departure until tomorrow fade with every smooth shift of the transmission. My omens are riding high. Why break the string?

In truth, Phoenix and every aspect of my father's life here feels like a furnace, and for both his sake and mine, I want to put it all in the rearview mirror. Ready or not Dad, we're leaving today.

10

Fortress del Calor

The U-Haul, with its greater height and shorter wheelbase, is a bit more unwieldy than the boat trailer I'm used to towing back in Minnesota. It takes a little getting used to. In my first attempt at backing into Dad's narrow carport, I miss. When I pull ahead for a second try, I notice a small audience of neighbors who have gotten wind of my father's imminent departure. A half-dozen of them are standing across the street in the shade of a neighbor's carport. One of them, a grouchy-looking old fart in a wrinkled tee shirt and cut-offs, waves his arms as he pads down the driveway.

"Hold on there, Sonny Jim!" he shouts, as if I'm some sort of cart-boy in a grocery store parking lot. He saunters up to the side of the car and begins commenting on my trailering ability, or lack thereof. His sermon ends with a question: "Just what the hell you trying to do here?" And without waiting for an answer he bends low in the open window to introduce himself. "Thirty years city delivery down some of the skinniest damn alleys in all Chicago," he says, all the while tapping his chest with two nicotine-yellowed fingers, his tee shirt stained with a dollop of dried ketchup. Am I supposed to be impressed? Also, like the shuttle driver from yesterday, Chicago comes out "Chi-cay-go," and what with his white hair and heavy-framed glasses I'm reminded of another Windy City know-it-all, Harry Caray. Next thing I know, Harry Scary's got one of his meat hooks on the door handle and suggesting I "jump out so's I can show you how a pro does it."

I force a smile. "Thanks, but I think I got this."

Nope. He's already announced to his fan base across the street he's going to give me a lesson, and so, without warning, he flings the door open, nearly taking my arm with it. Whoa. I wasn't expecting this. I'm not combative by nature but at the same time I'm not about to be buffaloed by some codger who's probably taken a few union-busting baseball bats to his head. Gripping the wheel, I reach out with my free hand and jerk the door shut again, nearly catching his fingers in the jamb. Now it's his turn to be pissed-off, and he leans in through the window so close I can smell his lunch. But before he can get started I stick my finger an inch from his nose and issue a warning.

"Look pal," I tell him. "No offense, but you need to get over there with everyone else. I Don't. Need. Your, Help. *Understand?*"

My admonishment is perhaps a bit more forceful than I intended, but maybe not. I am, after all, on a mission. He weighs my directive for a moment as he sizes up my considerable bulk, perhaps noticing for the first time the veins protruding in my neck. Apparently he's having second thoughts. He retreats an inch or two and then mumbles something about sparing me "the pain and embarrassment," after which he lets go of the door and saunters back across the street, his flip-flops slapping the warm pavement. In the meantime I slide the trailer into the shade of the carport as if I've been doing this my whole life. Harry Scary stands amidst his minions and glowers. I lift my chin in defiance; it's entirely possible I missed my calling.

I unlatch the U-Haul's trailer gate. Inside are the two wardrobe cartons I rented from the store, and also a pile of furniture pads which were included in the deal. I start with the utility shed and begin dragging things out to the rear of the trailer. A few of the onlookers from across the street wander up into the narrow space between the trailer and the side of the house, one of them expressing sorrow at the realization my father is leaving. Another inquires about Eunice's whereabouts, even asking if she's still alive; no one's seen her in awhile. I answer as noncommittally as I can, informing them that yes, my father is headed to a memory-care facility in Wisconsin and that, in the short term, Eunice will remain behind in hospice care. I tell them I'm sorry it all has to happen so suddenly but that we, Dad's children, felt something needed to be done now before things got any worse.

One of the neighbors—a small, stout woman wearing an Iowa State *Cyclones* tee shirt—marches boldly up past the U-Haul and follows me back to the utility shed. She points to the three-wheeled bike partially obscured behind the headboard.

"That's my bike," she says. "I loaned it to Russ nearly five years ago."

I nod and smile reassuringly. "We won't be taking it with us. I'm sure you can have it back."

"I bought that bike for my husband at an estate sale in Sun City for a hundred dollars. And then he died a year later."

"I'm sorry to hear that," I tell her. "I'm sure my Dad would like you to have it back. Can you come by and pick it up after we leave? Otherwise I'll have to move the trailer to get it out of here."

"Russ told me he felt like an old woman riding it. Don used to say the same thing. Don was my husband. He ate himself into an early grave, that one. Put too much salt on everything, put salt on his *watermelon*, can you believe it? And he didn't get enough exercise. I thought the bike would be the solution. But men ... I tell you, they think they're going to live forever. He had a heart attack, you know. And it's no wonder; he put butter on everything. I told him a week before he died, I said, 'Don, you keep buttering your Pop Tarts like that and one of these days—"

"*You can get the bike tomorrow!*" I tell her loudly. Too loudly. Jesus Christ.

She looks at me and blinks. Then she says quietly, "I'll bet somebody else in the park could use it."

I smile contritely. "No doubt." I push past her with the headboard and then return for the bag of sheets and linens, all the while avoiding her eyes. She eventually takes the hint and wanders back across the street.

I keep working from the list prepared by Kath when she was here, but now I'm beginning to wonder if I'm going to have room for all of it. Better to quit worrying and keep working. When I've finished wrestling everything out of the shed that needs to go, I'm dripping wet. Dry heat, my ass. And I haven't even started on the inside stuff. The crowd across the street hasn't grown any smaller, and now I notice a few of them have brought lawn chairs, like it's a party. The word must be out. In the sky beyond the park, the sun is beginning its descent toward the White Tank Mountains. Don's widow yells, "Russ used to ride that bike around the park with his little Tuffy in the basket! We'll never forget that!" And a quiet murmur goes up from the rest of them. I smile and wave, wishing they'd all just leave.

I go inside to start on the other things. The aide is cleaning the kitchen and Roseanne is in checking on Eunice. Thankfully, my father is asleep in his recliner, the TV tuned to Dr Oz. I head quietly into his bedroom and test the weight of the dresser; too heavy. After removing the drawers I start dragging the cumbersome cabinet out into the hall and that's when he awakens. The sight of his drawer-less dresser confuses him and he erupts.

"Put that back!" he shouts. "Godammit, put it back!" To make his point, he grabs his cane and starts swinging it wildly in my direction.

But I'm out of range and manage to wrestle the dresser past him unscathed. I succeed in getting it out the back door, down the steps, and into the trailer. When I return for the drawers he's struggling to free himself from the recliner, but Roseanne's got him pinned which makes him even angrier. She eases off for a moment, and that's when he swings wildly with his cane and knocks the box of photos off the coffee table, scattering the entire collection across the floor.

"*Russell Halter!*" Roseanne shouts, and from the tone of her voice I can tell she's growing weary of this. She gives me an exasperated look, to which I can only shrug. My father, left unattended for this brief moment, and flush with success at dumping the photo box, takes another wild swing with the cane and this time finds the back of my knee, just below the cuff of my shorts. The blow is unexpected, not to mention sharp.

"*Godammit!*" I shout, more in surprise than pain. My out-burst startles everyone, but especially my father, who suddenly begins to cry.

"Go, *GO!*" Roseanne orders, pushing me into the bedroom and slamming the door behind me. I hear the muffled sounds of my father's sobbing, his voice pleading with Roseanne to make me go away. I stare at the back of the door, disgusted at myself for the chaos I've created. I need to figure out what it is I have to do to make this work. For the umpteenth time I ask myself why our father couldn't have been sedated for a three-hour flight to Minneapolis, to be awakened at the end and carted by a skycap to the main terminal. I also wonder why one of the many medical professionals in our family couldn't have come up with a better solution than the one I'm trying to implement, and more impor-tantly, why the hell isn't *one of them* here now instead of me. Right now I feel no more qualified to do this than the grouchy truck driver from across the street. Kath had made it sound so simple—a nice three-day trip home through the deserts and mountains, stopping at all the historical markers along the way, listening to books on tape, and talking talking talking. What a crock of shit. I decide it's time she needs to be included in this, to hear what I'm up against, to come up with a few more of her great ideas. I step over to the bedroom window for better reception. Kath answers on the first ring.

"It's not working," I tell her abruptly. "He's fighting me every inch of the way."

"You don't seem very happy about it!" she replies, trying to sound cheerful.

"He just *whacked* me with his fucking cane!" I shout. It feels good to vent, but it's not accomplishing anything. I pause to breathe. "Got any ideas?"

"Hmm ... Well, you could tell him this is all *my* fault, that I'm the one who instigated the whole thing and it's me he should be mad at, not you."

"Like that's going to help," I reply sharply. "If you were *here* it might, but you're not. I'm the one he sees dragging all his worldly possessions out the door, carrying on like I'm about to kidnap him. He insists he's not leaving. And he'd like to beat the shit out of me with his cane to prove it!"

I pause to take to take another breath. "What else you got?"

She can't think of anything, other than it wasn't supposed to be like this.

"Why don't you call him?" I suggest. "Then get Betsey and Mark to do the same. He needs to be reminded again that this is a family decision, that it's not just me. Will you call him?"

She says it's worth a try and I hang up and return to the situation at hand. I wade into the closet and begin sorting through his wardrobe. As I had earlier feared, even with the two containers I brought from the U-Haul, there's simply not enough room for everything. So I begin grabbing things indiscriminately, not really sure of what I'm doing. I mean, who am I to decide what he's going to be wearing for the rest of his life? He's always been pretty particular about the way he dresses and he won't be happy if the things I choose are outdated or the wrong size. But then I realize I'm overreacting because where he's going it won't matter. I start filling the boxes with what's at hand and call it good. Everything else can go to Goodwill.

Meanwhile, through the door I hear the phone ring and then my father's voice over the sound of the television. From his angry questioning I can tell it's Kath on the other end. It doesn't take long before he's completely frustrated and hangs up, the old landline receiver banging noisily into its cradle. That didn't take long.

I open the door and begin sliding the wardrobe cartons out into the hall, one by one. There's confusion on Dad's face as he recognizes the boxes as nothing belonging to him.

"What the hell are those?" he asks. "What have you got in there?"

Without even thinking, I reply, "Grapefruit in this one, oranges in the other."

His eyebrows lift in wonder as his mind wrestles with the

notion of all this citrus coming out of his bedroom. Then he nods approvingly. "Take every one you find!" he says. "The goddamn things fall off the trees and rot all over the yard. *Take 'em all!*"

"That's exactly what I was thinking," I tell him, and I turn to hide my smile.

On my next trip I sneak around through the other side of the kitchen and start collecting things from the formal dining room: the oil paintings, my mother's knick-knacks, my father's carved bird displays, and an old steamer trunk full of more family memorabilia. He doesn't see me with any of it, his attention once again tuned to the TV and the flexible young woman doing deep knee bends for Dr Oz's studio audience. At one point the phone rings again; I'm guessing it's my sister Betsey calling from Michigan. But with her he's even more abrupt than he was with Kath and he hangs up with barely a response. So much for that idea; I'm on my own here. I sneak back out through the kitchen with my final loads, the last of which is a plastic shopping bag containing the cribbage board and the half-can of Spanish peanuts from last night. Was that really last night?

Now the U-Haul is crammed full. I've managed to get everything from Kath's list inside. I roll the door shut and secure the hasp, wondering what I'm going to do next. It's going on four-thirty.

In the kitchen, the aide has packed a Styrofoam cooler with fruit cups, bottled water, homemade muffins, and sandwiches. Still stalling, I carry the cooler out and wedge it in behind the front seats. I check the location of my travel atlas, sun glasses, pencils, pens, and anything else I can think of. I check the connection on the GPS I've installed on the dash. Both my bag and Dad's suitcase are on the back seat, flanking a paper bag of CDs I brought from home and also the red shoebox of photos that Roseanne insists I keep handy. I pop the hood and check the oil again and also the coolant. I squeeze the upper coolant hose and notice it feels a little soft. Maybe I should have had Juan change the hoses after all. Too late now. I check the trailer hitch, test the tongue weight and try the emergency lights. I debate changing out of my damp shirt, notice the people across the street watching my every move, and decide against it. I kick the tires again, go to pop the hood and realize I've already checked everything under there. The sun continues its descent toward the White Tank Mountains.

What if he flat-out refuses to go? Will I have to drag him out of the trailer kicking and screaming? What would the neighbors think of that? I look across the street; they're still watching me. I wave and head back inside.

Roseanne sits at the kitchen table with an uncertain look on her face. She looks up at me and says, "I wonder if it might be better if you stayed over one more night?"

"No way," I reply, shaking my head. "Everything's loaded."

She scowls. "Well, I hate to tell you this, but I have to leave in twenty minutes to pick up my brother at the airport. I thought you'd be gone by now. It really wouldn't hurt if you stayed one more night."

"You're *leaving*?" I say in disbelief. I certainly wasn't planning on this. This only compounds the problem; I'll never be able to get Dad in the car by myself. She needs to be here to comfort him. I give her a withering look.

"We'll have to hurry then," I tell her, and without waiting for a response I slip past her into the living room. Dad is still in his recliner, focused on the TV. I kneel down in front of him and he cranes his neck for a better view of Dr Oz over my shoulder.

"Dad, it's time to go," I say quietly.

He turns his head slightly to look at me, his eyelids veiled and his lower lip pushed forward in defiance. "Nope," he says abruptly, and then he closes his eyes as if to make me disappear. But then he has a second thought and opens them again to speak, his words laced with scorn. "I'm sorry you had to come all this way to sweat and carry my things out to the car, but I'm not going anywhere and that's all there is to it, buster." He closes his eyes again to assure me he's said all he's going to say.

"Dad ..." I begin again, but before I can say another word, he erupts.

"You goddamn asshole! *Get the hell out of my house!*"

I feel the presence of Roseanne behind me, and then her voice. "Russ! Please don't talk to your son like that!"

He looks up her, his eyes livid. "I'll bet you're in on this, too!" he shouts, his voice breaking. "Every one of you sunzabitches can kiss my ass!"

I take his arm. "Dad, calm down. We've been talking about this for a month now, me and Kath and Mark. You're in bad shape here. Don't you remember talking to us about it?"

"I am not going anywhere with you and that's final!"

Roseanne bends to my ear. "Leave him alone," she says quietly. "He's upset and it's only going to get worse if you keep talking. We'll have to think of something else."

"*We?*" I reply. "I thought you were leaving."

"In fifteen minutes. I can give you that."

"Great, Roseanne. Wonderful."

With no idea of what to do next, I get up and go back outside to the carport to call Kath. She picks up on the first ring again but before I can say anything she tells me she tried calling Mark but couldn't reach him. "Did Betsey call?" she asks.

"It doesn't matter," I tell her. "It's not working. He refuses to leave."

"Well, shoot ..."

"And now Roseanne just informed me she has to leave in fifteen minutes to pick up her brother at the airport, or some god damn thing."

Silence on the other end of the line.

"You still there?" I ask.

"Yes ..." she says uncertainly.

I tell her about the truck driver from Chicago and the lady from Iowa and how they're all congregating like vultures out in the street for one last look at Dad. But in mentioning the neighbors I suddenly remember something Kath told me last week.

"Hey, didn't you tell me you met one of Dad's neighbors

when you were here? A retired rancher or something like that? Didn't he offer his help if you needed it?"

She remembers. "Yes! Cliff … great guy. And yes, he did say I could call him if we needed help."

"Well, we definitely need help," I say. "Maybe you could get Cliff on the line and see if he's willing to come over and talk to Dad. Tell him it's an emergency. Tell him I would really appreciate it if he could come like… *right now*."

Kath says she'll give it a try. What have we got to lose? I have run out of options.

I wander around the carport for a few more minutes watching the sun inch closer and closer to the horizon, my departure time decreasing by the minute. But then across the street I hear a friendly exchange of greetings as someone approaches from the other end of the block. It's a guy in a cowboy hat walking like John Wayne down the streets of Laredo. He's heading for the front porch of Dad's house. It's Cliff. It's got to be Cliff.

I hurry inside to meet him at the door.

11

ESCAPE

It *is* Cliff. He steps in through the front door and greets me with a solemn "Howdy-do" before removing his Stetson and glancing around the room. He's dressed in a long-sleeved western shirt and blue jeans secured with a belt boasting a big shiny buckle. But it's the ugly, fresh-looking scar to the right of his widow's peak that sets him apart.

"Melanoma," he says matter-of-factly. "Guy my age should know better, wouldn't you think?" His voice is a slow drawl, reminiscent of a TV cowboy but at the same time entirely reassuring. I feel like the cavalry has arrived, that everything is going to be okay. Cliff is here.

"Kathy has explained the situation," Cliff informs me, and without wasting any time he walks into the living room and pulls up a straight-backed chair beside my father. Dad eyes him uncertainly, his expression one of, *What the hell are you doing here?* Both men are hard of hearing and right away Cliff lets Dad know he's without the benefit of his hearing-aids. The shouting commences.

"Russ, I hear you're headed back to Minnesota!" Cliff begins.

"Like hell I am!" Dad replies. He shakes his head defiantly.

Cliff glances up at me then nudges his chair a little closer to Dad, the two of them sitting at an angle to each other, ear to ear. In a softer voice he says, "Russ, after my wife died, the kids were concerned about me living alone down here. I tried to assure them I was okay, told them I'd be fine. I told the eldest boy, I said, 'Son, the day comes you think I can't take care of myself anymore, why you just come fetch me up and I'll go quietly. I'll trust your judgment.'"

Cliff glances up at me again, looks over at Roseanne, then

leans forward into Dad, his voice quieter and tinged with sympathy. "Now Russ, your son John here, he don't mean you no harm. Hell, Russ, he's just trying to do what's best for you. Maybe you should listen to what he has to say."

My father blinks a couple of times, works his lower lip, his indignation growing but so far held in check. He looks up at me, over at Roseanne, then returns his attention to Cliff whom he regards thoughtfully. Finally, he nods.

"So you're in on this, too," he says, quietly. "You sonofabitch. And all this time I thought you were my friend. Well, you can go straight to hell with the rest of them." And with this he fumbles for his cane as if he's going to use it on Cliff, his best friend no less. Cliff leans back and holds up his large hands in mock self-defense, a sad smile on his face. Then he gently lays a hand on my father's shoulder as he slowly rises up out of the chair. He reaches for the Stetson on the coffee table, turns it over a couple of times in his hands and gives me a mournful look across the room.

"Well, John," he says, "I tried, but your old dad here is tougher'n rusted barbwire, 'bout twice as stubborn, too. You got your work cut out for you, I'm afraid." He puts his hand again on Dad's shoulder, gives it a gentle squeeze. "I don't blame you, Russ," he says. "It'd scare the shit outta anybody."

I follow him to the front door where he turns to face me, his lips pursed. "Anyhoo," he says, "good luck. I'd be obliged if you'd give me a call once the two of you make it back home. That is, if'n you do …"

And with this he nods and turns again to the door. And then he's gone.

I stare after him, the door pulled firmly shut in his wake, like a shop door closed at the end of the workday. The desert sun has blistered the finish off the door's cheap veneer, the varnish peeled and flaky. The faux brass doorknob is weathered too, its surface tarnished gray from the sweat of too many hands. Dr Oz's mellifluous voice drones in the background—something about dry scalp and the miracle shampoo which moisturizes follicles. The studio audience applauds. I hear Roseanne saying something to the aide, who leaves and then comes through ferrying a plastic bedpan from Eunice's bedroom. Then I notice Roseanne staring at the screen on her phone, pausing to glance at her watch. My father sits in his recliner with his eyes squeezed shut, but I can tell he's awake.

If'n you do…

Cliff's parting words hang in the air like a challenge, like the disintegrating tape at the beginning of a *Mission Impossible* episode—"If you decide to take this mission, Mr. Phelps…"

So be it. I quietly walk over and slide the cane from my father's unsuspecting grip, then lower myself into the chair vacated by Cliff. His eyes slowly open. I smile to reassure him, my eyes never wavering from his. Then I say,

"I'm sorry Dad, but we're running out of time here. C'mon, get up."

Roseanne looks up from her phone, her mouth agape. "Oh, John … it's too late. I think you've waited too long. Let's everybody get a good night's sleep tonight and we'll try again in the morning."

Her interruption annoys me. "Aren't you on your way to the airport?"

She scowls, gives me a troubled look. I tell her, "It's not going to be any better in the morning, or the day after that, or even a week from now. We're leaving today."

I take my father's hands in mine and gently pull. "C'mon, Dad, time to go."

He pulls violently away, slapping at my hands and cursing. "Godammit! Why won't you leave me alone? *I* didn't ask you to come out here to do this. Who told you to do this? This is none of your God damn *business!*"

I stare at him. "None of my business? *None of my business, you say?* Really, Dad? Do you think I'm enjoying this?"

I hear myself shouting but I can't help it. I'm surprised by the hitch in my voice and I suddenly realize I'm on the verge of losing it, that if I don't get him in the car in the next few minutes, I'm never going to get him in it. Before he can answer I hear my voice again:

"Do you think I've enjoyed listening to your phone calls every Sunday night for the past twenty years, listening to you cry about your drunk wife, or how she's scared off all your old friends?" I wave toward the back door. "They're all out there right now, all your old friends waiting to say goodbye. They all remember how you used to be before you married Eunice, how you used to be when Mom was still alive. How you …"

I stop. This isn't right. None of this is making any sense to him, especially with the way I'm shouting. This is just me further confusing him and making a bad situation worse. I'm ranting at someone who's fixated on the notion that he's required by God and his Catholic faith to stay with his wife until the end. And also by the fact that she completely controls him.

Controls him?

Wait …

What if she left him?

Left him? Or allowed *him* to leave her?

"Dad?" I say, and this time I make myself speak calmly, for I feel I'm onto something, something that just might work. He notices the change and regards me with an inquisitive look, as if he's at least willing to listen. This is good, his expression implies. Let's begin again.

"Dad, "I say, "what if Eunice gave you permission to leave? I mean, what if Eunice agreed that the situation here is hopeless and that you'd be better off back home near your family? What if she said it was okay for you to go?"

Now his eyes turn sad and he looks at me as if he's about to cry. I can tell he's as tired of this as I am, that I've worn him out with my incessant demands. It's been an extremely long and tiring afternoon and now it looks as though he'd like to get it over with as much as I would. His expression is almost one of defeat or at least tired resignation.

"Would you go?" I ask him again.

His eyes move from me to Roseanne, then back to me. Finally he sighs and says, "I suppose so."

In the next instant I hear movement behind me and I look up to see Roseanne turning as she flees from the room. In the next moment I hear her voice in the bedroom imploring Eunice to listen to what she has to say. "*He needs to go home to his family,*" she's shouting. "*You need to give him your permission.*"

I don't hear Eunice's response but suddenly Roseanne reappears above us, pulling Dad from the chair and leading him into the bedroom. Things have changed dramatically and now there's a different vibe in the room. I stand up, uncertain of my role. Dad shuffles along in Roseanne's grasp, his eyebrows arched, his forehead weary. I follow behind, with the day nurse behind me and then the night nurse, Luna, who has just arrived, taking up the rear. We all file into Eunice's darkened bedroom and stand just inside the door as my father shuffles over and kneels down beside the bed. Eunice's eyes are alert as they dart around the room taking in the unexpected crowd of visitors. She's never had so many people in her room. But it's me she regards fiercely, as if she'd like to remind me one more time that she is not drunk.

Now Dad takes her withered hand between his hands and begins caressing it, at the same time speaking very softly, murmuring something about how much he truly doesn't want to leave her. Eunice listens impassively, her skin waxen, her eyes clouding over again as if she's given up. But apparently she's still listening, for when Dad is finished she mutters something none of us can hear, something not even Dad can hear. He tilts his head and nearly pushes his face into the pillow beside her ear.

"What did you say, Eunie?" comes his gentle query. "I didn't hear you, Eunie."

And then an explosion: "*I SAID GO HOME, GOT DAMMIT!*"

Her words pierce the room like a missile strike. My father recoils in shock.

"Do you mean that, Eunie? Do you really want me to go?"

"YES!" she roars again, her eyes now fierce. "*Go back to Minnesota!*"

He stares at her in disbelief, his shoulders beginning to shake, his voice suddenly an anguished sob. He's crying. Roseanne and I move forward to help him to his feet, and he stands before her completely bewildered. For the third time in his life he's to lose the woman he loved. And now I realize I'm crying too, not so much over my father's plight but more because Eunice has at long last released him from her toxic grip. Mine are tears of elation mixed with relief. It's been an emotional day, but now, thanks to Eunice, we can finally go home. With tears brimming in my eyes I bend forward to kiss her cold forehead. She regards me with a look of suspicion, perhaps wondering if she's made a grave mistake.

"Thank you, Eunice," is all I can muster. And then as an afterthought I say, "Goodbye."

The aides take Dad by the arms and begin leading him from the bedroom. I hurry ahead to clear the way, grabbing his cane from the TV tray, looking around for anything else I may have missed. Roseanne pushes one of the aides aside and is cooing in my father's ear, going on about how much she's going to miss him, how she'll call him every day. "Mark's farm will be such a wonderful place to visit this time of year," she tells him. "And the cows, Russ, oh the cows will be so happy to see you!" But my father doesn't seem to be listening. He appears to be in a trance.

We make our way into the kitchen moving as slowly as a funeral procession, Dad morose, Roseanne continuing with her babble in his ear, the aides shuffling along like pallbearers. I'm making for the back door, already in travel mode, my thoughts beginning to focus on how far we might get tonight before darkness sets in, where we might stop to eat, the availability of a motel rooms, etc. Suddenly everything comes to an abrupt halt by an urgent pounding at the back door:

BANG BANG BANG!

Everything stops. Who could this possibly be? The aides look

at each other in confusion. My father looks at Roseanne. Roseanne looks at me. My first impulse is that something has gone
terribly wrong. Something I've overlooked is about to throw a
giant wrench into my plans; someone across the street has noticed
gas dripping from beneath Dad's car, say, or the manager is here
demanding a year's rent for the vacated property. Maybe Harry
Scary is standing out there with a baseball bat ready to teach me
a lesson. I brace myself for the worst, my senses on full alert, and
then I slowly push the door open.

At the bottom of the stairs stands the woman from Iowa—
Don's widow. She's got a worried look on her face. She nervously
clears her throat, then begins: "I just talked to my daughter in
Cedar Rapids," she says. "She told me I need to come over here
right now and get the three-wheeler before you leave." She fidgets
with the hem of her tee-shirt. "I never told your dad he could
keep it. When I loaned it to him, I said 'Russ, this is just—'"

Roseanne shoots past me like she's just won the meat raffle at
the local muni, hovering above the poor woman like she's about
to claw her eyes out. "*Can't you see we're in the middle of something
here?*" she hisses, her cheeks flushed with color. "You can get your
stupid bike tomorrow!" Wide-eyed and speechless, Don's widow
stumbles backward a few steps then scurries away down the car
port. Dad stares after her, his eyes wide. I manage to help him
down the stairs and turn him toward the waiting car. He seems
startled by the sight of the U-Haul trailer coupled to his minivan, notices the crowd of people in the street, looks at me, looks
at Roseanne, mutters something to himself then turns the other
way. He jerks his arm free of mine and starts shuffling off in the
direction of the shed. "Dad," I say quietly. "You're heading the
wrong way."

No he isn't; he has something else in mind. I follow behind
as he makes his way to the open door of his beloved shed. He
stands in the doorway, taking it all in—the bare workbench, the
empty shelves, the dim corner where his radio once sat, all of it
gone. His voice is quiet, as if he's talking only to himself. "I spent

a lot of good afternoons out here," he says. He sighs and glances up at me, his expression dour. He takes one more look around, shakes his head and mutters, "Shit ..." And with this, I turn him again for the car.

It's not fair. In my haste to get him out of here I'm afraid I've overlooked his stake in all of this. In addition to everything else he's had to endure today—the abrupt upheaval of his life, the betrayal of his closest friend Cliff, the coerced farewell of a dying wife—he's also leaving behind the home in which he's lived and loved for the past forty years. All the memories of the early years with my mother; all those friends now gone or going; the outings they once shared, the parties, the dances, the . . . life, none of which he'll ever know again. To whatever degree of cognizance his mind is capable of right now, he must realize that this part of his life is finally over, finished. He must also think that this is all my doing, and that I have somehow tricked him into leaving. His own son betraying him. I wish it didn't have to be this way. I wish I had the power to let him die right now, to save him the agony of what lies ahead—none of which is going to be pleasant. I wish, I wish, I wish ...

Roseanne waits near the open car door and gives him an extended hug as she settles him into his seat, telling him one last time how much she's going to miss him. Dad is cursing and I can tell he's growing angry about the whole turn of events, now that everything is happening at once. Roseanne helps him with his seatbelt, straightens his sweater, kisses him on the lips. The neighbors are milling about in the street, and from their expressions I can't tell if they're sad to see him go, or wondering when the estate sale will begin. I climb in on my side, buckle my seat belt, and start the engine. He looks over at me. "What in the hell are we doing?" he says mournfully. "God *dammit,* anyway."

I ease the car into gear and pull ahead, the U-haul following heavily behind. As we descend the driveway the neighbors stoop and gaze in through the open windows, bidding Dad goodbye. Their sympathy is real, I decide, their emotions sincere. I slow to a crawl, nearly stopping, giving Dad ample opportunity to say his own goodbyes in return. But he doesn't seem to want to. He smiles at some of them, waves reluctantly at others, hides his tears beneath his trembling hand.

"Can't you go any faster?" he mumbles.

We clear the driveway, the trailer chains rattling over the dip in the gutter. The neighbors close in. "Goodbye, Russ, goodbye!" I don't dare look at any of them, my role in this too obvious. Dad is either humming or wailing, making a noise I've never heard before.

"Aren't you going to say anything?" I inquire. But now I can plainly see he's incapable of talking, that he's crying, overcome with grief.

"Goodbye goodbye you sunzabitches!" he suddenly blurts, his voice breaking. And with this he gives a final wave of his hand as we turn into the street and leave all of it behind.

By the time we reach the iron security gate the tears have stopped and he's seething. I absorb the worst of it as the gate opens dreadfully slow, every clank of the drive sprocket seeming to punctuate his words. He demands to know who gave me permission to drive his car. He insists that if he had a gun right now he would shoot me, but then quickly changes it to no, he would shoot himself. He pleads for me to turn around, "*Can we please turn around?*" to which I grit my teeth and stare straight ahead as the gate finally opens. "GOD *DAMN* YOU!" he cries in utter despair, his worst fear now realized as we clear the gate and leave the womb of Casa del Calor.

I turn north onto 91st Avenue and merge into the rush hour traffic racing past. The trailer feels a little tongue heavy, and did something just scrape as we turned the corner? The transmission shifts quietly through its paces but it's still cool and the real test will come later when we start climbing into the higher elevations. Too many things to worry about, I decide, so best not worry about any of them, except the most important one sitting beside me. He's removed his glasses and is wiping the tears from his eyes, his face a mask of desolation. I reach beneath my seat and extract the Rand/McNally road atlas stashed there, the page open to Arizona. I pass it across to my father and drop it in his lap.

"What's this?" he says angrily.

"How do we get to Flagstaff from here?" I reply.

"Flagstaff? How the hell do I know?"

"Well, you better know," I tell him. "You're the navigator on this trip."

He stares at me, confused. "I am?" he says, and suddenly the look of anger on his face is displaced by one of wonder.

"Yes, you are," I reply, and I nod toward the atlas. "Now, how do we get to Flagstaff?"

"Well, let's see," he says, and the weight of this unexpected promotion registers on his face as if he's just been handed night orders in the Sea of Japan. He licks his thumb and tips the page toward the afternoon sun.

"Flagstaff … here it is!"

12

ON THE ROAD

If I thought the worst of it was over once I got my father in the car, I overestimated my capabilities. With some 1,800 miles and thirty hours of driving ahead of us, the real challenge has just begun. When I came out for his birthday a year earlier, he had been lucid and attentive, and I got the impression that he had enjoyed my company, and also enjoyed himself. I had been imagining this much longer trip as an opportunity to expand upon that foundation, a chance to reexamine the past and consider together whatever remained of the future, while also having a little fun. Those dreams have vanished.

Having spent a stressful couple of days getting ready to go and coaxing Dad to cooperate, I realize my new challenge will be to keep his mind occupied. Making him the trip navigator was an act of spontaneous desperation, but it worked. Dad definitely needs to be distracted, to keep his mind focused on the task at hand and nothing else. He now truly believes it's up to him to get us to Flagstaff.

The change in his demeanor begins immediately. Even though our late departure from Phoenix has put us in the middle of the rush hour traffic, it is a huge relief to be underway at last. With Dad following our progress on the map, we crawl along the Agua Fria Expressway at a snail's pace. I strive to keep him focused.

"What exit is this?" I call out as we approach a ramp.

"Bell Road," he responds. "Keep going."

A little later: "What's this one? And how far to I-17?"

"This is 51st Avenue. Seventeen is still another mile or so."

"Ok good," I tell him. "Keep checking them off until we turn north."

He glances over as if to make sure it's still me sitting next to him and not some junior officer on the bridge of an aircraft carrier. "Aye aye," he says. And from the tone of his voice I can tell he's enjoying this.

A few minutes later he calls out, "This is it, I-17 north." I take the exit, round the cloverleaf, and merge into the traffic headed north. The U-Haul tows flawlessly, but even here the traffic is congested and I'm not able to bring her up to speed. It's another ten miles or so before things finally begin to loosen up. I accelerate to seventy, and when I'm satisfied everything is performing as it should, I begin looking for an exit ramp; I need to call my sister.

We exit on a ramp marked "Carefree Highway" and head for a strip mall along a frontage road. I feel a little giddy due to my success and begin singing the old Gordon Lightfoot standard: *Carefree Highway! Let me slip away, slip away on you.*

Dad looks up from his map with a worried expression. "Is this Flagstaff?"

"Not yet," I reply. "I'm going to stop here at this gas station for a cup of coffee and whatever you might need. What can I get you—a cup of decaf, candy, cigarettes? How about a cigar, a White Owl, perhaps?" At the mention of the White Owl he glances over at me and smiles, remembering an old navy joke he used to tell. His smile assures me he's okay. But there *is* something he'd like.

"Grab me a newspaper," he says. "Seems like I never got around to reading it today."

"One newspaper, yessir," I tell him, and I then I park and head for the convenience store. Because of the trailer, I've parked at the outer limits of the parking lot, a fair distance from the door. Walking across the asphalt I call Kath whom I haven't talked to since well before our departure. No doubt she's wondering what's going on. She answers on the first ring.

"Well, has anything changed?" she begins. There's the sound

of defeat in her voice, not to mention guilt. She must think we're still at Dad's.

"Just one," I tell her, barely able to control my glee. "We're on the road!"

"Oh my God!" she shouts, her voice now jubilant. She can't believe it.

While getting my things inside the store, I fill her in on the events of the afternoon, most of it focusing on the tearful good-bye at Eunice's bedside. Kath wonders how Dad is taking it now that we're on the road, and I tell her about his navigator duties, finishing with, "So far, so good." Unfortunately I have to cut the conversation short by reminding her I don't dare leave him alone for very long. I pay for my purchases, cupping the phone to my shoulder. "I'll call you tonight," I tell her, signing off, and then I'm out the door, hurrying across the parking lot to the car. As I feared, I have been gone too long; Dad's expression as I climb in the car is one of indignation mixed with fear.

"Godammit!" he curses. "Where the *hell* have you been?"

"Getting your paper," I assure him, and I drop the latest edition of the *Arizona Republic* in his lap. He stares at it, bewildered. He's in need of another job. "Take a look," I tell him. "Tell me if the Twins won last night."

"How the hell would I know?"

I nod at the paper. "Check the box scores. Tell me who was pitching."

I start the car and begin maneuvering out of the parking lot, concentrating on the signs that will lead us back to I-17 North. Dad, meanwhile, makes a holy mess of the newsprint trying to find the sports page. But he finally does and announces, "They lost. Somebody named Santana was pitching. Never heard of him." And then to my great relief he folds the section into a manageable size and raises it to his face, poring over every inch of the box scores. FUBAR avoided, we roll on.

Beyond the exit for New River the road begins to climb. I set the cruise control at sixty-five, as fast as I dare go until I'm sure the transmission can handle the steady climb. The engine purrs, the trailer continues to tow easily, and my fears about tongue weight begin to subside. The traffic is moderate but steady, with everything behind us coming up to pass. The mountain range to the east glows orange in the long rays of the afternoon sun, which angle through my side of the car and provide adequate light for Dad's to read by. I tune the radio to a quiet station—a little background music in our otherwise quiet sanctum. We climb through a few mountain passes and cruise past the exits for Prescott, Camp Verde, and the Montezuma Monument. Near the exit for Cornville, I spot a herd of cattle grazing along the highway, and I lower my window to do my best cow impersonation, mooing (or "bawling") the way Dad taught me when I was a kid. To do it right, the initial moan needs to come from the back of the throat, starting low but then building into a deep two-tone bellow delivered with the jaw thrust forward and accentuated, if possible, through cupped hands. Steering with my knees, I perform it to perfection, and Dad looks up from his paper. Taking my cue, he joins in, the two of us cupping our hands over our mouths and mooing out of both sides of the car. This gets us both laughing between bellows, and for just a moment it's almost like fifty years ago, except that now we're sitting on opposite sides of the car. The miles slip past easily and I can't help but think, *this is just how I imagined it would be.* We just needed to get on the road, away from Eunice.

Sometime later Dad finishes the paper and sits studying the atlas for our next route change, I-40 East to Winslow. He looks up and stares out the window with a worried expression on his face. We're still a good forty miles from the Flagstaff exchange but he stares as if the exit sign is fast approaching, as if he's afraid we might miss it. Up until now he's been well behaved and I don't dare lose him. Out of the blue, I ask him, "When was the last time you were in Flagstaff?"

The question confuses him. "Flagstaff? Can't say for sure."

"Really? You and Mom never drove up here for the day?"

Then he remembers something, apparently something amusing judging from the smile creeping over his face. "Oh Christ ..." he replies, and after a moment he gives me a sidelong glance.

"What's that supposed to mean?" I say. "Did something happen here once to you and Mom?"

"Not your mother, no," he says smiling. But he looks ahead at the road and offers nothing more.

"So, what are you smiling about?"

"Am I smiling?"

"Yes! Tell me!"

"Oh hell, I guess its water under the bridge now," he finally admits. He glances over at me. "Do you remember that old gal from North Dakota, the one I used to step out with? The one always pushing those goddamn vitamins?"

"Ava?" I say. "I sure do! She's the woman you *should* have married."

"Like hell," he says, chuckling to himself. "Anyway, she and I used to meet up here about once a month."

We ride along in silence for a few moments. "Is that it?" I ask

He looks embarrassed, but finally he says, "Well ... we'd meet up here after passing secret messages to each other."

"*Secret messages?*"

He smiles; the memory is plainly a happy one. "About once a month I'd find a note in my mail slot at the Rec Center, a note with a date and a motel room number written on it. If I agreed, I'd dial her phone number and let it ring once before hanging up."

"What were you agreeing to?" I ask. I'm surprised he's even telling me this.

"Christ almighty, I was agreeing to *meet* her up here in Flagstaff!" he shouts. "Once that particular date rolled around, we'd both drive up here separately and meet at the motel room she'd rented for the night."

"You drove up *separately?*"

"She didn't want anybody in the park talking about us behind her back."

"Talking about *what?*" I cry. "What exactly *were* you doing?"

"Well, we weren't pitching horseshoes!" he says excitedly. "I can guarantee you that!"

"You were *shacking up*!" I crow, using one of his expressions.

"By God, I guess we were!" he says, laughing. He's really enjoying this.

Up ahead, another mileage sign appears: Flagstaff 25, it reads. I tell him, "If you'd like, we can stop in Flagstaff for the night. We could even get the same motel room you and Ava used for your shack-jobs. Give me a few minutes to check-in, and then later you could call the room, let it ring once—"

"You shut up!" he shouts. "Knock it off!"

I shake my head. "You really should have married her."

"Bullshit," he replies. "She ruined any chance of that with those goddamn vitamins. The last thing I needed was some old broad filling me full of vitamins."

We ride along in silence again. But not for long. I'm beginning to understand that it helps to keep him talking, to keep his mind occupied. There's any number of subjects I might bring up but since he's the one who brought up Ava, I decide to stay with women. From his stories of the war, I know he had a few girlfriends in his salad days, one in particular. "Tell me about Twyla."

His head jerks around. "Twyla? Why would you ask me about her?"

Because Twyla was one of the main characters in his stories of the war, her exotic name lending a certain allure to the tale. Just before the war began, he had driven Twyla from Los Angeles to her home in Kansas, including a few stops along the way. I hoped the mere mention of her name might launch a story, another subject to keep him talking.

"Shack job," I reply. "Don't try to bullshit me."

His mouth drops open but then he starts laughing again.

"God damn you!" he shouts. "Pay attention to your driving!"

"Then tell me about Twyla!" I shout right back. "Start at the beginning."

13

ANCHORS AWEIGH

The attic in our home on Pleasant Avenue was accessed through a closet in my sisters' bedroom. The entrance had been built above the house's main staircase and was rather unusual. A narrow hallway contained hooks where my sisters hung their everyday clothing, above which ran a half-wall ledge ascending to the attic door. The attic's usable space consisted of wooden planking resting on rafters filled with a thick blanket of rock-wool insulation that muffled the acoustics and gave the space a secretive air, except when it rained and the patter on the roof became sensual, almost hypnotic. The light from two bare bulbs held in porcelain fixtures extended to the farthest recesses of the attic, including distant corners where my mother had pushed boxes containing things that might never be seen again—her wedding dress, Dad's

Seaman Apprentice, 1936

old uniforms, newspaper clippings, old Christmas cards, etc. On the hip wall directly across from the door, my father had screwed a section of plywood and fashioned a small shrine to his Navy career. An array of photos showcased the men and ships he had served with, most of them from World War II. He is easily identified in the long black and white photo from boot camp, Company 30, taken in December 1936 at the Great Lakes Training

Center in Chicago. Dad is kneeling far left in the front row, his left leg cocked at an awkward angle compared to those of the other recruits around him. A later photo reveals a much more seasoned sailor wearing faded dungarees, this time squatting with his division shipmates in front of a dive bomber on the flight deck of an aircraft carrier, somewhere in the South Pacific. Another photo of the same ship, the USS *Langley*, shows it at the mercy of a hurricane, with two sailors warily eyeing an enormous wave about to roll the ship on its beam ends. I grew up believing one of the men in the photo was my father, only to learn later it wasn't, even though he'd been aboard the ship at the time. The remaining photos were of the other ships he served on, all their names as familiar to me as the make and model of the cars he drove in those days—*Lexington, Leedstown, Tuscaloosa.* He was very proud of his time in the Navy, especially those years spent at sea.

In March of 1937, straight out of boot camp, he was ordered aboard the aircraft carrier *Lexington,* then in dry-dock at Bremerton, Washington. "It was mind-boggling to see such a huge ship out of the water," he wrote. But his amazement was short-lived, as he, along with the other thirty members of his boot camp company so assigned, were put to work chipping rust, swabbing decks, polishing brass and cleaning heads, the marine toilets used daily by a crew of over two thousand bean-eating swabbies. Just imagine the filth. It was mind-numbing work to which there seemed to be no end. At times he thought of jumping ship—deserting. A couple of fellow recruits had already done so. When they were apprehended and sent to prison, he changed his mind and decided to heed the advice given him by Egan High School pal and Navy veteran Jingles Jorgensen: "Take the easiest job you can find, and get out in four years."

One morning on the ship's bulletin board he saw a posting for Yeoman striker (apprentice) in the ship's clerical department and immediately signed his name to it. When the boatswain's mate in charge of the maintenance division learned of my father's plan to transfer, he tried to stop it but couldn't. Dad's ability to type sixty words per minute made him a prime candidate and he was awarded the job. The boatswain was furious: "Get your goddamn clothes out of that locker and get the hell out of here!" he roared. Dad didn't like getting yelled at. In a letter to his brother Bill he described the restraint he mustered to keep from taking a swing at the boatswain. This was a small turning point in his life: he was now thinking of his future and whatever career might await him beyond the Navy, and he had managed to escape the drudgery of manual labor, a fate he had known since childhood.

The *Lady Lex*, as she was known, homeport Los Angeles, spent long months engaged in naval war games, no doubt in response to the military buildup then beginning in Japan. In late spring of 1937 the ship anchored for a week in Honolulu where my father experienced his first "liberty" ashore amidst the yet undeveloped natural beauty of Oahu. He would return to Hawaii a few months later, in July of 1937, when the *Lex* joined the search for Amelia Earhart, the American aviator lost at sea on her historic 'round the world flight. (She's still missing.) He would remember his year and a half aboard the *Lexington* as a period of endless training for the impending war, followed by his regular duty in the ship's office where he was schooled in the Navy's methodic and at times redundant practice of record-keeping, every document and order typed in triplicate.

In late summer of 1938 Dad was reassigned to the Naval Air Station in Pensacola, Florida, to meet the demand for the rapidly expanding pilot training program. He worked in the crash-boat office, typing the incident reports of those unfortunate student pilots who wound up in the water instead of the practice aircraft carrier on which they were supposed to land. In his year and a half at Pensacola he made rate (Yeoman 3rd Class), for which he was required to return to sea. This turned out to be an unexpected stroke of good luck. In March of 1939, he reported aboard the heavy cruiser *Tuscaloosa*, homeport Norfolk, Virginia, just days before the ship departed on a two-month goodwill cruise around South America. Ports-of-call included Caracas, Rio de Janeiro,

Buenos Aires, and Lima, as well as a transit of the Panama Canal. Because the ship's southern route took it across the equator, any sailors not so initiated were subject to a rite of passage known as the "Line Crossing Ceremony." To hear my father describe it, this was a day of intense corporal punishment in which fellow sailors dressed in hula skirts beat him with belaying pins and mop handles. He was made to eat fish guts and drink bilge water (or so he said), got cursed at, spit on, and ordered to kiss the slimy foot of a sailor disguised as King Neptune of The Deep. At the end of the rite he was issued a proclamation declaring him *"Worthy to be numbered as one of our trusty Shellbacks..."* signed, *Neptunus Rex, Ruler of the Raging Main.*

He claimed he nursed the cuts and bruises of his shellback ordeal for weeks afterward and prayed that none of his children would ever have to endure such torture. None of them did, not even me, who would join the US Coast Guard some forty years later.

Despite the beating, the South America cruise would be one of the highlights of his first enlistment. Photos from the trip show him in the crowded streets markets of Caracas, Venezuela; standing at the base of the Christ the Redeemer statue on Corcovado Mountain in Rio de Janeiro; his ship in a heavy sea rounding the infamous Cape Horn; the hundred mile tour-car trip he made through the mountains of Peru; and finally the transit of the Panama Canal, the first of four canal transits he would make in his career. In a letter to his sister he described the beauty of South American women, especially those in Rio who, upon being asked to pose for a photo, might easily reply, "Weez pleasure!" He wrote his sister Adeline that he "has enjoyed the cruise very much, but will be glad to get back to English speaking people again."

Returning to Norfolk, the *Tuscaloosa* spent a month in the shipyard to be fitted with special boarding ramps, an elevator, and living quarters for a very important guest. Dad wrote Adeline to report that "none other than our president F. D. Roosevelt is coming aboard to make a cruise either to England or Alaska." He cautions her that there is "probably no truth to any of this" and that she "shouldn't mention it to anyone." But in fact FDR did come aboard and for the next few years the *Tuscaloosa* became his private yacht for clandestine fishing trips to both Canada and the Caribbean. In a later letter to Adeline written on a "beautiful Sunday afternoon" in August, of 1939, the ship is anchored off Halifax, Nova Scotia, where the president is at that moment fishing. His presence onboard has completely stunned my father, giving him "an awful surprise." He wondered how many people in America knew "just what physical condition that man is in…He is just as helpless as a three-day-old baby… with paralyzed legs no larger than my arm!" However, once the initial shock wore off, my father, a lifelong Republican, warmed to the old

Dad and his sister Adeline, Los Angeles, 1940

man. "You have to hand it to him," he remarked, that in spite of "his physical disability, he has kept coming and became President, with all of its worry and responsibility." He added, "As a man, he appears to be very common, wears an old pair of pants and a straw hat on his fishing excursions." And then he confessed, "Being around him the little I have, I think he is the right guy for now, and I hope that if he goes up for a third time [presidential election] you will cast your vote in his favor."

Tuscaloosa's sailors were ordered to be discreet about the president's appearance. As a reward, conditions on the ship improved remarkably whenever FDR came aboard. Special menus of gourmet food were prepared for every occasion, and every crewmember got to partake. "Smokers" were staged every evening on the ship's aft deck, with boxing, wrestling, and silly competitions held for FDR's amusement as he sat aloft in a specially constructed bird's nest, his wheelchair hidden behind a shroud, his trademark cigarette holder held jauntily. And since his sole purpose for being aboard was deep-water fishing, FDR had his own specially-equipped fishing dinghy and his own master chief boatswain's mate whose only responsibility was to help the president catch fish. My father loved to joke that among the rest of the crew the chief petty officer was known as FDR's "master-baiter," a pun I heard so many times growing up that it became tiresome. But to be sure, my father understood that his close proximity to greatness was a rare privilege and when he spoke of his encounters with FDR it was always with a degree of veneration.

When his four-year enlistment ended in late 1940, Dad was twenty-four years old, and had seen more of the world than any South Dakota farm boy could expect to see in a lifetime. And he was only getting started. In November 1940, now a civilian, he returned to Los Angeles where he took a job at the Lockheed Airplane factory in Burbank, doing inventory control on the revolutionary P-38 Lightning. On weekends he broke the monotony with trips to the infamous Santa Monica Pier, where he filled his dance card with the names of women like Evelyn, Ruth, Ann, and Twyla. Photos from this period suggest a quintessentially "tall, dark, and handsome" erstwhile sailor who favored nice clothes and new cars. Later that same year, when the war finally did begin, he knew it was just a matter of time before the draft board back in South Dakota hunted him down. And even though he'd already served four years in the Navy, he was looking at an additional four years in the Army, most likely in the infantry. He wrote the Navy Bureau of Personnel and convinced them to send him to Navy shorthand school in San Diego, in exchange for which he would give them four more years of his life. By the end of his first enlistment he had advanced as far as Yeoman 2nd Class. As such, he knew that by completing shorthand school, especially during wartime, it all but guaranteed a quick advancement to Chief Yeoman, which included all the honors and courtesies afforded the rank. The Navy readily agreed. Before heading to San Diego, he drove home to put his brand new Ford V-8 in storage, and also to escort the lovely Twyla to her own home in Enterprise, Kansas. Pictures of Twyla suggest a slender young woman with dimples and a fetching smile. I often stared at her photo in Dad's tattered scrapbook and imagined what life would have been like with Twyla as my mother. Did the onset of war interrupt any long-range plans my father might have had for her? He would never say. Maybe it's time I asked him again:

"You think you would have married Twyla had the war not broken out?"

He glances over at me, perhaps annoyed by the interruption. For the past twenty minutes he's been reliving his early Navy years, the narrative I've heard countless times before, getting most of it right. His mind sometimes gets a little jumbled with the names of places and people, but he rushes right past them as if they didn't matter. I've grown used to this in the past few years. But Twyla is different. He certainly remembers Twyla, and I've no doubt he had long-range plans for her.

"How the hell do I know?" he finally admits. "It was a crazy time in my life, running back and forth across the country. Jesus Christ ..." He stares ahead at the highway and then remembers something else. "She wasn't the only one, you know. There was a gal in Philadelphia a few years later. Kathleen... boy oh boy."

Yes, Kathleen. In 1943 he spent ten months in Philadelphia, assigned to a ship still under construction in the nearby Camden, New Jersey, Navy Yard. Granted lots of liberty, or time-off (I trust he didn't spend it chasing the whores he would decades-later accuse me of resembling), he did in fact begin a relationship with a woman named Kathleen, from the New Jersey countryside. A letter I discovered years later in his scrapbook is signed "Kathleen," and it suggests a deeper involvement: *Dear Russell,* it begins --

I still think of you sometimes and wonder how you are. If your ship is in port at Christmas, and you can get leave, etc, would you like to come down and spend Christmas with me?

I remember reading this at the time and thinking, *Here she is again, another woman who might have become my mother.* But by the time Kathleen's letter reached my father he was three-thousand miles away in Los Angeles, on a ship bound for some of the deadliest action of World War Two.

I turn to him now with a mock-serious expression on my face, my voice an octave lower. "I hope to God you behaved like a gentleman with young Kathleen," I tell him.

My statement catches him off guard. He gives me a surprised look, then blurts, "You're God-damned right I did!"

And now it's my turn to tell him a story.

14

A PERFECT GENTLEMAN

In our family, you had two options when you graduated from high school: enroll in college or join the service. No exceptions. The old man was pretty adamant about this. He made sure that we understood from an early age that a college education was the sure route to a successful and happy life—the type of life both he and my mother had struggled to attain without the benefit of higher education. Their plan worked. Every one of my brothers and sisters invested themselves in option one and realized tangible results. Kathy earned a PhD in education, Mark a masters in fisheries and wildlife, Betsey a BS in nursing, and Jim a BS in aeronautical engineering. I joined the service.

The decision was relatively easy. One of the stipulations of the college option was that we pay our own tuition. This was nothing new. We had all attended Catholic high schools, for which it was also understood we would pay our own way. The only financial help we received came from the tax deduction my father claimed for the tuition we paid to attend parochial schools. He divided the refund equally between us which, as I recall, amounted to something like $130 annually. By my senior year my tuition was $690. We all worked part-time jobs through the school year and full-time jobs throughout the summer, all of it going toward our tuition payment in the fall. I got my first job at age twelve working four hours a night at Marty's Kwik Shop, stocking the beer cooler, pricing the canned goods, sweeping the floors, etc., for a dollar an hour. In high school I caddied, sold soft drinks at the Minneapolis Auditorium, bussed dishes at the Normandy Inn, and checked merchandise in the sub-basement of Dayton's Department Store every night after school from four to ten p.m. for $1.35/hr.

After four years of such drudgery, I couldn't imagine enduring four *more* years of it to attend college, especially living at home where we were promised free room and board if we stayed in school. By then, my father and I were like oil and water, and I felt I needed to make a break. Option two presented the only possibility. By the end of my senior year in high school things in Vietnam were finally winding down to the point that joining the service no longer meant a likely death sentence. So I considered my options.

I can remember my resolve in making the decision to enlist, but also the uncertainty about which branch of the service to choose. The Army or Air Force? Nah, nothing about either of those two operations attracted me in the least. The Navy seemed the logical choice, what with my father's vivid stories playing such an important part in my upbringing. I gave it some thought. The Marine Corps had an exotic, if not fatalistic, flavor to it, but I'd heard they brainwashed young men into doing things not necessarily conducive to a long life. If I wanted that kind of action I might just as well have joined the French Foreign Legion.

Then a chance encounter on a fishing trip changed everything.

In the spring of my senior year, I joined some friends from work for a weekend smelting trip along the north shore of Lake Superior. Smelt are a small, sardine-sized fish, and in those days they returned by the millions each spring to spawn in their ancestral streams and rivers. In catching them, the idea is to huddle around a shore-side campfire and drink as much beer as possible before wading out in the frigid water to capture the migrating fry with the aid of a dip-net. An impaired sense of balance brought on by the consumption of the beer only heightened the overall experience. On this particular trip the fishing was slow, which seemed implausible judging from the number of pickup trucks and campers jamming coastal Highway 61 all the way to Canada. On the evening of our second night, the party atmosphere along our stretch of the lake was interrupted by a flashing blue light on the water. People stopped fishing to point at the oddly-comforting light as it emerged through the darkness, its purpose becoming more and more apparent as the white hull of the boat crept into view. Everyone left the water and moved en masse a hundred yards or so up the shore where the boat seemed to be headed. A rumor began circulating that a woman had gone into labor and required evacuation. Because the highway was too jammed with traffic for the swift arrival of an ambulance, the US Coast Guard had been dispatched.

Maybe it was the warm, windless night with the stars twinkling above and the glassy lake undulating over the smooth granite ledges below. Maybe it was the perfumed scent of wood smoke hovering in the coves and recesses, a thin layer of it running like a lace tether between the pine trees atop the bluff. Or maybe it was the simple fact that I'd drunk too much beer. Whatever the case, I closed ranks with the hushed throng along the shore and stood transfixed as the rescue boat idled in as close as it dared. The stark white hull rose and fell in the gentle swell, and the smooth slabs of rock glistened dangerously in the starlight. Presently, a blanket-clad woman was hoisted onto the shoulders of serious-minded men who proceeded to wade into the water and transfer her safely into the arms of the crewmen aboard the boat. One of the men in the water, presumably the woman's husband, was pulled by his arms over the bulwark, his rubber-clad legs kicking violently to assist. A lusty cheer went up as the boat backed away into the darkness, the blue light keeping a constant vigil as it grew dimmer and dimmer down the coast. I watched until it finally disappeared, the whole spectacle taking on a dreamlike quality.

Afterwards, I began to think of it as a God-sent omen, and I made my decision; I would join the Coast Guard.

My joining the service both baffled and pleased my father. He feigned betrayal when I told him of my choice. "The *Coast Guard?*" he howled. "Are you shitting me? You're joining the *hooligan* navy, the *shallow-water* sailors?" He joked about having to hide his face in public and complained that word of my decision was to go no further than the immediate family. What would he tell the neighbors, his relatives in South Dakota, the guys at the office? But one night I overheard him on the phone in his bedroom telling someone about my impending enlistment. He was laughing, but it was an excited laugh, as if he'd just won the church raffle. In truth, he seemed quite proud of my career decision. At dinner, he began rehashing old stories of his time at boot camp, putting a special emphasis on what I could expect. Now his stories seemed to be of a different flavor than when I was younger. These were change-of-life stories, father-to-son, man-to-man.

I had purposely chosen an enlistment date in late July, allowing me part of another summer of work as a Minnesota Teen Corps volunteer at the state mental hospital in St Peter. I'd worked there the summer before, and this summer I'd been asked to serve as the community leader, essentially managing the contingent of twenty or so other teenage volunteers. My father considered it another helping of the "hippie bullshit" he was not too fond of. He didn't understand why I hadn't enlisted sooner, when school was out, so I could get started on my military career. I had my reasons but they were certainly nothing he would have understood, so far apart were we in our ideologies. When I arrived home from St Peter two nights before leaving for boot camp, my hair was longer than it had ever been and my jeans were worn to holes in both knees.

"*Good God!*" he exclaimed. "I hope to hell you're not going to report to boot camp looking like that!" I assured him I was, with the excuse that I'd be getting my head shaved as soon as I arrived. Why waste money on a haircut now? He shook his head and scowled. As far as he was concerned I couldn't leave soon enough.

On the morning of my departure, I had orders to report to the federal courthouse in downtown Minneapolis. I'd been out late the night before saying goodbye to high school friends, and then up half the night thinking about what lay ahead. Mom was supposed to drive me downtown but it was Dad who shook me awake and insisted he would be driving me instead. He claimed it was nothing more than a small detour on his way to work, but I sensed there was another reason. I got dressed and wolfed down a bowl of cereal, grabbed my small duffel bag, then jumped in the front seat of Dad's car. He was dressed in his customary business suit, chewing Doublemint gum and puffing on a Salem cigarette as we headed downtown. Neither of us said much for the first few miles, my mind too preoccupied with the day ahead. So many new things were happening at once—my first-ever airline flight, my first-ever whiff of the sea, and my first-ever encounter with drill instructors who reportedly were as tough as those in the Marine Corps. I barely noticed when Dad suddenly veered off Glenwood Avenue and pulled to a stop in a vacant lot, but when he killed the engine the silence roused me from my reverie. I looked around at the unfamiliar setting, confused by where we were and unsure of why. Dad turned in his seat, his considerable girth in those years making it a bit of a challenge. Something was bothering him, this much I could discern.

"Now you listen to me, buster," he began, and I braced for the worst. He only called me buster when he was pissed off about something. What could possibly be so urgent that he had to stop the car *now*, on the most important day of my life? The look on his face was similar to one years ago when I'd nearly started the garage on fire.

But now something was burning inside of him. "One thing you need to know about being in the service," he said, starting again. "You see, well ... well you see, *dammit, you're going to meet a lot of women!* And when you do, well ..." He looked away, obviously agitated, obviously struggling for the words he wanted to impart.

I watched him nervously, unsure of what to do. I had no idea where this was headed. And I also feared we were going to be late getting downtown.

Finally, he seemed to find the words he was looking for and he leaned toward me again, his large frame filling the front seat. I could smell the Old Spice after-shave he'd splashed on that morning—part of his daily ritual—and he was working overtime with the chewing gum, snapping and popping it in his mouth as he began again. "Now I'm only going to tell you this once," he said, "so you'd better be paying attention."

"I am," I replied, nodding.

"You're going to meet a lot of women in the service, and Godammit, you'd better be a *gentleman* with every one!" The words came out quickly, angrily, as if I was already guilty of whatever it was he was trying to imply. And then just as quickly he turned and started the engine and we were off, underway again for my downtown appointment and the beginning of my new life.

I don't remember my response, if indeed I said anything at all. For that matter, I don't remember the remainder of the ride downtown, or getting dropped off, or even meeting up with the recruiter who surely must have delivered me to the airport. But later that morning I did indeed fly to San Francisco, where I was taken by helicopter across the bay to Oakland, and an island in the estuary—Coast Guard Recruit Training Center Alameda. I got my first whiff of salt-water, got my head shaved by an assembly-line barber, got more vaccination shots than I would ever have believed possible, and for next two months got screamed at day and night by any number of red-faced drill instructors. Women? There simply weren't any, so I never had the chance to behave "gentlemanly" or otherwise. Those opportunities would come later, of course, as my father predicted they would. And when they did I could not help but remember the terse lecture he had given me that morning on our trip downtown. In retrospect, I realized it was the closest thing to a sex talk we had in the first eighteen years of my life.

15

SUNDOWN

I've been talking long enough that we're now on the outskirts of Flagstaff. The exit signs begin appearing more frequently, including one for Winslow and I-40 heading east. Dad is sitting next to me shaking his head at my story about joining the Coast Guard. "You're so full of shit," he says. "I don't remember telling you any such god damn thing about being a gentleman."

We could easily begin arguing right now, as we used to in the past, but I've got other things on my mind.

"Hold that thought," I tell him. "Are you feeling okay? You want to keep going or would you rather stop here in Flagstaff?"

He looks around as if he's just been awakened from a dream, realizing he hasn't been paying attention to the map. He glances down at it and then looks up at a sign as we pass beneath. "Flagstaff," he says quietly as if he's never heard of it.

"Dad?" I say. "Would you like to stop here?"

He checks the map again, nods, and finally says, "Let's keep going. I guess I'm okay."

"Alright then," I tell him, "on we go." And suddenly I feel energized, like I could drive all night. So we exit on I-40 and head east, the sun now behind us, casting long shadows out ahead.

Curiously, after we turn, the mood inside the van grows noticeably darker. Odd how the absence of direct sunlight can do that. Before we turned, the low rays of the sun's last light streamed through the windows on my side of the van, basking both of us in a gilded glow. Now we sit in relative darkness, the sun disappearing behind the gray bulk of the U-Haul, blocking its rays. Now it's like we're at the tail end of a long dark shadow, pushing it forward, its shape and size changing with every bend in the highway.

The landscape on either side of the van becomes one of rolling hills, here and there sprinkled with Ponderosa pine. The sky is a deep azure, and the air looks fresh and feels cool in the vents along the dash. I adjust the vents to restrict the flow, retaining some heat for my senior co-pilot and navigator.

"How far to Winslow?" I call out. But the navigator doesn't seem to be listening. He's sitting a little more erect than he had been, his hands clenched in his lap as he stares at the road ahead.

"Dad?"

Nothing. But I decide to let it pass. He seems content enough; maybe his mind is still fixated on Twyla, Kathleen, or even Ava and their trysts in Flagstaff. Oh, the life he passed up for his stubborn pride!

But then, near an exit ramp marked "Cosnino Road," he noticeably flinches as we pass beneath the shadow of a towering utility pole beside the road. And now I'm concerned.

"You okay?" I ask matter-of-factly. But he continues staring out his side of the car, his sights fixed on something else. The road ahead stretches to the horizon, the Ponderosas finally surrendering to an endless patchwork of scrub. My own mind begins to calculate the miles ahead of us, the distances and hours we'll need to consume before this is over. I begin adding in the fuel stops, the lunch stops, the stops to rest and stretch. If we can make it as far as Holbrook tonight we'll have taken only a small bite out of our total mileage, but also a wide chunk out of Dad's former life in Phoenix and his new one in La Crosse. My mind is halfway to Albuquerque when Dad suddenly erupts beside me:

"Jesus Christ!" he shouts. "He's diving on us! *Hit the deck!*" And with this he lurches sideways in his seat, his shoulder and head tipping clumsily into my armrest. Startled, I swerve so far left our tires rumble over the warning strip on that side of the highway. I instinctively swerve back to bring us toward the middle of the road as my eyes frantically search the rearview mirrors for whatever it was that just missed us from above. But all I see is the rigid truss-work of a high-tension electrical tower standing mutely along the side of the interstate. I take my foot off the gas and let our momentum carry us to the shoulder. Our small rig slows and finally rolls to a stop, the tires crunching gravel along the edge of the pavement. I put the transmission in park and kill the engine, my trembling fingers clumsy with the key. Dad struggles to pull himself upright in his seat, groaning with the effort, and I reach to assist him with a hand beneath his elbow. A few cars fly past and then a semi, buffeting us in its wake. Dad stares down into the mirror on his side of the car, his hands working nervously in his lap, his hair disheveled.

"Sonofabitch," he says softly. "Son of a bitch."

I should have seen this coming. Both Roseanne and the public health nurse warned me it might happen. Sundown Syndrome they called it, something to do with the fading light. Well, the sun is definitely setting and here I am rolling along in complete ignorance of the obvious signs. God, I'm stupid. I mean, here I am in the middle of nowhere with night coming on and a ninety-six year old man on the verge of losing it. We should have stopped in Flagstaff, eaten at a nice restaurant, gotten a good night's sleep. But no, I had to push him. "On we go!" I told him. On we go. And here we are. I think they call this "senior abuse" and I think I'm guilty. Now what?

First order of business is to get him calmed down before it gets any worse. The look of panic on his face convinces me I don't have much time to waste.

"Wow that was close!" I say, trying to sound light-hearted. "I half expected to see a German dive-bomber coming in low across the desert. *Whew!*"

Dad checks the mirror again to determine if indeed that's what has happened. Another semi whooshes past.

"What did they call those German dive bombers?" I ask matter-of-factly. I'm determined to get a conversation going. "Wasn't it 'Junkers' or something like that?"

He glances over at me. "Yunkers," he says soberly, correcting my German. Then he gets an inquisitive look on his face, his eyebrows lifting. "How the hell would you remember that?" he says. "Did I ever tell you about German dive bombers?"

I feel myself relax a bit. From his expression I can tell I've talked him back a half-step from the ledge he was standing on a moment ago, the ledge on which his mind can so easily play tricks. It amazes me how that same mind can one moment be on the verge of hysteria, and in the next recall something from the past.

"I'm sure I heard about them in one of your stories," I tell him. "Wasn't it a Junkers 88 that bombed the *Leedstown* at Algiers?"

"That's right!" he says and he stares at me as his mind recovers something from nearly seventy years ago. He adds, "Have I ever told you about that night in Algiers?"

"I'm not sure," I reply, an outright lie.

"One of the worst goddamn nights of my life!" he says emphatically. "My first real exposure to war."

"How bad was it?" I ask.

"Oh Christ..."

"But you survived."

"Jesus," he says, almost whispering. "I'm a lucky sonofabitch. Always have been."

And then, without any further prodding from me, he launches into the story of Operation Torch and the sinking of his ship, the *Leedstown*. It's one of his favorites, and I've heard it countless times before, but I'm ready to listen again if it will keep him calm until we reach Holbrook.

I start the car and ease back out onto the interstate. My hand, I'm afraid, is still shaking.

16

North Africa

In World War II, the term "Post Traumatic Stress Syndrome," or PTSD, had not yet been coined. Back then, it was called "shell shock" or "battle neurosis," neither of which my father (as far as I know) ever complained of having. I also doubt he would have complained, given his stubbornness and also the pride he took in his service to his country. His stories, I now believe, were his way of coping with what he had experienced, and perhaps as good a therapy as any VA psychiatrist of the post-war era might have prescribed. As a boy I was often perplexed when friends told me their fathers made bare mention of their wartime experiences, though it was obvious to me some of those experiences had been traumatic. Mr. McDevitt, for example, had lost an eye in France and spent the remainder of the war in a German POW camp. Mr. Lamb had been an officer aboard a submarine in the South Pacific and saw plenty of action. Mr. Walch had been a hospital corpsman aboard a recovery ship, treating Marines wounded in the island-hopping campaign.

On the other hand, I heard stories of returning veterans who had been unable to cope with their wartime experiences, and eventually turned to alcohol or deserted their families altogether. One of my friends even suggested that my father's experiences couldn't have been as bad as he let on, or he wouldn't have been able to talk about them so openly. I didn't feel that way. My dad certainly never glorified himself in any of his stories, other than to mention his luck at having somehow survived. But his experiences were bad enough, I suspect, to compel him later in life, at the age of seventy-two, to write a memoir of his wartime experiences, ostensibly for his grandchildren but really, in my opinion, for himself. I found the memoir he produced to be great reading —an eyewitness account of history—and it also benefitted from my father's self-effacing sense of humor.

At one place in the memoir he wrote, "My time in the Navy was either super-good, or super-bad—there was no in-between." In the fall of 1942, upon completion of the shorthand training he had requested, he was sent cross-country by train to Brooklyn, where a former passenger ship, the *SS Santa Lucia*, now renamed the USS *Leedstown* was being refitted into a troop transport. Because it had been a luxury liner, the *Leedstown* had many creature comforts my father would never experience again—air-conditioning, for instance. Music was piped throughout the working areas of the ship, and his office came equipped with over-stuffed chairs, ornate desks, and floor-length mirrors. Day after day hundreds of workers from the Brooklyn Navy Yard scrambled to prepare the ship for the Invasion of North Africa. At night, on liberty, my father went ashore and explored the boroughs on both sides of the Brooklyn Bridge. In his scrapbook is a menu from the dinner he enjoyed at Jack Dempsey's in Manhattan, and also the dance-card from a Navy-sponsored soiree in a Brooklyn ballroom. The Navy invitation promised the attendance of:

"Fifty members of the female sex," all guaranteed to be "equal to, or better than, Madeline Carrol, Hedy Lamarr, or Ann Sheridan. So get there early and take your pick!"

There's a photo of him taken during this period in which he's standing arm-in-arm with a fetching young woman beneath the Brooklyn Bridge. But she's not Hedy Lamarr. And the romance couldn't have lasted long. The *Leedstown* weighed anchor in early September of '42, destination Europe and the invasion of North Africa. He would look back on his brief stay in Brooklyn as one of the "super-good" times of his years in the Navy. One of the "super-bad" times was about to unfold.

The invasion of North Africa (code-named *Operation Torch* by the Allied Command), was, at the time, the largest amphibious assault in naval history, deploying some 350 ships of all description and function. That the *Leedstown* was one of only eleven ships lost in the entire invasion makes my father's experience unusual. As mentioned earlier, he was already a veteran of four years naval service, over half of that time spent aboard fleet warships. The *Leedstown* was his third.

The operation was plagued by mistakes due to the crew's inexperience. FUBAR, a term common to service personnel in all branches of the military—Fucked Up Beyond All Reason—is how my father described it. The ship arrived in Belfast, Northern Ireland, in late September, where it loaded some four thousand GIs and then took part in a practice invasion along the Ireland coast. It later joined the much larger invasion fleet and arrived in the Mediterranean in early November, eventually breaking off into a smaller task force of four transport ships. On the afternoon of November 7 *Leedstown* anchored in a position a mile and a quarter off the Algerian coast near a rocky headland called Surcouf. That night, as the ship prepared to discharge its cargo of troops, along with trucks, ammunition, and a "hold bulging with supplies," it was discovered that the ship's electric winches were undersized for the job. The inexperienced crewmen had to improvise to get things moving, jury-rigging the winches and in the end unloading a lot of the material by hand. Meanwhile, German Junkers 88 dive bombers circled overhead while searchlights from Vichy-French batteries along the shore fixed the unfortunate ship in its sights.

My father's battle station was high up in the ship's bridge where, with sound-powered headphones, he collected and disseminated information from the various departments below, which in turn was relayed to the captain and bridge officers. From this vantage point and job description he got a pretty good picture of everything as it unfolded that night. It was his first real exposure to surface warfare and was no doubt terrifying. Whenever he told the story of that night—of how the shore batteries had fixed the ship in the cold glare of its searchlights, and how the dive bombers circled overhead with their lethal loads—his voice would break as he described the utter helplessness he felt and the dreadful feeling that in the next moment all hell might break loose. His narrative made me feel as if I was right there beside him, and it gave me goose bumps.

On this particular night, however, his ship would be spared. Gunfire from Navy destroyers knocked out the shore-based searchlights and eventually the inexperienced crew aboard *Leedstown* managed to get things moving. The invasion force landed on a beach left mostly unguarded, and by sundown the next day nearly all the troops and half the supplies were safely ashore. But that evening, just when my father believed he had survived the worst of it, a pair of Junkers 88s returned, flying in low over the water to drop a torpedo into the stern of the *Leedstown*, taking out her rudder and propeller. The torpedo, Dad wrote, created the "damndest explosion I have ever experienced … an initial blast [that] seemed to shake the ship violently for another 30 seconds." Miraculously, the ship stayed afloat and no one was killed.

Now disabled, *Leedstown* lay at anchor all the next morning while the remaining supplies were unloaded. A British Corvette providing security began to pick up U-Boat signals on its sonar and started deploying depth charges. And then, around noon, the dive bombers returned. Enter one of my father's favorite characters, a young gunnery officer named Wylie Smith. Ensign Smith spoke with a deep southern drawl, and my father doubted his callow cheeks had ever felt the sting of a razor. When the captain issued the order to "fire at will," Wylie, whose Alabama diction didn't include the word "fire," shouted "FAR!" with such authority that every gun on board began blazing at once. Moments later a lookout screamed, *"He's diving on us!"* followed shortly by the shrieking sound of a bomb zeroing-in on the ship. In between muttering a final Act of Contrition and cowering beneath his oversized helmet, my father was certain his luck had run out.

The bomb exploded five feet short of the hull, directly in line with Dad's battle station, and the resulting geyser produced a column of water that nearly drowned everyone on that side of the ship. Dad barely had time to thank the Lord when ...

"WHAMMO! we were hit with a torpedo, this one apparently from the submarine that had been lurking all morning."

He claims he doesn't remember much about the submarine torpedo. His "mind was so muddled" from the earlier percussion of the bomb explosion that he "just seemed numb as to what was going on." But before long he realized the ship had been hit and he began watching in horror as chaos unfolded. Water began surging through the torpedo hole so rapidly that the captain believed his ship might capsize within minutes. The order was given to "abandon ship." My father hurried off the bridge along with everyone else to save himself. In what surely must have been the result of shock, he suddenly noticed his shoes had filled with water from the bomb explosion. He stopped in mid-flight to remove them, along with his wet socks, which he neatly folded and placed inside the shoes. Then he ran off barefoot in search of a place to go over the side. He watched in silent horror as other shipmates made the twenty-foot drop into the water, only to have their skulls cracked open by the impact of their steel helmets. He saw blood on the water and men floating lifelessly in the debris.

He figured there had to be a better way off the sinking ship. He ran along the decks until he came upon the ship's Jacob's ladder hanging over the side, and on this he made his descent. Hand over hand he descended the rope ladder and upon reaching bottom he pushed off into the oily sea. Once safely in the water he began, "swimming like mad for two or three minutes thinking I would surely be a good long way away from the ship."

I'll confess here that as a child I often had my doubts about this part of his narrative. On the South Dakota farm where he grew up there probably wasn't a lake or swimming pool within twenty-five miles. Any swimming he may have enjoyed was most likely conducted in a pasture mud hole where grazing cattle and festering cow pies made access difficult. It's more likely he received the rudiments of swimming instruction at Navy boot camp, but to what extent, he never said. On our occasional child-hood outings to Lake Harriet, he swam with an awkward style of dog-paddling which he accomplished with no small amount of effort and sputtering lips. Could this really be the same stroke he employed to rescue himself from the sinking ship?

As the story goes, he had entered the water directly in front of the torpedo hole and was now inches away from getting sucked back inside the sinking ship. Dog-paddling or not, he did manage to save himself when he snagged the rung of the very same Jacob's ladder he'd just descended and pulled himself aloft to try again. This time he assisted a fellow seaman in deploying one of the last in-flatable life rafts aboard. They entered the sea on the non-torpedoed side of the ship and began at once picking up other survivors, some fifteen in all. By now the wind had increased, and the surging seas carried the fully-loaded life raft toward shore, aided by the thrash-ing arms and legs of the surviving sailors. As they neared shore, earlier survivors waded out in the surf and shouted terse warnings about the outcroppings they needed to avoid. But with no steering apparatus, the seaman were at the mercy of the sea, and it was sheer luck that carried them safely away from the deadly rocks.

"The surf was just horrible," my father wrote, "and we rode out one big wave before the next one picked up the life raft and flipped everyone out. I was in trouble—the water only neck-deep but each time I would get my feet under me another wave would knock me down. All of a sudden I looked in front of me and a sweet little 13-14 year old girl grabbed my hand and pulled me in to the beach. She had a bottle of wine and gave me a swig along with some sugar lumps ... I had drunk a lot of water and threw the whole thing up."

From *The Coast Guard at War: North African Landings IX*, a US Coast Guard eyewitness account of the sinking:

"The men of the torpedoed vessel [*Leedstown*] abandoned the ship and took to the life rafts which floated directly toward the beach. But a heavy surf was running and the survivors were thrown from their rafts into the sea a mile and a half from shore. There was bound to be trouble when those rafts hit the rocks offshore. We tried to get the survivors to steer the rafts before they hit the surf so as to avoid being battered...We swam out with lines we tied to the rafts which we could then pull to shore with the survivors clinging to the sides. The rafts had to be pulled, for the men on them could not steer clear of the rocks. The surf was throwing the rafts in the air, dumping their human cargoes into the water to be crushed as the rafts were tossed about on top. It was a struggle to keep afloat in spite of broken bones, concussions and shock... Some French and Arab natives came to assist in the rescue. The Arabs would cut down large reeds, about fifteen feet long, then wade into the water, extend them to the men and pull them ashore. Even the children were down by the waterfront, armed with bottles of wine and brandy which they'd offer the men as they were dragged ashore."

Eventually, Dad and some of the other survivors made it to a bakery in a nearby village where they peeled out of their oil-soaked clothing and covered themselves in discarded sugar sacks.

At some point during this ordeal, having realized their good fortune in surviving the sinking of their ship, the shipmates passed around one-dollar bills which they each autographed to commemorate their luck. One of these grim mementoes—called "short-snorters" by WWII memorabilia collectors—turned up on eBay eighty years later and was spotted by my brother Mark, who noticed our father's handwriting in the margin.

When the shipwrecked sailors were finally gathered up to be trucked to a staging area, the "grouchy baker," in my father's words, "made me return the sacks, and I had to put on my grimy clothes again." He would later recall that he had left a nearly-new set of dress-blues hanging in his locker aboard ship and often wondered if they were still hanging there. He also imagined his shoes and socks sitting neatly on deck, right where he left them before going over the side

(Decades later I would discover, by accident, his "abandon ship" clothing in a sodden box in the attic rafters. The limp denim was oily to the touch and still carried the dying aroma of a warship lying at the bottom of the Mediterranean, some ten thousand miles away.)

The staging area where they were bivouacked was actually the Algiers airport hangar, which was under aerial attack as the haggard sailors staggered in. They spent the night there and the next morning were trucked down to the wharf to board the US Coast Guard Cutter *Samuel Chase*. The *Chase* had performed admirably over the course of the invasion and was now tasked with the responsibility of carrying displaced seaman and soldiers back to Scotland for further deployment. Like so many ships pressed into service during the war, *Chase's* outfitting had been hurried and its sea-trials abbreviated to meet a schedule. In its short life at sea, it had broken down repeatedly.

The convoy it joined departed Gibraltar on the evening of November 14th and soon thereafter left the tropical waters of the Mediterranean for the frigid, storm-tossed seas of the North Atlantic. Sometime after midnight, November 15th, word went out that German U-boats had been picked up on sonar—a Wolf Pack reported to be as large as ten to twelve submarines. In formation some 600 yards behind the *Chase* was the British aircraft carrier *Avenger* with a full complement of 556 men. Suddenly the inky night exploded in horrific fire as a German torpedo ripped through the *Avenger's* hull and found her fuel tanks. The enormous ship went down in minutes taking all but a few of her crew with her. Other ships began exploding all around the horizon as the Wolf Pack fed on its easy prey. My father, huddled in a bunk deep within the bowels of the ship, said his prayers and waited for the torpedo that would finish it all. And just when he thought it couldn't get any worse, it did.

"When the going gets bad," he wrote, "it really gets bad. About an hour later the [ship] went dead in the water. The fuel oil had become contaminated and it could not proceed until they fixed up some [sort] of filtering system. All the other ships went on ahead without us and only one British Corvette was assigned to stay with us. We were dead in the water for three hours and, believe me when I say this, those were the worst three hours of my life. I had no hope of ever living through the night. The Wolf Pack must have been no further than five miles away and why they didn't come after us I will never know. It was cold, there were 25-ft waves crashing against the ship, it was pitch black outside, and there [was] no way we could have ever gotten off the ship if it was hit. I was disgusted, mad, and believe I cursed at the thought of 'what a hell-hole place to end [my] life.'"

(Irony of ironies, decades later Dad would call one night with shocking news from his lake home in northern Minnesota. The place next door had just sold to a former POW from the German navy, *a submariner*, no less! Dad was livid: "I've half a mind to go over there right now and kick the sonofabitch's ass!" He actually did, but the ass-kicking came on a horseshoe pitch, every Sunday afternoon for the next fifteen years, as the two WWII vets became close friends.)

Miraculously, the *Chase* engineers managed to get the filtering system repaired and three hours later the ship resumed its course for Scotland, sailing all the way to Edinburgh without further incident. From there, Dad was loaded aboard the converted troopship *Queen Elizabeth* (along with ten thousand Italian prisoners-of-war), which, with its exceptional speed, sailed unescorted to Halifax, Nova Scotia, in three days. From there, it was a train ride down the coast to Boston, where he arrived at 2 a.m. on a cold winter's night to partake of the "greatest display of food I would ever see in the military." In Boston he called home to tell everyone he was okay, and then was granted thirty-days leave—time enough to make it back to South Dakota in time for Christmas, 1942.

But for him the war was far from over. After Christmas, he was sent back east, this time to Camden, New Jersey, directly across the river from Philadelphia, where his next ship, the aircraft car-

rier *Langley,* was in its final year of construction. He would spend
ten months in Philadelphia, a period he would later call "the best
months of my life." I doubt he was referring to anything associated
with the Navy. His duties aboard the under-construction ship were
minimal, and in fact he spent most of his time there at the Navy receiving station in Philly where he was granted lots of liberty. It was
during this period that he met the lovely Kathleen, only to have
another ensuing romance torn apart by the war. Indeed, when
construction of the ship was finally completed in late November
1943, he wrote, "…we got underway [for the west coast]. I was
up on the bridge, very melancholy, wondering if I would ever see
Philadelphia again." He never did. He was headed for some of the
fiercest naval action of the war, and he obviously knew it. Before
departing Philadelphia, he took out a life insurance policy naming
his father as beneficiary, "payable upon death."

HE'S BEEN TALKING so long we missed the exit for Winslow a few
miles back. And that's okay. I actually saw the signs well in advance but decided to skip it. On my one and only visit to Winslow years ago I never saw any "girl, my lord, in a flatbed Ford."
As I recall, it was nothing but tourist traps and tee-shirt shops. Besides, Dad's reminiscing about the war has completely displaced
the hallucinations he was having east of Flagstaff. The talking is
doing him good. He did a few times trip up on some dates and
locations, but I never interrupted and he just kept talking as if it
didn't matter. And it really doesn't. His sanity is all that's important now, especially as it pertains to sundown syndrome. I need
to remember this.

It's quite dark inside the car, Dad's face barely visible in the
amber glow of the dashboard gauges. I break the silence.

"Why the hell did that Algerian baker need to have those
sugar sacks returned? I mean, weren't they full of oil and stink
after you took them off?"

"I'll be goddamned if I know!" Dad replies, his voice rising.

"I'd like to go back there someday and kick the sonofabitch's ass."
And from the tone of his voice I know he means it.

"I'll go with you," I tell him. "Tag team, just like the Crusher
and Bruiser." This gets him laughing. He used to love watching
Saturday night wrestling on TV. "How are you holding up?" I ask.
"Can you make it to Holbrook, another thirty miles?"

He doesn't respond. He might be confused, but in the dark I
can't tell. Best to get back to the war.

"When you left Philadelphia, did you have any idea what
you were in for?"

"Oh, god," he says, his voice trailing off. "Boy oh boy ..."

17

The War in The Pacific

The *Langley* didn't head directly to the action. It first stopped in Los Angeles to load its complement of fighter aircraft: forty-five Grumman F6F Hellcats. Now equipped for battle, it set sail for Hawaii, reaching Honolulu on Christmas Eve, 1943. Pearl Harbor was still littered with the carnage of the surprise attack two years earlier, and it must have been a sobering sight. "It was lonesome," Dad wrote in his memoir, "but carols were being played over the ship's loud-speaker system and I walked the flight deck looking at the beautiful city lights." For the next month the *Langley* put to sea for drills—the manning of battle stations, gunnery practice, take-offs and landings, damage control, etc. When it finally got underway, few on board would have guessed they would be in for seventeen months of continuous wartime operations, island-hopping across the Pacific all the way to Japan.

The routine was grueling and the stress all but unbearable. Every day carried the threat of death; the sailors were up each morning an hour before daybreak to man battle stations and launch the aircraft. Temperatures in the berthing areas rarely dipped below 110 degrees, and everyone was continually dopey from lack of sleep. "Tempers grew thin," Dad wrote. "Fist-fights were common as men fought each other for something as simple as the positioning of a fan."

In a letter to his sister Grace dated November, 1944, he confessed, "Have had some awfully hard days the last month but I know that from now on they are all going to be hard so I will just have to brace for it. I'm afraid that after two or three years of this I am going to be nothing but a bundle of nerves." And, "Mail is the most precious thing in one's life these days."

A month later he was no better: "It is so beastly hot and miserable... I am nothing but a stack of bones..." And, "I know we have a much tougher time ahead of us than what we have already been through, so there is nothing much to do but bear with it and hope for the best. Pretty tough on a person's nerves."

The aircraft were sent on daily sorties to bomb or strafe targeted islands, only to return later, often damaged, to crash-land on the deck, or, in some instances, not return at all. Sometimes, on longer missions, the planes would run out of fuel and were forced to ditch in the ocean, far from their home carrier, often in seas too rough to affect rescue. I've no doubt my father's fear of flying came as a direct result of his bearing witness to these tragic losses, something he experienced on a daily basis from the viewpoint of the *Langley's* bridge.

As if the incessant tension aboard ship weren't enough, later in the campaign the threat of Kamikaze attack added a new dimension to the war and kept everyone on high alert. By then the Japanese had lost most of their skilled pilots and the new, poorly-trained replacements were strapped into their cockpits with one objective: fly their bomb-laden aircraft into the first American ship they encountered. Some thirty-four US Navy ships were so destroyed, and countless others were damaged, including the *Langley*. One morning my father froze when a lookout screamed, "*He's diving on us!*" followed by the shriek of acceleration as a Zero kamikaze scored a direct hit on the flight deck. The plane missed the vital areas of the ship but found a nearly-empty berthing area below decks, killing a handful of young pilots as they slept between missions. It was terrifying and further frayed my father's already frazzled nerves.

On one such morning at battle-stations he snapped and got into a fist-fight with a fellow crewman. In Dad's sleep-deprived stupor he somehow stumbled into another man—a fellow chief petty officer, no less, whose battle-station was also on the bridge. The other chief made a crack about my father's clumsiness and an argument broke out. In full view of the captain and navigation

USS *Langley* leading Task Group 38.3 to anchorage in Ulithi Atoll, 1944; seventeen months at sea.

officer the two men commenced trading punches, and no one did a thing to stop it. At the height of the battle the other chief kept hitting the mouthpiece of my father's head-set, which bloodied his hands. Given the circumstances, it's entirely possible the blood Dad saw may have been his own, but he would never admit it, and in the end he declared himself the victor.

By "mid-1944," he wrote, "[the Navy] had quite a large number of big carriers in the fleet and it is most everyone's be-lief... that the war for the Japanese was lost on June 14th, 1944," in what came to be known as the "Great Marianas Turkey Shoot." The Japanese "were tricky and smart and brought every carrier they owned to the big showdown. They located their navy about two-hundred miles on one side of their island [chain] (The Marianas). We were two-hundred miles on the other side. The Japanese theory was that neither their planes nor our planes carried enough gasoline to make the round trip, so their plan was to launch air attacks and then land on an island on the way back [to] refuel."

The Turkey Shoot came to be regarded as the most intensive aircraft carrier battle of the war. The United States lost one hundred thirty aircraft in the fight, compared to almost five hundred Japanese land and carrier-based aircraft. Many of the American losses came as a result of planes running out of fuel on their return trips; some of the pilots were forced to ditch within sight of their ship.

In his memoir my father confesses that his "mind is blank as to which islands we were trying to capture." In his defense, he was taking part in world history, not recording it. But for the record, the *Langley* had a most impressive tour of duty in the Pacific Theater. Beginning in January of 1944, she conducted air raids at Wotje and Toroa, and supported amphibious landings on Eniwetok and Kwajalein. At the beginning of April 1944 she conducted raids at Palau and Woleai, afterward proceeding to New Guinea to assist in the taking of Hollandia and Truk. Throughout the summer of 1944, she saw action in the battles of Saipan, Tinian, Pagan, Guam, and Rota, and finally Peleliu. In October, the *Langley* was off Formosa and the Pescadores, and on October 25th took part in striking the depleted Japanese fleet in the battles of Surigao Strait and Southern Samar. From November 1944 through January 1945 she conducted raids on the Philippines and Formosa. Later that January she participated in a daring raid in the South China Sea, from which she returned in time to join in the early bombing runs of Tokyo on the Japanese mainland. At her furthest deployment of the war, she came within thirty miles of the coast of Japan.

And she wasn't finished. From February through March of 1945 *Langley* supported the landings on Iwo Jima, and also the airfields of Empire Island, where most of the Japanese Kamikaze flights originated. Well into May of 1945 she divided her attention between the Okinawa invasion and the support of the air strikes on Kyushu.

Among her other exploits during the war, the *Langley* survived "Typhoon Cobra," the deadly hurricane that slammed into Admiral Bull Halsey's Third Fleet as it prepared to invade the Philippines. For three endless days in mid-December of 1944, the *Langley* encountered winds to 160 mph and seas as high as 70 feet, which caused the 622-foot ship to roll as much as seventy degrees side to side. There was no escaping the terror. From his battle station some seventy-five feet aloft in the ship's bridge, a seventy degree roll would feel like a ship getting ready to capsize repeatedly in the next moment. Down below, where those not on watch were ordered to strap themselves into their bunks, a seventy degree roll is not as pronounced as seventy-five feet above. But escaping a capsizing ship from those depths would have been all but impossible. There was simply no relief from the constant anxiety.

The *Langley* survived but other ships were not as fortunate. Typhoon Cobra would sink three ships in the task force, severely damage another thirty-one, and send 790 sailors to their watery graves. Admiral Halsey would be brought up before a Court of Inquiry and reprimanded for "error of judgment," but otherwise exonerated. The storm became infamous in a movie called *The Caine Mutiny*, in which Humphrey Bogart plays the deranged captain of a destroyer whose crewmembers mutiny to save their ship from foundering.

My father had a similar regard for his captain aboard the *Langley,* a man whom he repeatedly refers to in his Navy memoir as "Old Shit-head." In my father's estimation, Old Shit-head was "the meanest bastard I have ever known, and I have often wondered why someone didn't push him over the side—he would have deserved it." It's not hard to understand why.

In July of 1944, at the height of the war in the Pacific, my father was promoted to Chief Petty Officer. There's an old saying in the service that goes: An officer may a command a ship, but it is the chief petty officers who run the Navy. "Chiefs," as they are commonly known, are those experienced sailors, often career men, who have risen through the ranks and perfected the skills peculiar to their field of expertise. And they are treated accordingly. Aboard ship, chief petty officers are afforded their own ward room, better sleeping arrangements, a private mess area, and cooks and stewards to attend to their daily needs. Upon making the grade, they also shed their faded work shirts and thirteen-button

Langley Captain's office personnel, Dad lower middle.

denim bell-bottoms for more sophisticated khaki uniforms. And they ditch the traditional "Dixie cup" for a blocked and billed CPO hat, the crowning glory of making rank.

Aboard the *Langley,* making chief meant assuming the duties of "Captain's Yeoman," which put my father in direct contact with the ship's commanding officer. The first captain he served under was a tough old Texan loved by everyone for his fairness and humility. Unfortunately, that captain's tour of duty aboard *Langley* came to an end not long after Dad made chief. He was replaced by Old Shit-head, the last sea-captain my father would ever know. The problem with Old Shit-head, in my father's opinion, was twofold. He had a complete lack of respect for the crew, and he was an idiot, severely lacking in intellect.

Every night at 2300 hrs (11 p.m. civilian time), as per his duties, my father was required to type up the ship movements— "night orders" in naval jargon—and bring them directly to the captain's cabin for signature. Running in combat mode, the ship displayed no outside lights at night, which could make movement about the decks treacherous. If a sea was running, there was a real threat of falling overboard. Climbing aloft to the captain's cabin, Dad would be stopped outside the door by the Marine Corps orderly standing guard. Per shipboard custom, all visitors were required to report to the orderly and state their business. With the former captain this was nothing more than a formality; upon arrival, Dad was immediately invited inside for the required signature, and was usually back below within ten minutes. But not with Old Shit-head. Invariably, even when it was stormy or raining, he was always made to wait outside the cabin door for up to an hour. He couldn't imagine why it always took the captain so long to let him in. He figured he was either in there clipping his toenails or finishing up the latest comic book his wife had sent him.

On some occasions, Old Shit-head would order my father to his cabin to take a letter, then to make five copies by hand and mail them to Old Shit-head's brothers, sisters, and cousins in Hicksville, Illinois. As Dad describes it, these relatives "would apparently write to him, *'do you really know Admiral Halsey?'* and he would explain how Admiral Halsey invited him over regularly for conferences."

Dad concludes the passage: "I think it amazed them all that he had ever [risen] further than Number Three man at a car wash."

Oh, how my father despised Captain Shit-head.

As the war in the Pacific continued to grind on in May of 1945, the *Langley* headed east to San Francisco for badly needed repairs. Since deploying in December of 1943, she had travelled some 180,000 nautical miles in pursuit of Japanese combatants. Her planes were responsible for the sinking of seven Japanese warships and twenty-seven merchant vessels, 119 enemy planes in the air and more than a hundred more planes on the ground. She had earned a total of nine battle stars, and the battle pennant fluttering behind as she sailed beneath the Golden Gate Bridge nearly dipped into the sea. In the entire year and a half his ship had been deployed my father had been ashore exactly two times for a total of four hours. *Four hours in seventeen months!*

In San Francisco, while his fellow sailors streamed off the

ship for some well-deserved liberty, my father, the only qualified court reporter on board, sat chained to a desk processing court-martial paperwork. Any other captain in the fleet would have encouraged his battle-weary men to have a good time while on their hard-earned liberty ashore. But Old Shit-head took it upon himself to court-martial each and every man who returned to the ship drunk. My father had reached his limit. He writes:

"On the day we were to be transferred off the ship everybody was out on the dock awaiting final orders. Luckily, I had packed my seabag the night before and had taken it out to the dock. I then went back aboard to try and finish up the court martial I was working on. Before I was through they passed the order *Last Call* over the ship's PA. I left that court-martial [paperwork] in the typewriter (I hope it's still there) and went out on the dock. [There] was old 'Ding-bat' walking up and down the ranks telling them all what a wonderful captain he was. I knew damn well that if he spotted me he would order me back aboard for two more weeks [of court-martial work]. So I hid behind a steel tool shed and stayed there until the order was given to 'march off.' I stepped into formation and thought 'goodbye, goodbye, goodbye *Langley* and Old Shit-head. *I am free at last.*'"

In my first recollections of him telling this story I was very young and so pictured him as one of Dorothy's companions in the Wizard of Oz, falling-in behind the witch's troops as they march into the castle. I was always so relieved that he'd finally managed to escape Old Shit-head.

Before returning to South Dakota, he went downtown and bought two new chief petty officer uniforms. Since his promotion had come at sea, this was his first opportunity to procure the uniform he was entitled to wear. He bought a khaki working outfit for everyday use, and then the beautiful blue gabardine dress uniform he wore for more formal occasions. I can just imagine him walking down Embarcadero Street in wartime San Francisco, stopping to admire himself in the reflection of every plate-glass window he passed. He was quite proud of that uniform, and when we were kids he would put it on every Fourth of July and parade around the house to the music of a John Phillip Sousa march blaring from the stereo. He could be sentimental, too. The uniform was the same one he was wearing the night he met my mother. When she died, he took it out behind the garage and burned it in a barrel, saving the brass buttons to give to his grandchildren as keepsakes. We were on the phone one night when he told me about burning the uniform; I was immediately skeptical and questioned his motives. When I heard his voice break I knew he was sincere.

It's PITCH BLACK in the Arizona desert by the time Dad finishes his story of the war, the umpteenth time in my life I've heard it. But this time I'm impressed by his ability to remember so many of the small details, like Wylie's Smith's Southern drawl, for example, or the letters Old Shit-head dictated home to his family. More importantly, his retelling of the story has kept his mind occupied for another half-hour, not to mention completely displacing the horror of the Sundown Syndrome I witnessed earlier.

Brilliant stars twinkle over the interstate ahead and soon the soft glow of an approaching town appears on the horizon. It's Holbrook, I'm guessing, and then a green highway sign confirms it.

"I'll bet you're getting hungry," I say.

"I guess I am," he replies, and then adds, "Where are we going to sleep tonight?"

"How about Holbrook? It's just ahead."

He doesn't say anything and it's too dark inside the car for me to gauge what he's thinking. But then he asks, "Would that be Holbrook, *Arizona?*"

"The one and only," I reply. "Do you know it?"

"Never been there," he says.

"I've heard its lovely this time of year."

He chews on this for a moment, then replies in the darkness, "You're full of shit. But I think I need to stop and take a leak."

"Well then, Holbrook it is," I tell him. And I disengage the cruise control as we glide up the exit ramp.

18

HOLBROOK

We cross the overpass and cruise a commercial strip on the fringe of town. I can't seem to find any restaurants and I turn to Dad for help. "Are you sure you've never been to Holbrook before?" I ask. "Never once in all your years driving back and forth to Minnesota?"

"Nope."

"And you're sure about that?"

"Are we lost?" he says.

"We're not lost, but Holbrook seems to be."

In the headlights up ahead I spot a half-dozen teenagers on bikes riding carelessly along the shoulder, and I swing wide to avoid them, my speed slowed to twenty. Finally, way up ahead, I see the neon signs of a few fast-food restaurants, the light casting a welcoming glow through the darkness. But I'd like to find something a little more substantial than a fast-food joint; someplace, at least, where we can sit down and get table service. And then, almost as if someone from the chamber of commerce had been listening, a family restaurant pops up on the left. I make a long U-turn into the parking lot, allowing ample room to maneuver the trailer later, when we leave. Dad groans audibly as he climbs out of the car, testing his legs before pushing himself to his feet. He refuses my help yet leans heavily on his cane, shuffling off towards the entrance.

As we settle into a booth near the windows I notice the kids on the bikes have made it to the parking lot, with a few of them circling the U-Haul. It's then that I realize the trailer isn't locked. In fact, I don't have a padlock in my possession even if I did want to secure it. I stare out the window and suddenly, as if by magic,

I spot the bright lights of a Tractor Supply store at the far end of the parking lot. I should write a letter to the Holbrook chamber of commerce.

"Don't move," I tell my father as I crawl up out of the booth. "I'll be right back." But he is too busy studying the menu to even look up. I head quickly for the door.

Ten minutes later the U-Haul is securely padlocked and I return to the restaurant to discover an empty booth. Where's Dad? But before I can panic, a gum-snapping waitress passes by to inform me, "Dad's run off to the restroom, hon, so sit your worried butt down."

But I can't. I just can't. I trot off to the bathroom where I discover him at the sink with a paper towel and an exasperated look on his face. He's trying to blot the front of his pants where he'd dribbled all over himself at the urinal. He's not having much luck. In fact, he's only making things worse. I clean him up as best I can before taking him back out in public, finally getting him settled again in the booth. He is inconsolable, loudly cursing himself for "pissing his pants," carrying on like a four-year-old. When the waitress arrives to take our orders he brightens considerably.

"I know you from someplace," he says, smiling up at her. And then he puts his hand on top of hers where she's rested it on the table.

"Don't you start anything, young man," she says. She wrests her hand out from under Dad's mitt, then looks at me and winks. "This guy a friend of yours?"

Before I can reply Dad begins running his hand up her arm, reaching for the grand prize. "You have nice boosums!" he blurts.

"*Dad!*" I cry. "*Stop it!*"

But the waitress is an old pro and grabs his wrist, playfully scolding him. "They ain't on the menu, hon," she says. "How about a hamburger instead?" She winks at me again. "He always this much fun?"

I smile grimly. "I'm afraid we've had a long day. We're on our way back to Minnesota."

"Minn-e-sooo-ta," she says, straight out of the Fargo movie.

"He's going into a memory-care home," I say quietly, as if to explain his behavior.

Dad interrupts. "Are you two talking about me?" He has a leering grin on his face.

"Yes!" I reply loudly for his benefit. "She wants to know if you'd like a hamburger."

His mouth drops open, the upper plate of his denture hanging loose. "You're damn right I'd like to hug her!"

The waitress laughs. "Gonna be an interesting trip!" Then she adds, "I can come back."

"No, no," I tell her. "A couple of hamburgers, French fries. Dad, do you want a Coke?"

He looks confused. "Don't I get to hug her?"

"No, you don't!" I say abruptly. I look at the waitress. "And two Diet Cokes."

The waitress departs. Dad looks crestfallen. "What are you having?" he asks.

"A hamburger, same as you."

"Listen here, buster, I saw her first!"

DINNER OVER, WE drive back down the strip and find a Super8 near the interstate. It's going on ten and I'm exhausted. I run in to check availability. The hotel is a two-story so I ask the desk clerk for something on the first floor to facilitate my elderly father. He's Pakistani and his smile is apologetic when he informs me the only room left on the first floor is a smoking unit. I'm too tired to go looking elsewhere, so I take it. When he begins processing the paperwork I go back out to get Dad. But he's not in the car. I begin to panic again, this time trotting out toward the highway. Then I turn and spot him in the darkness behind the U-Haul. He's leaning on his cane with his eyes fixed on the trailer's license plate.

"This trailer's from *Florida*," he says incredulously, as if it's full of cocoanuts.

"Dad, c'mon," I tell him, too tired for lengthy explanations. "I got us a nice room here. Time for bed"

But by now the trailer has captured his full attention. He lifts his cane and pushes its rubber tip against the corrugated tailgate, probing. "Say, what the hell's in here, anyway?" he asks.

I don't dare tell him the truth, not now, when we've just completed a long, long day. I grab his arm and give it a playful tug. "I'm going to put *you* in there if you don't come with me," I tell him.

Big mistake. His eyes widen and he pulls his arm away like he's afraid I might actually do it. I wrap my arm around his shoulders and lean into him. "I'm kidding, Dad," I tell him. "I'll tie you to the roof before I put you in there. Let's go to our room and see if there's a baseball game on TV."

The room reeks of stale cigarettes but he doesn't seem to notice—immune, I suppose, after twenty years of Eunice's exhaust. I help him remove some of his things from the suitcase Roseanne packed this afternoon (was it really just this afternoon?): his toiletries kit, the medication tackle box, his electric shaver, and a change of underwear. I help him out of his clothes, hang his sweater in the closet, run some hot water in the sink. As he goes into his bedtime routine I lie down on the bed nearest the window and turn on the TV: no baseball games, but the weather channel says something about severe thunderstorms tomorrow afternoon in the direction we're heading. I can barely keep my eyes open.

Dad, meanwhile, has finished getting ready for bed and now stands beneath the fluorescent glare of the vanity light rummaging through his suitcase. The expression on his face in the mirror suddenly turns sour. "God damn it," he says irritably. "Who the hell packed this thing?"

"Dad, it doesn't matter. Get in bed."

But apparently it does matter, to him anyway. He turns and shuffles out into the room, the expression on his face bitter.

"Say, what the hell is going on here?" he says. "Where exactly are we going tomorrow?" He stands at the foot of my bed in his wrinkled boxer shorts and loose tee shirt, his elbows and knees as bony and flinty-looking as sticks of white chalk. He's without his glasses and now his eyes have the same dark, menacing look I remember from my youth.

"Dad," I say quietly, "we're on our way back home."

"Home, you say."

"Yes. It'll be a couple more days of driving but it'll be fun. We'll talk and we'll tell stories, just like we did today."

"But we're going back home, right?"

It occurs to me that his idea of home and mine are two entirely different entities. But I'm simply too tired to explain the difference so I nod, and this seems to placate him. The bitterness on his face gradually turns to one of mild apprehension, and he shuffles back to the vanity to close his suitcase. His toilet ritual now complete, he shuffles back in and stands between the two beds.

"Which one is mine?" he asks.

I give him a dubious look. "Did you want to sleep with me?"

"No."

"Well, then how about that one?" and I nod at the adjacent bed. I get up and pull the covers back on it, throw the extra pillow aside, give the mattress a pat, and motion for him to come sit down. He shuffles up between the beds and collapses on the mattress with an audible sigh. Lying back, he groans even louder as he pulls his legs up off the floor. I reach across him for the covers, his toenails beneath me yellow and splintered, the skin dry and flaky. But he abruptly pushes me away, insisting he can do it himself.

"You don't want me to tuck you in?" I ask.

"No," he says.

"Are you sure? It could get chilly in here tonight. I don't have the heat on."

His eyes flick on me, then back to the ceiling. "No."

"Okay, then. I'm going to leave the light on for a few more minutes while I look over the map for tomorrow. You go to sleep, okay? Good night."

He doesn't respond. He lays on his back staring up at the

ceiling, his body uncovered. I lay on my bed studying the road atlas for the exit in Albuquerque we'll need to take north tomorrow. Soon, the page begins to blur and suddenly the unwieldy book slips from my grasp. I sit up and put the atlas on the nightstand between the beds, then go in to brush my teeth. When I return, Dad is still lying on top of the covers, staring at the ceiling. Without asking, I pull the covers up over his legs and tuck them in mid-chest.

"How's that?" I ask.

No response. He continues staring at the ceiling, completely ignoring me. I kill the light, the TV, then crawl into bed, where I feel myself drifting off within seconds.

What a day.

Sweet dreams …

19

TEMPER, TEMPER

I'm awake. Lying on my side, facing the window. I've got an eerie feeling someone's watching me. I stare into the darkness, my eyes adjusting to the faint glow of light emanating around the perimeter of the curtained window. Instinctively, I roll onto my back, and in the faint light I discern the looming shape of someone standing over me. It's my father, I suddenly realize. What's he doing? He seems to be staring at something on the ceiling.

"Dad?" I call out. His looming presence is a little unnerving. No reply.

"Dad," I call again. "What are you doing? What's wrong?"

Now I see him pointing at the ceiling, his bony white arm lifted in the darkness. He says, "Are you going to fix this?"

"Fix … what?" I reply, and I reach over to turn on the light. The harsh glare makes both of us flinch, but he keeps his eyes on the ceiling.

"You said you were going to fix this," he says.

I rub my eyes and look at the clock. It's 12:30, barely two hours since we turned in. If there's one thing I don't like, it's being roused from a deep sleep.

"What are you talking about?" I say quietly.

"*This!*" he replies angrily, and he dramatically waves his hand at the ceiling as if he's Vanna White. I rise up on an elbow and stare at the ceiling for a good ten seconds before I decide there's nothing wrong with it—no cracks, no flaking paint, no falling plaster, nothing.

"Dad, there's nothing wrong with the ceiling."

"Like hell!" he shouts. "You promised me you were going to fix it!"

"Dad, get back in bed," I say sharply. I feel a little punch-drunk, woozy.

"Jesus Christ," he mutters. "You told me you were going to fix this."

"I'll fix it in the morning!" I tell him through clenched teeth. "Now get back in bed."

Which he does, albeit reluctantly. He lays there in his boxer shorts and tee-shirt, once more refusing to pull the covers over himself.

"Dad, pull your covers up."

"You told me you were going to fix it," he mutters again.

I jump up and jerk the covers from beneath his legs, pull them up tightly around his chin, tucking the ends beneath the mattress. I lean in, my nose inches from his. "Now you go to sleep," I order, in much the same way he used to order me to bed when I was the child and he was the dad. Well, things have changed, buster. I turn off the light and crawl back into bed, my mind stirred up by his nocturnal antics. I really wish he hadn't awakened me. Now I know I won't be able to sleep.

He's mad at me. I can tell that much; I can feel him brooding. Is this his subconscious way of getting even? God knows he can be tough. Not to mention angry. He has a volatile temper and I've seen it erupt on more than one occasion. Never on me, though, never physically on me. Except for that one time, that is, and that was my fault, not his. I don't hold him accountable for that. I was careless and he reacted, that's all. I wonder if he even remembers it?

I was probably eleven or twelve at the time, and growing like a weed. I was one of the taller boys in my class and desperately try-ing to improve my skills at basketball, to make the "Gold" team at Incarnation Grade School where the legendary Jack Marton was coach. Every day after school—and every Saturday and Sunday, too, for that matter—I could be found practicing jump-shots and free-throws on our driveway court. Years ago Dad had fastened a rim above the garage's old-style barn doors and installed a homemade backboard. The garage doors opened horizontally, sliding in each direction along a track. Almost every afternoon the doors remained closed to keep the basketball from rolling into the far recesses of the garage, but on weekends, the doors were kept open shoulder-width to allow adequate passage for my father as he worked on his various remodeling projects around the house. On this particular Saturday afternoon he'd been going in and out with the lengths of lumber he was sawing to size in his garage workshop. I was alone on the court practicing my jump-shots and had just "swished" a beauty when Dad suddenly emerged in the open doorway, laden with lumber. The ball went cleanly through the net and made a glancing blow off his forehead, sending his work hat (a paint-stained fedora), his pipe (unlit) and his glasses to the concrete apron. In the confusion he also dumped the load of lumber from his shoulder.

"*God damn you!*" he cried as I hurried in to grab the rebound. What happened next is something I've thought about at length over the years, and I've come to believe it was unpremeditated and therefore innocent. The basketball lay in the tangle of lumber strewn at Dad's feet, and as I bent to pick it up he kicked me as hard as he could in the seat of my pants. It didn't hurt, or at least I don't remember it hurting. But I do remember grabbing the ball and retreating a few steps to recover from the shock of his attack. It was so unexpected. It must have surprised him, too, because in the next few moments his scathing profanity took on a conciliatory, almost apologetic tone as he bent to retrieve his lost articles.

"Help me pick this up," he finally muttered. And this was all the apology I needed. He had calmed down. As requested, I helped him load the boards back onto his shoulder, and a few minutes later he continued on into the house as if nothing had happened. Whew.

But make no mistake; he had a temper. He was the youngest of five brothers in a motherless household ruled by an autocratic father. He knew how to take care of himself. Once, when I was very young, he loaded the entire family into Mom's old Plymouth for a Sunday outing to buy a Halloween pumpkin. Baby Jimmy sat untethered between Mom and Dad in the front seat, with Kath, Mark, Betsey, and me riding loose in back. (Seatbelts and car seats were still decades in the future.) We had just come to a stop at a red light when our car was suddenly hit from behind by another car. I remember the impact – a sudden jolt -- and then my father's startled eyes in the rearview mirror. He muttered a curse as he set the hand brake. Then he told Mom, "I'll be right back," and climbed out.

Those of us in the back seat turned around on our knees to watch through the rear window as Dad walked past. He paused at the rear bumper long enough to examine the large crease in the car's trunk, put there by the garish, chrome bumper of the other car. We could see he was not happy, his eyes taking on the malevolent quality I had witnessed a few other times in my short life. Then he turned and walked back to the offending car, which had retreated a few feet. Behind its windshield two young men watched with what appeared to be amused expressions as Dad approached their car, the driver rolling down the window as Dad bent to question him. Judging from the look on Dad's face, I don't think he said anything funny, but in the next moment the two young men started giggling and laughing like a couple of school-girls. And that's when my father reached in and slugged the driver, hitting him squarely in the jaw. I remember not only the look of shock mixed with pain on the driver's face, but also the one of as-tonishment on his buddy's face as he realized their afternoon had turned suddenly serious. Dad leaned through the window for a few more minutes, lecturing both of them before finally returning to our car. As he climbed back inside I couldn't help but notice the subtle look of satisfaction on his face. He glanced at Mom and smiled. "Those two sunzabitches are drunk," was all he said. And then he released the handbrake and drove away as if nothing had happened. He never did repair the damaged trunk.

SATURDAY NIGHTS, BEFORE the *Lawrence Welk Show* came on, Dad loved to watch *All-Star Wrestling*, a local show broadcast live from the Calhoun Beach Club, not far from our Pleasant Avenue home. He had his favorite wrestlers: Vern Gagne, of course, the hometown hero who had played football at the U of M and was the quintessential "good guy" in every match he ever fought; The Crusher, a barrel-chested beer drinker from Milwaukee who smoked fat cigars and made the most outlandish faces before the TV cameras; and Tiny Mills, a half-breed lumberjack from the north woods who liked to rake his opponent's faces with the spiked soles of his logger's boots (or so we were led to believe). Dad would never acknowledge the fact that it was all staged because to do so would spoil the fun. Thus I grew up believing it was real, which made what happened one night even more memorable.

Dad got tickets to attend the live broadcast. This was not uncommon as he was a big fan and I'm certain we went more than once. I can recall other nights when we sat at various spots around the small studio, all of the seats close to the ring as the venue was nothing more than the Beach Club's dining room cleared of tables. But on this particular night Dad had gotten seats on the main aisle, down which the wrestlers paraded on their way to the ring. I had the seat directly on the aisle, with Dad next to me, and Jimmy on his other side toward the middle of the row. One of the first matches headlined a resident "bad guy," a towering, heavily-muscled wrestler who called himself "The Great Dane." His identifying feature was the length of platinum blonde hair that, once displaced from its combed glory, covered the side of his face like a silk curtain. I would never learn the nature of Dad's particular aversion to the Great Dane—perhaps he reminded him of Old Shit-head, his commanding officer on the *Langley*—but for whatever reason, he seemed to despise him. As the Great Dane sauntered down the aisle, close enough to touch, Dad suddenly leaned over me and shouted, "*You're a horse's ass!*"

Almost as if on cue, the giant wrestler spun on his heels and made a threatening motion toward Dad, his powerful arms swinging wildly over my head. "*Dad!*" I screamed. "*Stop it!*" To my relief the Great Dane turned and resumed his walk to the ring. I begged Dad not to do that again but he just sat beside me watching steely-eyed as the wrestler strode away. He had bought popcorn, of course, and his mouth worked overtime on a mouthful of kernels as he watched the Dane make his grand entrance over the top rope.

When the match began, the Dane locked arms with his opponent—one of the show's perennial losers, either Scrap-iron George Gadaski or The Capable Kenny Jay. As the clinch broke, the opponent landed a cheap shot to the Dane's jowl, which reverberated through the studio like a sharp slap. What I remember next comes back to me in slow motion, so perfectly was it choreographed between the two professionals. Upon impact, the Great Dane's head jerked sideways and his veil of platinum hair lifted like a curtain as a virtual downpour of saliva sprayed from his mouth. I've no doubt he had aimed it directly at Dad, for in the next moment we were showered with what felt like a gallon of wet spit. To this day I'm certain he'd been holding it in his mouth as he made his entrance, waiting for some fool to challenge him, some fool like my father. The saliva rained down all over us— in my hair, on my face and even into the open box of popcorn on Dad's lap. Dad stared down at it with a disgusted scowl, the half-eaten box now ruined. When the match was over—the Great Dane the victor, of course—Dad accosted him one last time as he strode past. "You sonofabitch!" he shouted, loud enough for the wrestler to hear. But the Dane just smirked, confident he'd won two matches that night.

☙

ONE HUMID SUMMER night a thunderstorm erupted over the Twin Cities and straight-line winds toppled boulevard trees throughout our South Minneapolis neighborhood. We awoke to find Pleasant Avenue blocked by an enormous elm lying diagonally across the middle of the street. Dad somehow made it to work that morning but Mom later got a call from Public Works informing her it might be days before they could clear our street; trees were down everywhere. The word went out and by lunchtime every kid on Pleasant Avenue had equipped him- or herself with an axe or saw from their father's garage. We started with the smaller branches stretching clear across the Bensons' front yard and worked our way back toward the street where the heavy timber lay. By the time Dad got home that evening we were down to the main trunk and a few heavy limbs still blocking passage. We were determined to get it done by nightfall. Dad lit his pipe and sat down on the front steps of our house to watch the young lumberjacks in action. He seemed genuinely amused if not impressed.

Around the corner of our block, halfway down 42nd Street, lived a retired railroad man known throughout the neighborhood as "Tex." A bachelor, Tex was one of those neighbors Dad described as a "grouchy old fart," and wanted nothing to do with him. Every evening after supper Tex could be spotted making his way west along 42nd Street with a bag of empty beer bottles, heading to Marty's Kwik Shop to exchange them for a fresh supply. He wore bib overalls and a railroad cap, and stopped periodically to spit long strings of plug tobacco juice on the boulevard grass. Every kid in the neighborhood avoided him whenever possible.

On this particular evening Tex was on his return trip from Marty's when he happened to look north up Pleasant to see the volunteer woodcutters hard at it. He turned and ambled up the street for a better look, stopping on the sidewalk in front of the Bensons', which we'd already cleared of branches. We all ceased chopping and sawing long enough to look at him, as it seemed he had something to say:

"Who told you kids you could do that?" he growled. "Go on home before I call the police!"

As a matter of fact, the police had already been by earlier in the day to inspect our work and had actually thanked us for our efforts. So we felt pretty safe on that front. But just then I noticed my father getting up from our front steps and heading in our direction, his expression ominous. Holding his pipe like a pointer he aimed it across the street at Tex and shouted, "You go on home yourself, you old fart! These kids aren't bothering you."

Tex's eyes narrowed and he puffed up his chest, acting like he was going to do some serious damage. But this only further infuriated my father, at the same time frightening me as I saw the anger in his eyes.

"I told you to go on home!" Dad shouted again, and this time there could be no doubt as to his intent. He started across the street, heading straight at Tex. We all watched, waiting for what was surely going to be a real fist-fight between two adults—more real even than All-Star Wrestling. But to his credit (and my relief) Tex turned-tail and started for home, grumbling over his shoulder as he went, the beer bottles clinking in the paper bag. From that day on, I began to see him in a different, more diminished light, now completely harmless. And I began to see my dad in a different light, too. He was certainly no one to be messed with.

℘

I LOOK AT THE clock again; it's going on 2. Good God. I've been awake all this time. I need to get some sleep or tomorrow is going to be an even longer day. Then I chance a look over at Dad. Even in the faint glow from the curtains I can see that his eyes are open and that he's lying there awake, probably as long as I have. I sigh and roll over again, this time toward the window. I can only imagine what he's thinking: "Who's this asshole in the other bed, the one ruining my life? And why won't he fix the goddamn ceiling?

20

ALBUQUERQUE

It's still dark when I hear him get out of bed. His bare feet scuff across the carpet as he makes his way to the bathroom, his hand sliding along the wall for balance. He turns on the fluorescent light over the vanity and this, along with the rattle from the exhaust fan above the toilet, is enough to wake the dead. He slams the door to the bathroom behind him and now I'm convinced it's all for me. A few minutes later he emerges and goes about his morning routine in front of the mirror, none of it quietly. I sit up and swing my feet to the floor, my head heavy and thick. The clock says 4:40. I doubt that either of us has slept much more than the two hours I got before the ceiling repair dilemma.

I sit bleary-eyed on the edge of the bed watching as he gets dressed. He changes into the underwear I laid out the night before, the clean slacks, fresh shirt, and the cardigan from yesterday that he somehow remembers is hanging in the closet. Then he is standing at the foot of the bed looking at me, his silhouette dark against the florescent glare from behind.

"You're taking me home today, right?" he says. It's more of a statement than a question. His voice is strained. I can tell he's already upset.

"That's right," I tell him. "And it looks like we'll be getting an early start." In spite of my lack of sleep, this suits me to a tee. We've got somewhere around fifteen hundred miles ahead of us, and I'd like to finish it in two days, if he's able. I get up and go through my own routine in the bathroom, and fifteen minutes later I'm carrying our bags out to the lobby, my father in hot pursuit. He shuffles along as fast as his feet and cane can carry him, buoyed by the notion that we're headed back to Phoenix.

In the lobby, to my surprise, we find a couple of tables already occupied by a handful of men dressed in dark work clothes, their ballcaps embroidered with the same company logo. They're helping themselves to the continental breakfast, slurping down bowls of cereal and buttering waffles hot off a do-it-yourself griddle. A TV high in the corner is blaring FoxNews stories about the Trayvon Martin investigation and also decrying the rising price of gasoline. As if I didn't know; everywhere we've stopped so far the gas has been at least $4/gal. I turn with the bags and wait for Dad to catch up. "Would you like to get something to eat?" I ask. "It's free."

"Free?" he says, wrinkling his forehead and staring at the men sitting at the table. "The hell you say."

I drop the bags and get him situated at a table near the TV, pour him a cup of coffee (one cream, one Sweet n Low) and grab him a doughnut from the plastic display case. I tell him I'll be right back, and then I run the bags out to the car where I pop the hood and check the oil. The sky glows faintly pink in the east with a few faded stars still visible above the lights of the parking lot. The temperature, I guess, is about thirty degrees cooler than it was in Phoenix. I'm wearing the same shorts and sandals I started with yesterday, but this is by choice; loose and comfortable is my idea of smooth sailing.

Back inside, Dad is sipping his coffee and staring up at the TV, the doughnut untouched before him. "How about I make you a waffle?" I say. "Some of those guys over there are eating them and they look pretty good. I'm going to have one."

He shifts around in his chair and again wrinkles his forehead as he studies the men in the blue work clothes. They are mostly silent and seem more intent on eating their breakfast than anything else.

"Okay, I guess I'll try one of those," he says solemnly. Then he adds, "Is there any milk?"

I pour him a plastic tumbler of milk, a necessity to facilitate the lengthy process of swallowing his meds. Returning to the counter, I begin making a waffle, following the directions affixed to the top of the iron. While it's cooking, an elderly couple emerges from the hallway and takes a table next to ours. My father ignores them, focusing on his med doses while keeping an eye fixed on the TV, which is now broadcasting the baseball scores from last night. He seems totally engrossed. When the waffle is done I fork it onto a plastic plate, add a couple pats of butter, a packet of syrup, and put it down in front of him. I begin to help him with the syrup packet but he slaps my hand away, insisting he can do it himself. He seems determined to be a grouch today. I return to the counter to start on another waffle and have just finished pouring the batter onto the iron when I hear a commotion behind me. I turn to discover my father has spilled his milk, not only on the waffle, but all over the table in front of him where it is now dripping onto his lap. He's swearing a holy fury, effing this and effing that, which causes the elderly woman beside him to stare wide-eyed at her hands. Her husband begins pulling napkins from the tabletop dispenser and throwing them into the puddle creeping across our table. I rush over with more napkins and build a dam along the edge, at the same time tossing the plate of soggy waffles on the table behind. The blue uniforms have turned as one to watch, and the Pakistani desk clerk (the same guy from last night) hurries out from behind the counter with a large towel. "It is okay, sir, it will be fine," he says calmly, wiping up the mess, and a minute later the table is dry. My father's swearing subsides to an angry mutter.

"Goddammit, whose stupid idea was this anyway?"

"I guess that would be mine," I tell him, and then, "Okay, I think it's time to go."

With a little more callousness than is perhaps necessary, I haul him up out of his chair and shove the cane into his hand. He's got a thin line of spilled milk across the lap of his khakis and for a second I consider taking him back to the room to change into something dry. But then I remember that Roseanne has allotted for only one change of clothes per day and decide this damp

pair will have to do for now. Right now I feel it's more important
to remove him from the scene of his humiliation. I wrap the uneaten doughnut in a napkin and grab a couple more for myself on
the way out. They're free, you know.

We idle down the frontage road toward the interstate and I
pull into a gas station to fill up. The price on the lighted marquee
is again over $4 a gallon and before I can get out of the car Dad
demands to know who's paying for it. I insist it's nothing he needs
to worry about, but from the expression on his face I can tell he's
getting angrier. I climb out before he has a chance to elevate his
rant, pump the gas, clean the windshield, and then run into the
store to grab something I know will calm him. When I get back to
the car I hand him a morning newspaper and a fresh cup of coffee—one cream, one Sweet 'n Low. Maybe like yesterday the box
scores and fresh coffee will calm him down. I turn on the reading
lamp over his seat, check his seat belt, and pick up some of the
trash that's accumulated on the floor around him. (I never knew
him to be such a messy traveler!) As he studies the front page of
the paper I start the car and find our way back out onto the interstate. Again, the trailer pulls easily behind, and just like yesterday
it is soon forgotten. I set the cruise-control at 68, tune the radio
to the morning news, and settle in for a long day of driving. I have
it in my mind to make mid-Nebraska by nightfall.

Straight ahead, the sun is making its first appearance of the
day, flashing like a welder's arc through gaps in the distant mountains. I flip my visor down to block the glare and glance over at
my father to see if it's bothering him. But it's doubtful he's even
noticed; it appears he's got something else on his mind. The newspaper lies unopened on his lap, and he's staring at the dashboard,
his lips moving in a silent conversation with himself. He catches
me looking at him.

"Say, who the hell gave you permission to drive my car?"

I scowl. "C'mon, Dad, stop it ..."

"Don't you have your own car?"

I don't look at him. "You know I do. I have a Dodge pickup

truck. Remember? We drove it down to Mark's farm a couple of years ago. We sang Mitch Miller songs all the way home. You must remember that!"

He glares at me, steely-eyed. "I don't give a *shit* about Mitch Miller. If you have your own car, why are you driving mine?" Before I can reply, he adds, "Jesus Christ, I wish somebody'd give me a *goddamn* straight answer around here!"

Oh boy. We ride along in silence for awhile, my father stewing with this new perceived injustice, his own son refusing to tell him the truth. But there is no reasoning with him at this point and I decide it's better that we not argue. I point at the newspaper on his lap. "Did the Twins win last night?"

"How the hell do I know?"

"Check the box score," I tell him. "It's in there someplace." And for a few minutes he is distracted while he rustles through the paper in search of the box scores. But he can't find the sports page and in his frustration he throws the whole disheveled cluster on the floor. I can tell by the look on his face we're back to Square One. Whatever nirvana we achieved on the road to Holbrook yesterday is now completely gone. I'll need to try something else.

"Tell me about your teeth," I say.

"My teeth? What about my teeth?"

"Until last night, I never knew you had a full set of dentures. I knew you were having some problems with a bridge a few years back, but when did you get the full set?"

For most of his adult life he's been a tooth grinder. Asked a question he needed to think about, his first course of action was to grind his front teeth together, his lips parted for the world to see. Decades ago a dentist warned him he would eventually grind them down to nothing, and sure enough, he's succeeded. He was fitted with an upper bridge for a number of years, which he managed to break in half on more than one occasion, repairing it himself with a dab of Super Glue. The glue *"tastes like shit,"* he once confessed over the phone when I inquired about its flavor. But then he added, "I'll be goddamned if it doesn't work!" Or at least it worked for awhile, until he broke the plate again. At some point in the past few years he went through the total tooth extraction process and had an entire set of dentures installed, both upper and lower.

"They're a pain in the ass," he grumbles now. He then proceeds to spit both plates into his hand, which he holds before his nose, one at a time, to scrutinize them for God knows what. When they've passed inspection he deposits them in the pullout tray beneath the radio alongside a St. Christopher statue, a plastic spoon, his travel-size box of Kleenex, and the uneaten doughnut.

"You going to eat that doughnut?" I ask.

"No."

"Can I have it?"

"No."

"How about a fruit cup then?" I ask. He had gotten into the fruit cups yesterday and seemed to enjoy them. Roseanne and the aide must have loaded a couple dozen into the cooler, along with bottled water, a loaf of banana bread, a few cranberry scones, and a bag of homemade cookies. I remove one of the fruit cups and peel the top back. Dad is poised with his spoon and wastes little time as he begins scooping. Watching him slurp the fruit off his spoon, his mouth concave from the removed dentures, he looks every minute of his ninety-six years, like someone from a depression-era documentary.

"You want to try a little of this banana bread?" I ask, and before he replies I steer with my knees and begin unfolding the layers of Saran wrap from the tightly wrapped loaf. I hand him a thick slice. He holds it in his lap and eats it by breaking it into chunks with his fingers. Before long, his sweater and pants are littered with crumbs, which he brushes to the floor. His side of the car looks like a hamster cage. But now, with a little food in his stomach, he seems somewhat placated. I silently pray that he'll be in a better mood for the rest of the day.

As the sun rises the scenery beyond the windshield grows more spectacular with each passing mile, painted buttes and soar-

ing cliffs emerging around every bend of the highway. For awhile
we find ourselves in step with an eastbound Amtrak train, our
paths at times converging at bridges over the interstate. When it's
close enough, I roll down the windows and listen for the sound of
the train's whistle at distant crossings, offering my own rendition
in return. I'm hoping Dad will enjoy this as much as our mooing
at the cows. At first he seems amused but soon begins to complain
about the cold breeze, warning me he'd "better not catch a goddamn cold."

We lose sight of the train anyway, in Gallup, New Mexico,
and I ask Dad to check the distance to Albuquerque, but he's no
longer interested in playing navigator. He grabs the atlas out of
a side pocket and shoves it at me. "Look for yourself," he says. I
don't have to. Our ETA on the GPS suggests we'll make it to the
back side of Albuquerque after the morning rush hour is over.

Just after eight my cell phone rings; it's Roseanne wondering
how things are going. She starts telling me how much she misses
my father; how this is the first morning in as long as she can remember that she hasn't stopped by to visit him. There's a pause
and then her voice breaks as she asks if she might talk to him. I
pass him the phone. "It's for you," I tell him. "It's your girlfriend."

"Hello!" he shouts, lifting the phone clumsily to his ear, the
black case all but disappearing behind his thick fingers. I can hear
Roseanne's voice plainly enough, her sentences slow and clear, her
tone comforting. But my father doesn't seem to be responding.

"Hold it closer to your ear!" I shout at him. "It's Roseanne,
she's talking to you!" But he just sits there with the phone clutched
to the side of his face, his eyes staring vacantly ahead. A minute
later, he tosses it in my lap.

"Why the hell did you give me that goddamn thing?" he says
with a look of disgust. "There's nobody on it!"

I glance down at the screen: Call ended. It's just as well; in
a day or so he probably won't remember Roseanne anyway. He's
already having trouble remembering me.

We drive along in silence for awhile. Then Dad spots some

cattle high on a rocky slope out his side of the car. The landscape has turned windswept and rough, with sparse vegetation growing in green tufts here and there along the hillside. The sight of the cattle bothers him.

"What a godforsaken place to be a cow," he mutters.

"You think they have a choice?" I counter. This only makes him madder.

"What the hell's the matter with people grazing cattle in a place like this? Cows need green pastures and a goddamn watering hole. You see any waterholes out there in this shit? Jesus Christ!"

Yep, he's definitely pissed-off at the world this morning. I realize I'd better find something to keep his mind occupied or this could get bad. At my wife's suggestion I've brought along a number of CDs I checked out of the Saint Paul library, things he might enjoy listening to. Reaching behind, I start digging through the bag they're in and manage to grab the one on top. It's called *Musical Memories of WWII,* and I immediately cue it up on the van's CD player. A moment later Vera Lynn is singing "The White Cliffs of Dover" and I join in on the chorus:

There'll be bluuuue-birds o-ver

The white cliffs of Do-ver ...

"What the *hell* is this?" Dad snaps.

I stop singing and look over at him. "It's Vera Lynn singing 'White—' "

"*Bullshit!*" he says. "*That's* not Vera Lynn."

"It is too!" I say.

"Like hell it is!"

I grab the CD cover and examine the back side. *All songs performed by the Greater Bloomington Community Choir,* it reads. Well I'll be damned. He's right; it's not Vera Lynn.

"Turn it off," he says.

"No wait," I say. "I've got other stuff you might like. How about an audio book?" And again my right hand rummages through the bag behind and emerges with *In My Time, A Memoir* by Dick Cheney. Dick Cheney? Did I really bring this? I'm not sure why, but it's no secret that my father has voted Republican for as long as I can remember. Once during a Sunday night phone conversation, he practically begged me to vote for George H. W. Bush in the next election, pleading that HW might be the *last* of the Greatest Generation to run for president. And wasn't Dick Cheney HW's secretary of defense? Maybe that's why I brought it along. I decide to play Dick's CD, hoping he'll get caught up in the long narrative.

Mr. Cheney himself reads the opening prologue, which is a minute-by-minute account of the events on the morning of 9/11. His voice is a reserved western drawl, subdued so as to show a man in complete control of his surroundings, both now and on that fateful day years ago. I turn the volume up a notch as we are now approaching the outskirts of Albuquerque and the traffic and noise are rising. The morning rush hour I had hoped to avoid is still heavy.

My father's forehead wrinkles as he bends to hear the program. "What the hell is this now?" he demands. "What happened to *Bluebirds?*"

"It's Dick Cheney," I reply. "You like this guy, right? You once told me so yourself." I pass him the CD cover, which he studies for all of two seconds before tossing it on the floor. I turn the volume up and we ride along listening to the former vice president describe the moment the planes crash into the Twin Towers of the World Trade Center, then the Pentagon, then how the brave patriots took back the plane headed to destroy the White House. Dick describes how he fled to the secret bunker beneath the White House; how he was able to maintain his mental acuity under times of such great duress; how he—

"Do we really have to listen to this shit?" my father shouts.

I glance over to find him muttering to himself, his eyes dark with anger. A sign over the freeway ahead announces our proximity to downtown Albuquerque and the ramp to the I-25 North exit I need to take for Santa Fe. Dad notices the sign too as we pass beneath it.

"Santa Fe?" He spits it out like a curse. "Where in the *hell*

are we going?"

"Dad, calm down," I tell him. "Let's listen to what Dick is saying. He's about to start making command decisions that will change the course of history."

"*I don't give a goddamn about the course of history!*" he shouts. And now there's a desperation in his voice I hadn't noticed before, something almost fatal in its tone. The traffic is heavy on both sides of us but I chance a quick look at him. He's agitated, worked-up into a froth and on the verge of something drastic. I begin to worry. The traffic is bumper to bumper all around us, everything moving at a frantic clip. I turn the CD volume up but it doesn't seem to help. My father is onto me.

"You told me we were going back home!" he wails.

"Dad, we *are* going home. We're going to your *new* home in La Crosse, where Mark lives on the farm with cows and tractors and dogs. Remember his nice dogs? Remember how Eunice said it was okay for you to leave? She said so yesterday, don't you remember?"

Somebody behind me starts flashing their lights and somebody else coming up on the right lays on the horn, the blaring of which completely drowns out Cheney's monotone. I glance down at the instrument panel to discover I've somehow slowed to 45, way too slow for this mess. The voice on the GPS announces: "In one mile, exit left." Dad is having a fit. "God *damn* you!" he shouts, his voice breaking. "I'm not going back to… goddamn it, *wherever* the hell it is you're taking me! Stop the god damn car! *Stop the GOD DAMN car, I'm telling you! LET ME OUT!*" And with this he begins fumbling with his door, from which I feel a sudden whoosh of air. My god, he's opened it! The dashboard warning light flashes DOOR AJAR – DOOR AJAR, and then the alarm goes off – DING DING DING. I lean across to pull the door shut while Dad struggles to free himself from his seatbelt, the two of us fighting for control. The car on the right looms dangerously near, its horn blaring, the driver screaming at me through the window, his face livid. "RECALCULATING …"

says the GPS. "RECALCULATING…" I've missed the I-25 exit.

"*I don't want to live!*" Dad cries out in anguish. He's trying to open the door again but I've finally succeeded in setting the electric lock from my side, something I should have been doing from the start.

"Dad, *stop!*" I shout. But he's turned sideways in his seat again and is gripping the door handle with both hands, prying at it, shaking it, trying to tear it completely off. That's when I spot the red shoebox behind me on the seat, nearly hidden behind everything else, the red shoebox filled with old photos. I strain to reach it and manage to hook a corner with my pinkie, the car swerving into the right lane which brings more honking and another angry driver in the window. But I succeed in pulling the box to the floor beside me where I pluck a photo—any photo—from the collection. It's a picture of his dog, his beloved dachshund. I hold it up in front of his face.

"*Whose dog is this*?" I shout, my voice more pleading than questioning.

And suddenly, all is calm.

"Why, that's *my* dog," he says. And he's smiling now, his face as serene as the Mona Lisa's as he takes the photo.

"That's my little Tuffy!" he says. "Where did you get this?"

I take a breath, relax a bit, check the mirrors.

"I think God just handed it to me," I say quietly.

Then I wait to for a story to begin.

21

WOOF!

Dad can talk dogs for hours. He loves dogs. There was a time in my life when I wondered if he didn't love dogs more than he loved Mom, or for that matter, me. He didn't always understand me. But he certainly understood dogs.

He told me once that in all his years as a salesman he'd never once been bitten by any of the hundreds of dogs he'd encountered. Which was uncommon. Rural contractors often kept dogs on their premises to ward off thieves and other ne'er-do-wells, like salesmen. A lot of his contemporaries, Dad claimed, were scared shitless of dogs and carried mace or a chain, or some other deterrent whenever they had to call on a contractor in a remote setting. But not Dad. "You have to show a dog who's boss," he said. "Let them get a good whiff of your hand and show them you're not afraid. If they sense you're afraid it stirs something in their primal instincts and you've lost. A vicious dog will bare its teeth and try to show you how tough he is. You've got to call his bluff and show him you're tougher."

He claims the only time in his life he'd ever been bitten was when Curly, a favorite dog from his childhood, was run over by a car in front of their farmhouse. In his retelling of the tragedy, the dog's back was broken and when a tearful young Russell ran to lift him off the road, Curly, in his dying anguish, bit him on the left shoulder. This is another one of those stories he's told a couple million times, and at this point in the narrative he would stop and search the faces of his listeners, almost always children.

"I still have the scar," he would say grimly, and then clutch his shoulder as if it still bothered him. "If you want, I'll let you feel it."

He never failed in luring one of his unsuspecting listeners to step forth and reach for the injured shoulder. As soon as the tentative fingers of a young child touched his shirt, he would *bark* in a sharp shrill voice, frightening everyone but himself, and then laugh at his own joke.

Curly, Rastus, Stub, and Adolph—he had stories about all his childhood dogs. Rastus was a good dog, but because he spent the majority of his life playing second fiddle to the more dominant Curly, he was considered meek. Stub was a toy bulldog with a friendly disposition and a stub tail. He actually belonged to a neighbor three miles down the road but refused to stay there. Every time my father brought him back to his rightful home, he returned. The owner didn't seem to care much, and eventually Stub was allowed to settle in on George's farm, finally dying of old age beneath a bush during a snowstorm.

Adolph was an Eskimo Spitz and a menace to every living creature that dared show its face in the open barnyard. Of the fifteen or so cats known to keep the farm free of mice and rats, only one was still alive when my father departed for the Navy in 1936, thanks to Adolph. Dad's sister Adeline wrote to him in boot camp that George had finally shot Adolph after he'd found their last remaining cat murdered. My father had to admit that for once in his life he was in full agreement with his father's decision; Adolph was a beautiful but bloodthirsty hound.

Dad didn't wait long after marrying my mother to buy the first of our many family dogs. In the few photos of him I've seen, Snoozie appears to be nothing more than a scrawny runt He didn't last long. Left alone in the house while his master and mistress went off to work every morning, Snoozie grew anxious and one day got into my mother's closet, chewing the hems off all her skirts. My mother, who was never a great lover of dogs in the first place, must have demanded the dog's removal, and Snoozie became nothing more than a vague memory in the history of the burgeoning Halter family.

We didn't have a dog in the early part of my childhood, but

there were plenty of other dogs in our South Minneapolis neighborhood, most of them running free, as was the custom of the time. A neighborhood dog named Teddy used to chase cars up and down Pleasant Avenue, and more than once he received a well-placed boot from an angry motorcyclist. My father called Teddy a "nervous little shit" but would nonetheless scratch his rump whenever Teddy stopped by to say hi. He knew just where to scratch a dog's rump and also the exact spot on a dog's ear that, when rubbed, would make the dog's rear leg jerk spasmodically, something he never tired of doing. The Westlins, our neighbors two doors down, kept their dog Bootsie fenced in their backyard—a rarity in those days. On those warm Sunday nights when Dad grilled a flat slab of round steak for dinner, he would separate the circular chunk of bone and announce, "Who wants to give the bone to Bootsie?" My sister Betsey, a dog-lover in training, was always the first to respond, but I'd be right beside her as she held the bone through Westlin's fence for Bootsie to snatch from her fingers. Betsey begged and begged for a dog of her own, but Mom wouldn't give in.

Betsey wouldn't relent, and in the summer of 1965 we finally got a dog of our own. Snoopy arrived as a puppy but soon grew into a big black-and-white mutt resembling the Peanuts Cartoon character, hence the name. He was mild-mannered and friendly, and posed no threat to the neighborhood as he roamed at will, like almost every other dog we knew. Dad built a doghouse identical to the one in the cartoon strip, and for awhile he tried to get Snoopy to sit on the roof, same as the fictional dog. But Snoopy wanted nothing to do with it; he preferred to sleep in the house, usually in the back hall off the kitchen. We never locked our back door (nor the front one for that matter), but every night it was someone's responsibility to make sure the back screen door was latched so that Snoopy couldn't get out. One morning we awoke to find the back door unlatched and Snoopy gone. Betsey blamed me, claiming I was the last one to bed the night before and had neglected to check the latch. I was fairly certain I had. But looking back on the episode, I've started to wonder if Snoopy had simply gown wise enough by then to jump up and unlatch the door himself. In any event, he was gone. Betsey made posters and hung them all over the neighborhood, cried herself to sleep at night, and shamed me at every opportunity. One night, in an effort to console us, Dad made up a story about how Snoopy had most likely ventured south, out past the Minnesota River, where he was now running free with the cows and horses, chasing squirrels and chipmunks to his heart's content. He could paint such amazingly pastoral pictures with his stories that I truly believed Snoopy was better off in the wild than he was living with us. But not Betsey; Dad's story only increased her despair, and she would not be consoled until we got another dog. She eventually developed such an infatuation with dogs that as soon as she left home for good she acquired more dogs than might be considered normal. And I think she trained every one of them to growl at me on sight.

When we moved to Saint Louis Park in 1970, Dad bought our second family dog, this one a dachshund/terrier mix he named Tuffy, later to be known as Tuffy I. The new house had an expansive backyard that bordered a pond and was infiltrated with gophers, hundreds of them. One of my father's favorite Saturday morning pastimes was to shove a garden hose down one of the gopher holes, turn on the water, and then allow Tuffy to do what he was bred to do. It didn't take long for the flooded rodents to scurry up a distant escape tunnel where Tuffy stood watch, ready to pounce. He snatched an unsuspecting gopher in his quick maw and obediently laid it at my father's feet, where it was readily dispatched with the flat side of a garden spade. Oh, the fun! Later, the victorious hunters would retreat to the kitchen table where they sat beside each other, Tuffy rewarded with braunschweiger sandwiches. One winter when my brother Jim was still in college he brought Tuffy along on a snowshoeing expedition through Theodore Wirth Park. At some point the dog took off after a rabbit and when it didn't return Jim hung around the parking lot for a couple hours waiting for it. Finally he went home and informed

Dad that his favorite dog of all time had run off. Dad was furious and drove with Jim back to the park where the two of them
searched until well after dark, suffering frostbitten noses and toes
for their efforts. But Tuffy was nowhere to be found. Three days
passed—three of the coldest days in the history of cold weather,
as my father would have you believe. And then one night, as he
and Mom were getting ready for bed, they heard a whimper at
the door. Poor little Tuffy, half frozen and nearly starved to death,
had found his way home, a journey certainly more incredible than
anything Walt Disney could ever have dreamed up. And a legend
was born. (At least in my father's telling.)

    How he loved that little dog. Tuffy lived to a ripe old age,
and in fact was the last remaining member of the family still at
home when my parents retired and moved up north. Dad bought
an old pickup truck in which Tuffy rode shotgun, propping his
forefeet on the passenger armrest and flapping his ears out the
open window. Sometimes Dad carried him in the wide pocket of
his coat as they made the rounds of hardware stores and gas stations, Tuffy nearly invisible with his dark fur against the darker
fabric of the coat. Other times Dad simply carried him under his
arm like a loaf of bread; they were pretty much inseparable.

    When my mother died in 1984 and Dad headed south for
the winter, Tuffy was his lone travelling companion. On their last
night en route, at a motel in the middle of the New Mexico desert,
he let the dog out to pee and it didn't return. Perplexed, Dad ventured out with a flashlight and began searching beneath every bush
and cactus plant within a hundred yards. Still no Tuffy. The next
day he went to the police station to see if anyone had turned in a
stray dog, but no one had. He stayed an extra night in the motel
hoping Tuffy might perform an encore of his Incredible Journey
of years before. But the dog never returned. Eventually, Dad came
to accept that Tuffy was just old and had probably wandered off to
die alone, as dogs sometimes do. But at the time, Tuffy's loss was
as almost as unbearable as the death of my mother, especially since
they had occurred nearly back-to-back. When he told me about it

afterwards, in one of our Sunday night phone conversations, it was the first time in my life I'd ever heard him cry.

He acquired Tuffy II sometime after he married Eunice. It's possible he was trying to recapture some of the happiness he'd known with his first Tuffy, and also his first wife, my mother. But it didn't work. Tuffy II was a purebred Dachshund and possessed all the traits peculiar to the breed. He was low-slung and lazy, preferring to spend the bulk of his day sleeping on the couch or staring out the window. He was friendly enough but in a stupid sort of way. He would happily lick someone's bare toes until it became embarrassing, to both the person being licked and my father, whose sharp reprimands couldn't make the dog stop. Apparently he liked the taste of toe-jam. Worse, the dog refused to be house-broken. But that may or may not have been true. Tuffy I had been housebroken by Betsey, who had the patience and understanding it took to train a dog. Not so my father. He lacked patience in a lot of things but he took peeing on a rug as a personal insult and was known to inflict corporal punishment on violators. Apparently Tuffy II had been peeing on the rug for years and had been made to suffer my father's wrath. One day Eunice, in a moment of clarity, decided she'd had enough of it. The dog had once again fouled the hideous, lime-green shag carpeting that, in my father's estimation, was more sacred than anything in the sacristy of the Sistine Chapel. He grabbed Tuffy II by the scruff and threw him out in the yard, threatening to get rid of him if he ever did it again. Eunice, whose brother-in-law had a friend visiting from Montana, sneaked the dog out of the house and by noon the next day Tuffy II was on his way to Bozeman. Dad thought Tuffy had run off, and when Eunice told him the truth he didn't talk to her for weeks.

Later, I asked him if it was true that Eunice was only following through on something he'd already threatened to do. "I say shit like that all the time," he replied angrily. "She had no right getting rid of that dog. God damn her!"

❧

HE'S BEEN TALKING for over an hour about his fondness for dogs and it has had a calming effect on him, except for this last part. He's angry about Eunice. I wonder if he even remembers his tearful farewell from yesterday, much less considers the fact that he will never see her again. But I don't dare ask. Better to change the subject.

"Do you need to stretch?" I ask.

"No, not really."

"Do you have to pee?"

He looks at me, an eyebrow arched. "Yes, I suppose I should."

"It's a little early," I tell him, "but maybe we should stop for lunch, too. You hungry?"

"I guess I am. Yes."

Up ahead is an exit for something called Clines Corners, New Mexico, and the promise of a twenty-four-hour restaurant. I disengage the cruise control and head for the exit ramp. What a morning it's been, what a crazy, heart-stopping, fucked-up way to see the world. I glance down at the fuel gauge.

We'll need gas, too.

22

CLINES CORNERS

When we missed our exit in Albuquerque, the GPS kept imploring me for the next half hour to "turn right at the next exit, turn right at the next exit, turn right at the next exit." I finally turned it off. I don't need it. The interstate runs straight to Oklahoma City; one left turn and I-35 will take us all the way to Minnesota. No problem, just boring as hell.

Now, as I exit to find lunch and a place to pee, a fierce wind from the southwest buffets our rig as we cross the bridge over the interstate. Unbeknownst to me, the same wind has been pushing us along all morning and explains the good gas mileage we're getting. We've gone nearly three hundred miles on this tank, much better than our mileage from yesterday in the mountains. The trailer is catching wind like a reefed mainsail, and also a lot of sand; I can hear grains of it ticking against the windows on my side of the car as we head across the bridge.

Clines Corners, New Mexico, is not so much a town as it is a sprawling rest stop/service station. The gas pumps are arranged on islands surrounding an oasis of restaurants, souvenir shops, and a 24/7 truck stop. I pull up to an island within walking distance of the restaurant and climb out, the windblown sand immediately stinging my bare legs. I should be wearing the jeans I flew down in, but I prefer the comfort of shorts while driving. As I begin fueling, Dad struggles to free himself from his side of the car, but finally manages it. He bends and pivots around the axis of his cane in his version of stretching exercises and then starts down the side of the van.

"Don't go wandering off now!" I shout over the wind. "Stay where I can see you!" But he pays me little mind. Over the top of the van I watch as he slowly makes his way down the other side, probing here and there with the rubber tip of his cane. Tractor/trailer rigs rumble back and forth across the expansive lot, heading to an island of diesel pumps about fifty yards away. I again remind Dad to stay close but he doesn't seem to hear me, disappearing beyond the far side of the trailer.

"Hey!" I shout, but I get no reply.

"DAD! God damn it!" Again, no response, only the sound of the wind and the sand as it ticks against the car. I hurry to finish, slopping gas down the side of the van and onto my sandals. I jog down to end of the U-Haul where, to my relief, I find him once again staring at the license plate, transfixed.

He shakes his head. "How in the *hell* did you get this thing here all the way from Florida?"

"Dad," I reply patiently, "like I told you yesterday, it's a U-Haul. They come from everywhere. C'mon, let's get something to eat."

But he resists; the trailer continues to hold his rapt attention. He lifts the rubber tip of the cane to the padlock on the sliding door and tests it with a gentle prodding. "What's in here, anyway?

Dad with Tuffy II

Not this again. I want to tell him, "Your entire life is in there, the residue of ninety-six years of existence reduced to the capacity of a five-by-eight trailer, all of it going to a secure memory-care unit in a city you barely know. A place where you'll be spending the rest of your life."

Instead, I roll my eyes in mock disgust and slowly shake my head. "I'm not supposed to tell you this, but it's your birthday present."

He turns to me with a look of utter astonishment, his feet

scraping the asphalt as he takes a step backward. "My *birthday present?* Jesus Christ, I hope it's not a horse!"

"*Who told you?*" I shout, stifling a smile.

"Goddammit, it *better* not be a horse!" he says, and now he's laughing, too, excited that he might be the recipient of a horse for his 96th birthday. "What the hell am I going to do with a horse?"

"It's just a little horse," I assure him. "A pony. Wouldn't you like a pony?" And before he can respond, I wrap his arm in mine and turn him toward the restaurant.

"I guess a pony wouldn't be so bad," he says, the two of us bowing to the wind. And we both begin laughing as we make our way across the parking lot. A pony, sure.

Safely inside, I walk him back to the restrooms, then run outside to move the car up closer to the building. Upon my return, I find him shuffling back from the restroom, his fly open, his gait uneasy, his cane nowhere in sight. I shepherd him into a booth beside the windows, and when the waitress arrives he immediately goes into his Valentino routine.

"Oh my, haven't you got some nice boosums," he remarks.

"Dad, stop," I warn him. Unlike last night, this waitress is not amused and turns to me with a tired look.

"Tell pops here he better watch it. I been on duty since four a.m. and I ain't in the mood. Now whatchyagonna have?"

"*Dad...*" I say forcefully, reaching across to grab his hands before he tries anything stupid. "Dad, I'll bet you're getting sick of hamburgers. How about we try a BLT this time?"

He stares at me blankly. "Sure, I guess so." But then he looks up at the waitress with a fierce expression on his face. "A BLT but I want the bacon fried crisp and not burned. Nothing worse than a goddamn piece of burned bacon ruining a sandwich—"

"Okay, Dad, good," I tell him. I grab his menu and pass both of them back to the waitress without looking up. Once she's gone I excuse myself and head off to the restroom to find his cane. I discover it in one of the stalls where he's left a holy mess—the floor wet, the bowl unflushed, the toilet paper roll running down the wall and into the puddle on the floor. I take a few minutes to clean things up then return to our table where I'm surprised to find our lunch orders already on the table. "That was quick," I say, lowering myself into the booth. "How's the BLT?" He's already taken a bite of his sandwich.

"Horseshit," he mutters. He's got a sour look on his face and his jaw is working like he's chewing a piece of shoe leather. Then his expression turns bitter and he suddenly spits the entire contents of his mouth into a napkin, his tongue searching the recesses of his lower lip for every last bit. "That's about the toughest goddamn BLT I ever ate," he says morosely.

But something about his face seems strange and I ask him to open his mouth. Without hesitating, he bares his teeth. Or what's left of them; I immediately see the source of his problem. "Where's your lower plate?" I ask incredulously. "You're missing half your teeth!"

He looks at me in panic, his fingers reaching for his chin. "Jesus Christ!" he sputters. "How the hell do I know? They were here the last time I looked!"

And then I realize that in reality they weren't, that he's been talking a bit strangely since we stopped. I remember him removing both plates earlier, working them over with a napkin in one of his habitual cleanings. He must have left the lower plate on the center console.

"Don't take another bite," I tell him. "I'll be right back."

Out in the car the teeth are not where I expect them to be, and now I'm in a panic, wondering what he's done with them. Suddenly I feel like an angry young father scolding his four-year-old over his knack for losing things: *What did you do with your teeth? I told you to leave your teeth in your mouth and not play with them. And now you've lost them!*

But then I spot something on the floor mat, up in the shadow where Dad's feet have been and, sure enough, there's the lower plate, looking as if it's been beer-battered and dredged through sand. I grab a bottle of water from the cooler and stand in the open passenger door rinsing the false teeth over the asphalt. When I look up, the occupants of two booths inside the restaurant are watching me in a bemused silence. I nod grimly, then carry my prize back inside where I present it to my father. A small cheer goes up from the adjacent booths. Dad stares at his audience with a look of mortification, replants his lower teeth, then shoves the remainder of his lunch across the table at me.

"I must be losing my goddamn mind," he mutters. "Let's get the hell out of here."

I wolf down my own sandwich, which is actually quite tasty, and then attempt to take his arm again as we head for the door. But he's in a sour mood now and slaps my hand away, insisting he can walk on his own. I get him settled in the car, bag-up some of the trash around his feet, then climb in beside him. We travel on. But back out on the interstate the afternoon has grown as overcast and chilly as the mood inside the car. The loss of his lower plate, albeit temporary, has pitched him into a funk and he once again begins questioning our destination:

"You've been lying to me," he says. "You know goddamn well we aren't going back to Phoenix and you've been telling me we are. My own son is lying to me."

"I said we were going *home*," I say tiredly, "home to Minnesota, or La Crosse, or wherever the hell ..." I hear my voice trailing off. What's the point? He's right; I have been lying to him and I'm as tired of it as he is. I suddenly feel the weariness of a bad night's sleep, coupled to the stress of the past two days and the grim prospect of the long road ahead. We're not even halfway home and suddenly I'm so tired I can't bear the thought of going another mile, let alone the twelve-hundred miles we have remaining. I've half a notion to call my sister and inform her I'm turning around. Why was it so important that Dad had to leave at once, to abandon the dying wife that his Catholic principles command him to stay with "until death do us part?" I feel like I'm only making his situation worse by burdening his mental capacity and undermining his physical health. I have a genuine fear that the scene from Albuquerque this morning might easily happen again. But will I be ready for it next time?

I need to talk someone. Not my sister; I need to call my wife.

As evidenced earlier, my father has never quite grasped the miracle or convenience of a cell phone. For the last of the cross-country trips between Minnesota and Arizona he made with Eunice, Kath had outfitted him with a prepaid cell-phone to carry along in case of an emergency. I tried calling him on it a few times and got no answer, later discovering that he'd never even turned it on, claiming it was "too goddamned complicated." Now, he more or less ignores me as I talk quietly to my wife, Jan, back in Saint Paul.

"You sound tired," she says, and she can immediately sense from the tone of my voice that this trip is not the one I imagined it would be. She suggests she might easily catch a plane to Oklahoma City that evening to relieve me at the wheel. I mull this over for a moment while she goes on to fill me in with news from around the neighborhood, which is a nice respite from the news inside the car. When she's finished I feel a little better about things and decide to tell her no. Actually, I tell her to hold off, that I'll call her this evening with an update, after we've stopped, at which time I'll make a final decision. In the meantime, she suggests we pull off the highway for a nap. "From the sound of it," she says, "I think you're both just tired. And who wouldn't be after a night like that? Give your dad one of those Advil PMs and push his seat back. And then you take a nap, too. I'll bet you'll both be asleep in about two minutes. Then, after you've had your nap, he can keep sleeping while you drive. You might make it all the way home like that."

Dad suddenly interrupts me. "Say, who in the hell are you talking to over there?"

"I'm on the phone," I tell him, and I hold the phone up to show him it's the same one on which he couldn't hear Roseanne yesterday. "It's Jan," I tell him. "My wife."

He gives me a disgusted look. "You have a wife? Who the hell would marry a liar like you?" I hear Jan laughing on the other end. I say goodbye and end the call.

Up ahead is an exit ramp—not a rest stop, but at this point I don't care. We leave the interstate and come to an overpass, beside which sits a few abandoned commercial buildings, a few forlorn-looking houses, and a windswept landscape. I pull onto the cracked concrete apron of an abandoned gas station, kill the engine, and get out of the car. I open the sliding door on my side of the van and rummage through my travel bag until I find what I'm looking for—a bottle of over-the-counter sleep aids, the Advil PM my wife suggested. I shake a couple into my hand, grab a bottle of water from the cooler, and walk around to his side of the van. Opening his door, I crouch down out of the wind and hold the pills out to him. "I want you to take these," I say, my voice edgy. He stares at the two blue pills and then, without a word, puts them in his mouth and swallows them with a swig of water. I suspect he's so used to taking pills, regardless of their purpose, that a couple more are just part of the routine. But he's nonethe-less still angry and regards me with a malevolent expression, like he's about to take my head off. I reach down and release the latch on his seat and gently guide him back into a reclining position. Even on his back, he continues staring at me. "I need you to take a nap," I tell him. "We are both going to take a nap."

I close his door, walk around to my side, and crawl in, reclin-ing my own seat to the same position as his. I close my eyes and fold my hands across my stomach, take long, deep breaths—relax-ing breaths—counting the logs as they go over the waterfall. In the distance I hear the drone of the diesel semis on the highway. The relentless wind peppers the side of the car with grains of sand. I feel the sun on my eyelids as it emerges from behind a cloud, warm and sensual. I'm drifting, my body beginning to float off the seat, my brain going numb…

"Jesus Christ …" my father mutters.

I open an eye and glance over at him. His own eyes are wide open, staring at the ceiling liner.

"Dad, please," I say quietly. "Can you just close your eyes and try to sleep? Just a short nap then we'll be on our way." He acts as if he doesn't hear me and continues staring at the ceiling. A few minutes pass but he remains quiet. I can tell he's still mad but at least for the moment he's stopped bitching about it. I close my eyes again and try to let the feelings from before wash over me. The diesels drone, the sand goes tick tick tick, another log disappears over the waterfall ...

"This is bullshit."

"Dad," I say quietly, "you're supposed to be sleeping."

"God dammit to hell."

"Really, Dad? Really?"

It's no use. It isn't working. As exhausted as he has to be, he refuses to sleep. I jerk my seat to the upright position and glare at him. "All right then," I tell him, "this is how it's going to be. I'm going to drive but you're going to stay right where you are because I *need* you to sleep. Okay?" And then I start the engine. My hope is that my driving, along with the effects of the Advil, will be enough to put him to sleep. At least one of us will sleep, I hope, and then maybe things will get better.

We head back out onto the interstate, the road stretching long and straight all the way to Texas. I sit behind the wheel like a zombie, keeping the nose of the van pointed between the lines. Dad lies beside me, staring at the ceiling, his hands folded in his lap. A half-hour passes, then an hour. Every time I dare glance down at him his eyes are open. After an hour, his voice suddenly breaks the silence:

"How long do I have to stay like this?"

I sigh; he is *so* stubborn. "Okay, you can sit up but only if you remain quiet. I will not tolerate any bitching." He agrees to this and manages to pull himself to an upright position. But within minutes we pass beneath a sign displaying the distance to Amarillo, Texas.

"*Texas?*" he hisses, spitting the word like venom. "Jesus goddamn Christ!"

"Don't start," I warn him.

"Where are you taking me?"

This again. I feel punch-drunk, worse than I did last night when he woke me from a deep sleep. I need to turn this conversation in another direction, which will mean lying to him again.

"You're going to ruin your birthday party."

"My birthday party?" He looks surprised.

"You heard me," I tell him. "Everyone's coming."

"Who's coming?"

"Everyone. And they all want to see your face when you open your present."

He laughs. "I told you, it better not be a horse!"

"It's *not* a horse," I remind him. "Remember? It's a pony."

"Oh, Christ! What am I going to do with a pony?"

"Well, for one, you'll have to give him a name. Will you name him ... *Topsy* ?"

Now he's nodding, staring at me with a look of wonder. "We had a pony on the farm named Topsy," he says. As if I didn't know.

"Did you ever ride Topsy to school, you and Ernie?"

"Oh, Christ, did we ever," he says. And I relax a bit, feeling as if I've bought myself another helping of worry-free driving. I'm such a convincing liar. And we've only got another eleven hundred miles to go.

23

HORSES

In the other memoir my father dedicated to his grandchildren, the one titled "The Way We Lived, 1916 – 1936: A Farm Childhood and Young Adulthood in Moody County, South Dakota" he wrote:

"I wish each of you could have spent four or five years on a farm. You would have found it a very good life with the peacefulness that comes only with the rural life, and above all, the chance to become acquainted with animal life. Those beautiful animals will always be in my memory; in particular, the horses. After fifty-two years I can still visualize going into the barn: in the first stall stand Jewel and Fanny, the second stall Jimmy and Jerry, third stall Fred and Pet, fourth stall Dick and Baker, and in the last stall our beautiful pony Topsy. What memories of Topsy!"

Dad's father, George, bought Topsy at an auction shortly after his wife died. And while it's not clear what George's original intentions were, it's possible the purchase of a pony may have been an expression of sympathy to his children after the loss of their mother. Whatever the reason, he did experiment using the pony as part of an auxiliary workhorse team—a little reserve horsepower, if you will—when he needed it. But those plans didn't work out. Topsy was a beautiful animal, bay-colored with a white star on her forehead, and legs of white hair, like boots, adorning the tops of her hooves. But she was also headstrong and spirited, refusing to be teamed with any other horse, draft or otherwise. As such, she was awarded the privilege (and safety) of her own stall at the far end of the barn and became, in effect, a plaything, or pet, for the family—especially my father, the baby of the family.

Topsy endeared herself to him early-on, when he was still

quite young. One morning while riding her bareback over an open meadow, my father was thrown off when Topsy made a sudden move—startled, perhaps, by the appearance of a gopher. I can well imagine Dad's reaction at the time: lying on his back in the field wondering if he'd broken anything, then watching the spooked pony to see if she might gallop away. Would he have to chase her down? He spent a great deal of his youth chasing stray animals, cattle mostly, herding them from pasture to pasture as part of a seasonal grazing plan. It was hard work and a chore he didn't much care for. But Topsy surprised him. Instead of galloping off she stopped dead in her tracks and didn't move until my father climbed safely back aboard. He later speculated she'd done it out of the remorse she felt for throwing him, and at that moment his affection for Topsy soared. He loved that pony more than any car he would ever own, and he would own many.

Dad's closest sibling, his brother Ernie, was a schemer. The daily walk to Shady Lawn, the country schoolhouse both boys attended, was a mile. Some of their classmates rode to school on horseback, tying their mounts in a small barn located on the school property. A few others took it a step further and arrived by horse and buggy, which made an impression on Ernie. Although the Halter farm had long ago gotten rid of its buggy, it still had a "stone boat," the use of which presented a possibility. A stone boat is a flat-bottomed wooden skid dragged behind a draft animal to haul boulders and rocks from the fields. Ernie thought it would make a suitable, albeit rough-riding, conveyance for the trip to school. One morning he and my father hitched it behind Topsy and headed off to Shady Lawn. As my father later recalled, the first three quarters of a mile went slowly as the independent-minded pony displayed her aversion to manual labor. But then, as they neared the driveway of a neighboring farm, an enormous dog raced out from the barnyard, barking a challenge at the noisy apparatus. Frightened, Topsy reared back and bolted, galloping down the gravel road with the young brothers bouncing along behind and hanging on for dear life. Ernie finally managed to get

Topsy stopped, and when he unhitched her from the stone boat, she deserted them and ran all the way home.

Undaunted, the boys tried again, this time leaving the stone boat behind and riding Topsy bareback. They made it to school without incident, but on the return trip Topsy "smelled the barn," so to speak, and took off at a full gallop. Ernie was at the reins, my father clutching their lunch pails and struggling to hang on behind him. The empty pails slapped against Topsy's haunches and spurred the pony to an even greater speed. In desperation, Dad wrapped his arms around Ernie's waist; Ernie apparently thought his brother had something else in mind. "Quit tickling me!" he shouted. Topsy wouldn't let up and galloped into the barnyard full-stride, heading straight for the barn door. Both boys were nearly knocked-off in the door's narrow opening but managed to hang on, heads intact, suffering only scrapes. They never rode Topsy to school again.

With only two years separating them, Dad and Ernie experienced life together at the bottom of the pecking order and were often left to their own devices. Fighting came naturally, and even though Ernie was the bigger of the two, Russell sometimes managed to connect with a "sneaky right" and make Ernie's nose bleed. On one such occasion, Ernie pinned Russell to the floor and let his bleeding nose drip onto Russell's face until he'd sufficiently extracted his revenge.

Ernie was also an early riser, and every morning, usually before 5 a.m., he made it a habit to rouse his brother from bed in an odd way. Sneaking into the bedroom Russell shared with his father, Ernie would pinch his toe until he stirred and then drag him out of bed. Straight out to the barn they went to begin the morning chore of milking cows. But my father was a sound sleeper and claimed it wasn't until he milked his third or fourth cow that he realized he was even awake.

I've no doubt Ernie initiated my father into the long tradition of Halter profanity at an early date. There's even proof. As part of the Catholic rite of making their first Holy Communion, the two brothers had each taken a solemn oath to refrain from sinning in the week leading up to the ceremony. One morning while on their walk to school, they began talking boisterously, as they often did when out of earshot of Adeline, who enforced strict rules in the house. But apparently coarse language had become such a natural part of their everyday speech that on this particular day they couldn't help themselves. From my father's memoir:

"Ernie and I were making our mile-long walk to Shady Lawn school, and of course doing quite a bit of talking. I don't know who, but one of us let out quite a profound swear word that just astounded both of us terribly. Ernie quickly came up with, 'God-dammit, we are going to have to stop doing this,' so we decided that we should walk about two hundred feet apart, and we did this for the rest of the week."

It must have worked; both boys received the Blessed Sacrament on schedule, with no account of a lightning strike, nor the rending of any sacred cloth.

In their teenage years the brothers began to experience the world beyond the farm. Their father was still of an age when he would go off for a few days with a threshing crew—time enough for his sons to experience the sweeter side of life. The boys would liberate two or three bushels of oats from George's granary and sell them at the elevator in town. This might net them the grand total of forty cents, but it was money enough to buy three candy bars apiece and an ice cream cone to boot. Another source of income was Adeline's chickens, a few of which they would sell in town to finance another sugar spree. Using a broom to sweep the driveway of the tire tracks of the car used for this petty larceny seemed, in retrospect, stupid to my father. The broom marks were more obvious than the tire tracks had been, but Adeline never seemed to notice. Or at least she never let on.

All three of my Dad's surviving older brothers left home at an early age. Harold, the eldest (after Leo's unfortunate death in 1921), tried farming on his own in the early thirties but eventually quit and spent the rest of his life as a hired hand on farms throughout the area. He was a quiet, simple man who never married, and my father confessed that the two of them never got along. When Harold died in 1993 at age 89, his only worldly possessions were a 1947 Chevy and a mobile home sitting vacant on a city lot in Flandreau, South Dakota. But he also left behind a mutual fund portfolio valued at $125,000, which he'd never told anyone about. It was divided equally amongst Harold's surviving siblings. My father was stunned by the revelation of Harold's small fortune, and in the new car he purchased with his share of the inheritance he installed a bronze plaque to honor his brother's memory.

Older brother Bill stayed on for a year after being denied school beyond his sophomore year. He too "hired out" on adjacent farms for an average pay of $30/month, working 5 a.m. to 8 p.m., seven days a week, with every other Sunday off. In 1936, the same year my father went into the Navy, Bill was able to purchase (with George's co-signature) his own farm for $1,100, which included livestock and machinery. The farm's horses, in my father's opinion, may have been ready for the "glue factory," and the tractor may have required "two hours of cranking in the morning" to start, but Bill was on his way. In 1942 he married Anna Mergen from nearby Dell Rapids and acquired a bigger, more prosperous farm near Ward, South Dakota. Their five children became my closest cousins growing up, and Bill would prove to be the favorite of all my South Dakota uncles, a hardworking gentleman possessed of an earthy wisdom and a unique sense of humor. He called his wife, "Tooti," which to me seemed so much more expressive and loving than the "Ma" with which my father addressed our mother. Once, when I was in my teens, Jim and I had spent a week at Bill's farm, where we got to help our cousins with the chores. One day at "dinner," (which was the same meal we called supper, but which Aunt Ann served at noon; for Bill and Ann, a much less extravagant "supper" came at the end of the day) Uncle Bill confessed to his assembled brood that he'd found marijuana growing in a ditch beside one of his fields. We all laughed nervously and one of my cousins asked if he'd ever tried it.

"Sure, I tried it," he said. And he grinned mischievously, his teeth small and square like my father's but rimmed with gold. "I figure, if it grows on my land how could it possibly be bad?" I liked his way of thinking, and I often wished my dad could be as cool as Uncle Bill.

Ernie left the farm early, too, heading west with his buddies in his Model A Ford to seek his fortune. This was during the height of the Depression, and Ernie ended up back in South Dakota to take up farming again.

A "red-headed lady by the name of Ethel Mae Cameron was on the 'wanted' list" of every available bachelor in town," my father wrote. And Ernie managed to capture Ethel's heart by convincing her he came from money. In February of 1937, my father arrived home from boot camp to be the best man at their wedding. "It surely must have been a revelation to [Ethel]," he wrote, "when on their wedding night [Ernie] had a tough time coming up with the buck-and-a-half for the honeymoon suite at the fashionable St. Vincent Hotel in Flandreau." But the marriage would prove successful in the long run, and Ernie and Ethel would raise four kids on a farm near Colman, South Dakota. Upon retiring, the ever-opinionated Ernie got into politics and ran for the state assembly on the Republican ticket. He lost.

It was Uncle Ernie riding shotgun in my father's Buick in 1993 when the two brothers decided to take a flood tour of Flandreau, where Ernie had retired. The Big Sioux, along with about every other Upper Midwestern river, went over its banks that spring and flooded most of the low-lying areas of the town. Ernie suggested they take a drive through the town park to gauge for themselves the extent of the floodwaters. Disaster struck when my father missed an important turn at a place where the road disappeared beneath the rising water. Before he knew it his car was floating with the current in the main body of the river. The elderly men had to climb out of the windows up onto the roof of the car, where they were later rescued. The story made the front page of the local paper, with a quote from Ernie

Off to boot camp (l-r): unidentified, Ernie, Bill, Dad

admonishing his younger brother. "I told him to turn left but he turned right instead."

My father never visited Flandreau again, convinced that Ernie and all the other "old farts down at the bakery" were still talking about him.

cx/o

THE TWO SLEEPING PILLS I gave Dad earlier seem to have had no effect. His farm stories finished, he's staring out the window at some grazing cattle, something he's been doing the whole trip. He certainly has a fascination with cows. It's getting later in the afternoon and the dreaded hour of the Sundown Syndrome is approaching. But there won't be a sundown today, I notice. The sky behind us is dark with clouds. I don't dare let the mood inside the car return to the darkness it was earlier, so I start to kid him, hoping to lighten the mood.

"How about it," I say. "Do you *really* think they're still talking about you down at the Flandreau Bakery?"

He gives me an amused look. "What do I care?" he says. "Bunch of goddamn old women."

I nod in agreement. "Old Ernie ..." I say, "he could sure bullshit with the best of them." Ernie had died last September and Kath and I had driven to South Dakota for the funeral. By then, Dad's health was such that he couldn't have attended even if he wanted to, and for once I think he really wanted to. Afterward, Kath wrote him a long letter detailing the ceremony and the names of the old neighbors and relatives who'd shown up. There weren't many, especially those from his generation. Except for his brother Leo and his infant sister Ruth, all his siblings had lived well into their eighties or nineties, and passed away in nearly chronological order.

"You're the last one left," I remind him.

He nods grimly, but now he seems distracted. Something else has caught his attention. He's staring out the window at the passing high tension towers, and I have a sudden fear we're about to encounter the German dive bombers again. I need to keep after him, keep the stories coming.

"Do you think it was the hard work?" I say loudly, trying to keep him focused on me.

He looks confused. "Hard work?"

"On the farm. You all worked so hard, it must have been good for your physical health, your longevity. You all lived into your nineties."

"I suppose that's right," he says. "Sure."

"Like threshing," I say. "Wasn't that awfully hard work?"

"Oh, Christ, was it ever," he replies. And I breathe a little easier; he seems to be rising to the bait. He begins again, this time with a story about threshing.

From his memoir:

"Cutting grain was surely the hardest part of the summer season. Late July and early August were the hottest part of the year: temperatures in the high nineties and sometimes a hundred degrees. It took four horses to pull the binder and we had eight good horses to do this. Dad did most or all of the cutting and he was a driver, to say the least. He would change the four-horse team about every three to four hours. I can still hear the horses coming from their tour of duty—they would be blowing so hard and loud you'd wonder why some of them didn't have heart attacks. Shocking the grain was an extremely hard job, too. You had to keep the water jug close at hand and use it real often. The wages for all this hard work was the picture it produced: going to town on Saturday night, seeing those beautiful golden shocks all in a row. The better the crop, the more shocks, and the more beauty. One of the best memories of farm life."

He was fortunate enough to witness steam-engine threshing once in his life, when he was perhaps five or six years old. When the shocks of wheat had sufficiently dried, a meeting of the neighboring farmers (usually six in my father's recollection) was called to plan the threshing. Threshing—the separation of the grain from the stalk—required (in my father's earliest memory) the use of a ponderous steam engine and lots of men and horse-power. Each farmer estimated his yield and decided how many hay-racks he would need to haul the shocks and the number of wagons required to haul the grain. The coal-fired steam engine lumbered from farm to farm, with men walking alongside and running ahead to brace bridges and culverts for the heavy load. The pecking order for the use of the steam engine was decided at the threshing meeting, and not everyone was in agreement. My father remembers an old German who registered a complaint: "Seems like I tresh last ever got-dam year!"

Once the steam engine arrived at its predetermined place, the work began in earnest. While George and the other farmers concerned themselves with the operation of the engine, the younger men and boys (later in life, my father), got to test their skill with the horses. Racing out to the fields with an empty hayrack, they slowed the team to a steady walk through the wind-rows, and everyone jumped off to follow along with pitchforks. The trick came in pitching the shocks properly—heads in, butts out—so they didn't later slide off in transit, or were difficult to unload for the men at the steam engine. George's horses were so well trained they walked the rows untended, stopping when they sensed a slowdown, always keeping perfect pace with the men behind. Working efficiently meant a short break back at the barnyard where teams and hayracks lined up at the steam thresher waiting to be unloaded. The big break came later, at noon, when everyone stopped to partake of the "dinner" put out by the farmwives and their helpers. On George's farm this incredible task fell on the shoulders of Adeline and her younger sister Grace.

The two teenage girls had been awake since sunrise getting everything ready. Roast beef and fried chicken, sweet corn and green beans, ripened tomatoes and cucumber salad, homemade bread and preserves, fresh-baked pies and cakes and cookies, all of it cooked on the wood-burning stove in a kitchen hot as a sauna. For a week beforehand my father had been enlisted to haul wood (*dry* wood, as Adeline demanded) from the grove, enough to feed the cooking fires for the day, and also to heat the wash water in stands set up around the yard. The men sat at tables beneath the trees, the two sisters running back and forth to the kitchen with fresh platters of food and pitchers of Kool-Aid, and later, urns of coffee for the cake and cookies. Burning calories required extra fuel, and in the afternoon more food was brought to the field by car or coaster wagon—more sandwiches and cakes and cookies, more coffee and more Kool-Aid. At the end of the day the threshed grain lay loaded in heavy burlap sacks aboard wagons ready to be taken to town. The steam engine stood idle and cooling in the barnyard, awaiting its early morning passage to the next farm on the schedule. The horses were fed and watered in their stalls, the tack hung to dry along the walls of the barn. The men turned in early, exhausted after the long day of work. But Adeline and Grace returned to the kitchen to finish with the dishes, heating more water as

necessary, carrying leftover food to the cellar to cool, and ener-
gizing the 32-volt light plant as the evening darkened.

It was a day of work, in a lifetime of work, unimaginable in
today's mechanized and digitalized world. More importantly, it
reveals much about the character of my father's and his siblings'
life on the farm. Without the presence of a mother to temper the
brooding nature of a tyrannical father, everything about their life
must have seemed like slavery. What should have been an evening
of quiet introspection after a day of such labor—with a mother's love to soothe sore bodies and weary minds, and comforting
words promising better tomorrows—were instead prolonged sessions of silence in which my father and his weary siblings were left
to make of their labors what they could.

It explains so much about Dad's personality, some of which,
I'm beginning to realize, he may have passed along to me.

24

El Reno

I have made a serious mistake. In my quest to keep Dad talking—to keep him distracted from the eventual outcome of this odyssey—I've ignored the world outside the car. I should have paid more attention to the darkening skies behind us and the arrival of raindrops on the windshield. At one point I did turn the wipers on but still I wasn't paying attention. Dad was talking and I was listening, and as far as I was concerned the world outside the car could go on without us for next few hours. But now, a lightning strike on his side of the car stops everything. And it has begun to rain *hard.*

I chance a look in the rearview mirror. It's roiling dark behind us, the sky an ominous green in some places. We're totally exposed—nothing but grassland stretching for miles in every direction with nary an exit ramp in sight. Worse, I notice for the first time that the traffic has thinned considerably, and I begin to wonder if the other motorists know something that I don't. Another bolt of lightning streaks across the sky, followed by a crash of thunder. My father wrings his hands, his head tipped toward the window and his eyebrows arched. "That sonofabitch was *close,*" he says, his voice full of concern. A gust of wind hits us and I can feel the drag on the trailer as it threatens to pull us sideways into the ditch. *How could I have been so stupid?* Here it is, springtime in Oklahoma, the epicenter of tornados in North America, and I've carelessly driven myself and my ninety-six-year-old father into the heart of a storm.

This morning in Albuquerque, after things quieted down, I had turned off the Dick Cheney tape, and never bothered to turn the radio back on. Now I do, and the first thing I hear is the harsh buzzing of the Emergency Broadcast System, the one that warns listeners to take immediate shelter before a funnel cloud sucks them into oblivion. My father glances down at the source of the buzzing and then up at me. His face is pale. I know he's heard enough of these warnings to understand their importance, and right now he's probably thinking we better do something to save ourselves. "Sonofabitch," he says lowly, more like a groan, as another bolt of lightning splits the sky beyond his window. The windshield wipers can't keep up and I'm crawling along trying to find the painted lines. Then, to compound matters, the right-of-way is suddenly reduced to a single lane, with orange construction cones separating us from the oncoming traffic, or what's left of it. A pickup truck hisses past in the opposite direction, its headlights distorted in our flooded windshield and its horn blaring above the sound of the torrent. Am I over too far? One of the orange cones skids sideways across the pavement and disappears into the gloom. I should pull off now but there's no shoulder and we'd be sitting ducks for a semi-truck running blind behind us.

"*Godammit!*" Dad curses beside me, and I pray he's not about to lose it again, not now, *please* not now. I don't know what I can do to distract him without killing us both. A quick look tells me his hands are locked in a death grip on the armrests, and his face in the fractured glare of the lightning is one of pure fright. I'm going as fast as I dare in the restricted lane, the rain lashing down heavier and heavier. All I can do now is hope there's not a funnel cloud in the terrible gloom surrounding us, and pray that there will soon be a bridge to hide beneath. But in the terrible flashes of lightning I see neither. Then another strike explodes so close I feel the hair lift on my neck and smell the ozone in the air. My father moans. I'm afraid to look at him. Has this last strike stopped his heart? A semi roars past in the opposite direction, and in the glare of its headlights I catch a glimpse of Dad's face. Huh? His face is surprisingly serene, relaxed almost, and he turns to me with a curious smile, which is even more unnerving.

"You okay?" I shout over the drumming on the roof.

"I am now," he says mysteriously. And the thunder rolls again.

But we make it. In a little while the storm abates, the lightning moving off to the northeast, the rain on the windshield diminishing to a light shower. If there was a tornado included in all of this, I never saw it. But I'm exhausted and decide I've had enough of this for today. I had hoped to make Oklahoma City but now my only goal is to get off the freeway at the next opportunity and take whatever motel room I can find. At an exit marked "El Reno" I see the high marquees of at least a half-dozen motels. I pull into the first one beyond the exit ramp. Motor idling, I dash inside through the puddles only to be told by the desk clerk that there is no vacancy. Nonplussed, I head across the road to the next place and find the same result—"Sorry, we're full." I drive back across the interstate overpass to the motels along the commercial strip and am given the same answer at every one: They're all full. At my final possibility, the desk clerk, an extremely polite gentleman of East Indian origin, senses my frustration and explains that there's an oil boom going on and the wildcatters are in town. I'll be lucky to find a motel room between here and Oklahoma City. I tell him I've got my ninety-six-year-old father out in the car and I doubt we can make it that far. He nods serenely, then holds up his smooth-fingered hand and slips into his back office. He's on the phone talking quietly in Hindi, but finally looks up at me, his hand over the receiver: there's been a cancelation at one of the places I stopped earlier.

I'm ecstatic. "I'll take it."

He murmurs something in the phone, then looks up again and quotes me a price, which is almost triple what I paid in Holbrook last night.

"*Seriously?*" I say.

"Oh, yes," he says. "Welcome to the oil boom."

I'm in luck: the room is on the lower level and I'm able to park directly in front of the door, though the expansive parking lot is largely filled with tool-laden pickup trucks and monstrous maintenance rigs. It's still raining as I unhook Dad's seatbelt and tell him to wait. I hustle our bags inside then come back out to retrieve him. He seems in no great hurry to get out. As I help him up, I immediately see the reason for his reluctance to move: he's had an accident. The seat is soggy, his khaki pants are saturated, and the smell of urine is now obvious against the cool fresh air outside. So. The thunderstorm was indeed terrifying and the mysterious smile at its height was actually one of relief.

"I need a bath," Dad says meekly.

"It's okay," I tell him. "We'll get you a hot bath and I'll lay out some clean clothes and no one will ever know the difference."

Once inside, we head straight to the bathroom where he insists on undressing himself, pushing me out the door and then locking it. I grab a towel from the vanity and head out to the car to blot the seat where it's wet, later starting the engine and turning the fan on full blast. When I reenter the room, I'm surprised to find him peering out from behind the bathroom door.

"I guess I'm going to need a little help in here after all," he says, his eyes downcast. "I'm worried I might slip getting into the tub."

"Don't move."I'll be right there." I try to sound upbeat, to reassure him he needn't feel embarrassed. I slip out of my sandals and squeeze through the bathroom door, careful not to bump him sideways into the toilet. He stands naked beside the tub, his skin white and withered, his torso completely hairless. His body is so remarkably different than the one I remember from my childhood that I have to pause. He was always such a physical presence, a man used to hard work and not afraid of getting dirty, with the body to prove it. His perpetually dark skin and thick, calloused hands always hinted at a deeper masculinity, one with which I had an early encounter.

I couldn't have been more than three at the time, old enough apparently to begin toilet training. My mother thought I might have a better understanding of how it all worked if I were given a few up-close-and-personal lessons from my father. One morning, I accompanied both him and my mother into the bathroom. Dad took his regular stance before the toilet bowl while Mom installed me at a 90 degree angle to his right, facing the side of the bowl.

"Now you watch how Daddy does it!" she said, and then she left us to our lessons.

As I recall, the level of my vision was on a plane with the opening in his wrinkled boxer shorts. I always imagined they were the same shorts he wore in the Navy because to me they looked as old and tattered as the sugar sacks the Algerian baker had loaned him, and about as comfortable. He was forty years old, broad and hairy and in the prime of life. When he freed the purple-headed monster from its cave, its maw gushed forth a stream with the intensity of a fire hose, and I stood transfixed by the sight of the incredible torrent. When he'd finished, and it was my turn, my own attempts were feeble by comparison, my tiny appendage barely clearing the cold porcelain rim, my reluctant stream dribbling and unfocused.

"Aim for the water, goddammit," I remember him shouting. "Look at the mess you're making. Ma!" he finally shouted, "Get in here!"

Now, fifty-some years later, Ma's not here to help. It's only us. I glance down at his nakedness where I can see at once that things have changed. Is this is what I have to look forward to, should I live this long? Do I even *want* to live this long?

"What do you need me to do?" I ask.

"I think you're going to have to pretty much hoist me into the drink," he says, reverting to his navy jargon. He's a bit embarrassed. "I can't lift my legs that high anymore."

"Okay, stand by." And with this I step over and lower one foot into the hot, ankle-deep water and straddle the side of the tub, my dry foot planted firmly on the tile. "Here we go," and I wrap my arms around his delicate torso, lifting him bodily over the rim. He's lighter than I imagine, nothing like his younger self. For most of my life his physical presence was always something to be reckoned with, the heavy force behind his sometimes imperious demands. Now it's me with the weight advantage and the strength, and I realize I need to be careful with this transition of power. I shuffle sideways and gently lower him into the water until he's comfortably situated. I remove my wet foot, unwrap a bar of soap, and grab a washcloth from the rack. I kneel down beside the tub and slip the soap into his hand, soak the washcloth in the bathwater beside his thigh.

"Is there anything else you need me to do?"

He stares into the water as if he's considering it, or maybe he's just humiliated by the prospect of his son giving him a bath. "No," he finally says, and I gather up his soiled laundry and leave him to his business.

"Call when you're ready to get out," I tell him as I slip through the door.

"I will," he replies, his voice barely audible. "And, thank you."

A little while later he summons me that he's ready to get out. He's in a much better mood now and when I deposit him on the dry floor mat he playfully grabs my arms like he wants to wrestle. "Watch it, buster," he says in a moment of mock machismo. "Wouldn't be surprised if I could still knock you on your ass."

"Fine," I reply. "But let's get you into your shorts first." And I help him into a fresh pair of boxers.

"I've laid out your clean clothes on the bed. The TV is on, Sports is coming up." Then I add, " While you're getting dressed I'm going to run across the road and grab some hamburgers. How does that sound for dinner? A couple hamburgers, French Fries, you want something to drink?"

He looks confused. "We're going to eat here?"

"Yes. It's getting late and I'm too tired to go to a restaurant. You okay with that?"

He looks worried. "Well, I guess so…"

"Good. I won't be gone ten minutes. There's a McDonalds right across the road and I'll use the drive-through."

"Okay, then," he replies, but he's still got a worried look on his face as I depart.

The drive-through order comes quickly and I'm back in the motel parking lot in ten minutes, as promised. But just as I'm about to exit the car, my phone rings; its Kath calling from Saint Paul. "How's it going?" she asks innocently enough. And suddenly I'm like a giant balloon deflating, my words escaping in a continuous rush as the world, if only for a few moments, returns to normal. It feels so good to be talking to someone who understands what I'm going through, someone who knows firsthand the extent of our father's dementia and the peculiar way it works. I talk and talk, filling her in on the gory details—his attempted escape from the car in the Albuquerque rush hour, the lost teeth, the sleepless nap, the violent storm, and his unfortunate accident. I'm about to mention the experience of giving him a bath when I notice the clock on the dashboard. I've been talking for a good twenty minutes and Dad's been alone in the room the whole time.

"Jesus Christ I have to run!" I announce and abruptly hang up. I've done it again, and I curse myself as I race for the motel-room door. Another stupid mistake; two in one day. Am I subconsciously trying to kill him? I burst through the door and my worst nightmare is confirmed. He's lying face down on the carpet at the foot of the bed, wearing only his boxer shorts, with his trousers bunched-up around his ankles.

"Dad!" I cry, and I toss the bag of hamburgers on the bed as I drop to my knees. He's still breathing, deeply in fact, and when I grab his arm he snorts, mumbles, snorts again, then groggily lifts his head.

"Were you sleeping?" I ask. I'm so relieved I hear my voice break, surprised by my emotion.

He blinks and looks around, his damp hair sticking out in spikes. "Where am I?" he finally says. "Jesus Christ! I must have rolled off the goddamn bed trying to put my pants on, and, and, godammit, I might have laid here 'til tomorrow for all you give a shit!"

"That's not true, and you know it," I tell him. "Kath called and we got to talking and, and ... well, I got you a couple of cheeseburgers. Are you hungry?"

I help him to his feet, we get his pants buttoned, and I wrestle a tee shirt over his damp head, then sit him on his bed facing me on mine. I spread the food out on the night stand, squirt some ketchup on a hamburger wrapper, dump the fries out on another. He starts in immediately, wolfing everything down as if it were his last meal. When he's finished, he asks me if that's all there is and I hand him my second cheeseburger, which he takes without comment. He chews quietly, apparently still upset that I abandoned him.

"Have some more fries," I tell him, and I push the rest of the pile to his side of the nightstand. Then I add, "We should be home tomorrow. No more of this shit."

He glances up, his forehead wrinkled. "To Phoenix, right?"

"No, not Phoenix. We're going to Mark's. Remember?"

He stops chewing, his mouth slightly ajar. "To Mark's…"

"Yes, to Mark's," I say firmly. I'm done bullshitting him.

He thinks about this for a moment, and then finally says, "If you say so."

"I say so."

DAY 5

25

OKLAHOMA!

Another interrupted night of sleep, as Dad spots another crack in the ceiling above his bed. This time I'm sleeping more soundly, however, and he has to nudge me with his knuckles, prodding my shoulder to wake me up. Once again I open my eyes to find him standing over me, his voice urgent: "Are you going to fix this?"

I turn on the light, not even bothering to look at where he's pointing on the ceiling. Someday, I'd like to ask a psychiatrist about the subliminal trauma that causes this particular delusion, but for now I don't dwell on it. Right now my sleep deprivation is the only issue that concerns me. I glance at the clock. It's 1:30. At least he's allowed me a little more sleep than the night before.

"We fixed that crack last night," I say tiredly. "Now would you please get back into bed?"

Which he does, albeit reluctantly. He sits down on the edge of the bed with his hands flat on the mattress for support. His bony knees protrude from the folds of his boxers, his droopy tee-shirt hiked up on one side of his belly. His hair is sticking out at angles and I realize he never combed it after I discovered him on the floor earlier. He's always been self-conscious about his hair, preferring it neatly combed. He sits looking around the room as if he's never seen it before, and I wonder if he's about to have an awakening as to why he's here.

"You need me to tuck you in?" I ask.

"No," he says, and he falls back on his pillow, at the same

time swinging his legs up over the side, groaning with the effort. I turn off the light and roll over to face the wall.

I sleep, but for how long, I'm not sure. Sometime later I'm awakened by the light over the vanity and Dad's noisy rummaging through his toiletries kit. He's angry again, same routine as yesterday morning. But this time the source of displeasure seems to be his dentures. He's run out of PolyGrip and he wants to know why there isn't another tube in his kit. More importantly, he wants to know who in the hell is responsible for packing his suitcase in the first place. Propped up on my elbow, I assure him it wasn't me and then try to convince him we can get more Poly-Grip in the morning. I look at the clock; its 4:30.

"Why don't you get back in bed?" I suggest.

"*No!*"

Great. Here we go again. He angrily informs me he can't sleep knowing he is out of adhesive. Apparently, his whole sense of well-being rests with the proper installation of his teeth.

And then, in case I didn't hear him the first time: *"Who the hell packed this suitcase?"*

"It wasn't me!" I yell. And then I fling my covers back. "Get dressed," I order him. "I guess we need to find you some Poly-grip before the world ends."

By 5 a.m. I have checked us out of our room, inspected the car, loaded the luggage, and I even have the presence of mind to grab coffee and a few pastries from the continental breakfast kiosk as we head through the lobby. No waffles today. As a precaution, I "borrow" one of the bath towels from our room and tuck it in across his car seat, still a little damp from last night. I'm afraid the smell also lingers, but Dad doesn't seem to notice. Now, as I buckle him in, his attention is focused on the Poly-Grip crisis and I assure him it's at the top of my list. We head immediately down the frontage road to a gas station-convenience store where, in the pre-dawn darkness, the pumps are already busy with the oil field traffic. I manage to find an opening at a distant island. Gassing-up, I feel the chill of the morning air on my legs and wonder if it's finally time I switched to my warmer Minnesota attire. I could do it here, but trucks are waiting in line and I decide I'd better not dally. I pull ahead to make room then go inside for supplies.

Inside the store it's even worse. The place is filled with hardhats and coveralls, the ruddy-faced roughnecks clearing the shelves of Mountain Dew, microwave sandwiches, potato chips, beef jerky, candy bars, and snack cakes. They form a line at the cash register where a quick-witted woman with red lipstick and a tight tee-shirt seems to know everyone by name. Her voice carries as she grabs cigarettes and chewing tobacco from the overhead display cases, loads purchases into plastic bags, and sends everyone on their way with a smile and a caution: "Yew all be careful out there today, promise?"

In what passes for the pharmaceutical aisle I am amazed to find Dad's Poly-Grip. I fully expected to spend half the morning driving around town in search of it, wasting precious travel time. But here it is and I grab a couple tubes, then a newspaper, and finally a bag of ice for the cooler. I step up and take my place at the end of the line. The smell of nicotine and dried petroleum permeates the air. The guy in front of me, his greasy hardhat adorned with Chiquita Banana stickers and an array of union decals, turns to say something but then notices I'm not dressed like everyone else and decides against it, a curious smile curving the corner of his mouth. I want to say something in return, inform him that there was a period in my life when I dressed like he's dressed and spent my days crawling through the bilges of boats and barges, dragging a welding lead, holding a flashlight in my mouth, breathing noxious fumes like he probably has. I want to tell him that I, too, once ate my lunch in a makeshift space, everyone sitting shoulder to shoulder in greasy Carhartts, our gloves drying above a propane heater on hangers fashioned from welding rod, all of us eating our soggy Stewart sandwiches with paper towels covering our filthy hands, later tapping Marlboros or Camels from the bottom of the pack to keep our toxic fingerprints off the filters. I want to say to him, "I've been there, buddy, and I know where you're headed this morning."

But I don't. Instead I just stand there and smile like a dork in a Hawaiian shirt and sandals, my only concern the ninety-six-year-old man sitting patiently (or not) outside on a damp towel, waiting for his tube of denture adhesive, the fix-all wonder goop that will get him through the day. And that's all that really matters to me right now.

The line moves quickly enough and soon it's my turn at the register.

"Well, now ...," says the attendant as she puts her hand on the boxes of Poly-Grip, notes the bag of ice, the newspaper, and then me. Her glasses are propped on the end of her nose, tethered to her neck with a fluorescent green ribbon. She tips her head and regards me over the rims of the glasses, takes in the loose Hawaiian shirt, the shorts, the sandals. Her jaw drops just enough to part her lips, but she recovers quickly, narrows her eyes and says, "Now I'll just go ahead and guess you ain't working on no rig around *here* today. Am ah right?"

"Check his union card, Cindy!" someone shouts from the back of the line, and everyone laughs. I realize then that Cindy is on stage, that this is theater. I give her a serious look.

"Ma'am, I'll have you know that these sandals are steel-toed and OSHA approved."

Cindy doesn't think I'm funny and abruptly runs my credit card, hands me a receipt and dismisses me with a curt "Thank yew." As I turn for the door she's already working the guy behind me. "Did y'all git wit in that rain last night, Dale? Whatn't that sumthin'?"

Dad is ecstatic at the sight of the Poly-Grip and wastes little time in refastening his plates. He examines his work in the light of the visor mirror, baring his teeth like a grinning chimpanzee. This puts him in a much better frame of mind. We head east on the interstate, the sky beginning to glow over the eastern horizon. On a tollway west of Oklahoma City, I head north to avoid the rush hour traffic downtown. By the time we connect with I-35 North the sun is peeking over the suburban buildings lining the freeway, and we're running free, all the heavy traffic heading the other direction. Dad moves his visor over to the passenger window and grabs the newspaper. The omens are positive; I feel like it's going to be a wonderful day.

He reads the paper while working on his coffee and donuts. He takes his medication and seems especially adept at performing the daily blood-sugar test, the one the public health nurse taught him specifically for this trip. He seems to be in a much better mood about everything. I'm beginning to wonder if our role reversal over his pants-wetting last night has something to do with it. Maybe he's beginning to trust me.

I turn the radio on and flip through the stations, not finding much more than modern country all around the dial. The best I can do is a classic country station and soon we're listening to Johnny Cash singing "Hey Porter." Dad likes it; I can hear him faintly humming along to the melody. The miles roll by and the sun makes its steady ascent in a clear blue sky. The GPS unit on the dash informs me we'll roll into my brother's farm around 8 p.m. tonight, some 840 miles from where we are now. But that's without taking into account any attempted suicides, severe thunder storms, or driver-related accidents caused by falling asleep behind the wheel. I resolve to stay awake, and also to play things by ear, to stop more often if Dad requires it or continuing on if I think he can handle it. I call my brother and give him our estimated ETA , then tell him we may or may-not be there tonight. Either way, he assures me, he's ready for us. He's been spending time at the memory-care facility getting Dad's room ready, familiarizing himself with the staff, feeling the place out. Once we arrive with the trailer he'll need a day to set up the bed and move in whatever furniture I've brought, unpack the clothes, hang some pictures. Did I bring the picture of his mother? he asks. I did. Dad will stay at Mark's place until his room is ready.

"The memory-care unit," I ask. "Is it decent?" I'm still plagued by the feeling I'm delivering my father to a life-sentence in prison.

I imagine a bleak cinder-block building smelling of dried urine masked with Lysol, tasteless institutionalized food, folding chairs in front of snowy TV screens, lifeless shells of people slumped over in their wheelchairs. Mark assures me it's better than anything else we've looked at, and besides, Dad will be a frequent guest at his farm, a place he's always enjoyed. I pray he's right.

When I hang up I glance over and am surprised to find Dad staring back at me. "Who were you talking to?" he asks.

"Mark," I reply.

"Mark?"

"Your son Mark. In La Crosse."

"I have a son in La Crosse?"

Uh oh.

The box of photos is on the floor between us and I lift it to my lap, quickly flipping through the contents until I locate one of Mark and his family taken from a Christmas card years ago. I hold it in front of his face. "This guy," I tell him.

"Why that's Mark!" he says.

"Imagine that. How would like to visit his farm tomorrow?"

"Tomorrow? Won't we be home by tomorrow?"

"Yes, but we should have time for a visit to Mark's farm. Would you like that?"

"Yes..." he says uncertainly, "but..."

"Hold that thought," I tell him. Something on his side of the highway has caught my eye. I check the rearview mirror and disengage the cruise-control, easing us towards the shoulder as the car begins to slow.

"What's the matter?" Dad says. "Did we hit something?"

I smile. "No, but would you move that visor? There's something you need to see."

As instructed, he pulls the visor around from his side window and clips it into its normal position. I check the mirror again—nothing coming—and then pull completely over onto the shoulder and kill the engine. It's suddenly quiet inside the car.

"What's going on?" Dad says nervously. "What's wrong?"

"Look!" I tell him and I power down the window on his side of the car. He glances at me uncertainly, then turns to look.

Beyond his window lies a glorious landscape of verdant greens and azure blues, the colors so brilliantly beautiful they about take my breath away. The smell of spring is in the air, the gentle breeze carrying the scent of wet grass from yesterday's rain. The birds are twittering, and from way off in the distance comes the peaceful lowing of cattle. Dad hears it too, and now he's smiling, his eyes searching the distant hillside until he finally locates the herd, their heads bent to the business of eating.

"Oh boy," he says. "Oh boy."

According to him, this is the way God intended cattle to graze, and for a few minutes we sit side by side, taking it all in, talking, speculating, breathing the fresh spring air. We could easily sit here indefinitely but a semi blasts by, buffeting us back to reality.

"We better keep moving," I tell him.

He nods in the affirmative. "Where exactly are we?" he asks.

I check the GPS. "This is still Oklahoma," I say. "I had no idea it was this beautiful." I start the engine and accelerate out into the slow lane.

Oklahoma. The mere mention of the name seems to have triggered something in his memory and a moment later he starts singing the opening line of the song "Oklahoma" from the musical. His voice is as weak as I remember it, but right now he's as happy as he's been on this entire trip. It's corny, the two of us singing, but we've done this before. Once, a few years ago, on a trip home from Mark's farm, I put a Mitch Miller CD on the player and we sang together for over an hour. Now, he's clearly enjoying himself in our father and son duet:

"Ooooo-klahoma, where the wind comes sweeping down the
        plain,
And the waving wheat, can sure smell sweet
When the wind comes right behind the rain!"
Ooooo-klahoma..."

His voice trails off as we both begin humming.

"What's the next line?" he asks.

"Damned if I know."

"Well, shit ..."

So we sing the same lines again and then I switch to an-other song from the same musical:

Oh what a beautiful moooorn-ing
Oh what a beautiful day!
I've got a beautiful feeling
Everything's going my way.

We stop again. "I suppose you don't know the rest of this one, either," he says.

"Do you?"

"*Goddammit to hell!*" he shouts, but now he's laughing, and suddenly I reach over and grab the inside of his knee, squeezing the tendon like he did to the kid riding up front between him and Mom. It would hurt but feel funny at the same time, and we'd laugh and scream until he stopped. Now he's pawing at my hand, begging me to stop because he knows this is payback and there's nothing he can do about it. Now I'm the dad and he's the kid.

But I do stop and we settle down, riding along in content-ed silence for a few miles. After awhile I glance over at him and notice he's looking at something up ahead along the highway, a sign: Welcome To Kansas. I keep a surreptitious eye on him, fearful of how he might react. I've been lucky so far today, but with him you never know. We pass the sign as if it wasn't there.

A little later, he says, "I need to tell you something."

"Okay ..."

He looks at me, hesitating.

"What?" I ask.

He blurts it out: "Your mother was pregnant when we got married."

I glance at him but don't say anything because, in fact, I already know this. He himself told me this on the Mitch Miller ride home from Mark's farm. Obviously he's forgotten that now. But even before that, I've known it for years. Kath—the "love child" of this confession—did the math of her conception decades ago. But I think it's interesting that he feels it necessary to bring it up again, here on this breathtaking morning in Oklahoma cum Kansas. I don't want to interrupt this story he obviously feels compelled to share, but maybe there's more to it than I know.

"Do you remember the first time you ever met her?" I ask. "Mom, I mean."

"Oh boy, do I ever!" he replies. And that's all it takes. He's nearly laughing as he says, "Spring of 1946, the NCO Club at Fort Snelling. Christ, she asked *me* to dance! Can you imagine? I about shit myself. She had that dark red hair, those beautiful blue eyes. And did you ever know a woman with such beautiful hands as your mother's? My God, she had beautiful hands!"

"Yes, she did," I tell him. She was quite a looker, my mother.

"What else do you remember about her?' I ask.

"Oh boy," he says. "Let's see ..."

26

Ma

The woman who would one day become my mother was born Lois Ethel Carlson in Duluth, Minnesota, a city she soon grew to dislike. The cold winds off Lake Superior, the daily trek in winter up and down the steep, icy streets to Central High School, the blue-collar nature of a rugged seaport city—all of it convinced her from an early age that Duluth would not figure in her future. Born of strong Swedish stock (with the exception of a maternal Irish grandmother) she spent her childhood in a house her father ordered from a Sears catalog and built on a hillside overlooking the big lake. Some of my own early memories take place in that same home on 9th Ave East, a half-block above Skyline Boulevard, where I can only assume some of my own experiences mirrored those of my mother's.

Her father, H. C. "Henry" Carlson, was a fastidious man, a bookkeeper by trade, but trim and fit from leisure hours spent in his garden or working on his house. And also adventurous: as a young man of twenty-one he rode his Harley-Davidson west to Spokane, Washington, with his best friend Harvey MacFarlane relegated to the sidecar for the entire journey. In Spokane the two adventurers found temporary employment working for the Great Northern Railroad. Henry later hocked the motorcycle and used the funds to buy an engagement ring for my grandmother, Louise Nelson Carlson, whom he had met while both were employees of The Standard Oil Company. They were married in Duluth in October of 1921. My mother came along in December of 1925 and her brother Richard, my Uncle Rich, in July, 1928.

Grandpa Henry entrusted me at an early age with the heavy binoculars he kept on the sill of the large picture window overlooking Lake Superior. I could stand for hours on the cushions of an overstuffed couch and study the traffic in the busy ship canal below. The lower shelves of the living room bookcase held volumes indicative of Grandpa's fascination with the moody lake: *Great Lakes Shipwrecks and Survivals, Ghost Ships of the Great Lakes,* and *Lake Superior's Shipwreck Coast.* All of them were kept well within the reach of someone like me, who liked nothing better on a rainy afternoon than to lie on the floor and study the old black and white photos. I've often speculated that my grandfather's fascination with the lake, along with my father's stories of his experiences at sea, instilled in me some sort of romantic notion about ships and maritime life in general. Grandpa Henry was a huge early influence, and I used to wonder how my life might have differed had his and my father's interests not run parallel.

Grandma Louise was a strong yet cheerful woman who could nonetheless be firm in her childrearing. Once, when Mom and Dad attended a wedding in Duluth, we were brought along and left overnight in her care. She was a wonderful cook, and for dinner that night she served us fresh Swiss chard from Grandpa's garden. I was perhaps four or five at the time and had never before experienced the flavor of chard. After taking one bite I decided it was a little too earthy for my liking and gagged, timidly asked Grandma if I might spit it out. *"Absolutely not!"* she thundered, and then abruptly dismissed me from the table, obviously insulted by my reaction to her cooking. I retreated to the living room where I waited for my siblings to join me in front of the TV to watch the Friday night programming: *The Flintstones, My Three Sons,* and *The Twilight Zone.* I can still remember the *Twilight Zone* episode all these years later because of my own dilemma with the chard. The plot concerned the residents of a uranium-mining town who were all going blind due to radiation poisoning. I feared something equally unhealthy was happening inside my mouth due to the lump of chard in my cheek. Later, when Grandma finished clearing the table, she joined us at her regular spot on the couch, working the daily crossword puzzle from the paper. I sat at the other end of the couch masticating the mouth-ful of chard, though the slimy leaves had long since taken on the consistency of a wet cud. At 9 p.m. she ordered us to get into our pajamas, wash our faces, and brush our teeth. The tooth-brushing part presented a special problem. There was something I needed to know.

"Grandma," I asked meekly, "does this mean I can spit out the chard?"

I could see the utter astonishment behind her glasses as she looked up from her puzzle, amazed that after three hours I had continued to hold the forkful of chard in my drooling mouth.

"*No!*" she replied angrily, and to press her point she swatted my behind with the folded newspaper. The chard went down in one quick gulp, pretty much liquefied by then and completely tasteless. I hurried off to join my brothers and sisters in front of the bathroom mirror, free of my terrible burden.

The next morning Grandma was her cheerful self again, busy in her kitchen, serving us fresh raspberries from Grandpa's garden—an extra scoop added to my cereal bowl—with nary a mention of the night before. And I began to appreciate both the nature and limits of my mother's childhood.

I have no doubt it was a generally happy one. Old photos show a healthy, cheerful child surrounded by a loving family with strong roots and a stronger work ethic. Her report cards from Grant Public School indicate she was an apt student from grades one through six, but her grades take a noticeable dip as she enters junior high, and it's possible a burgeoning social life may have distracted her. She enjoyed a large circle of friends with whom she skied, skated, and swam, was a willing participant in the Blue-birds, Brownies, and Girl Scouts, sang in the church choir and also the high school Glee Club. And she loved to travel.

In 1939, she experienced the thrill of her then thirteen-year-old life when she rode the Burlington *Zephyr* on a cross-coun-try trip to the New Jersey home of her married cousin Lorraine and her husband, the Reverend Dave Searfoss. Ostensibly, she was there to babysit the couples' young children, but the nearly month-long sojourn also exposed her to the larger world beyond Duluth. Twice she got to visit the World's Fair in New York City; she spent a day at the Jersey Shore where she got severely sunburned; she toured Princeton University for an inspection of the campus and a whiff of higher education; she spent an afternoon at a dairy farm, where she learned to milk a cow; and she made the acquaintance of some older kids in Cousin Lorraine's neighborhood who invited her out at night for rides in a 1929 Ford. It was more fun than she'd ever had in all her summers in Duluth put together. But it was also expensive; she blew her entire allotment of travel money before the month was half over. A small scrap of paper added as an afterthought to a regular letter home announced, "All my funds are gone." It's not known whether or not her money supply was replenished, but in a subsequent letter home she pleads with her parents to, "Please let me go West…" this in reference to an upcoming train trip to California Cousin Lorraine had invited her to join. She must have instinctively known that Henry and Louise would say no because she ends the same letter, her last from the East, with an amusing comment to her father: "Don't wear the lake out. I want to swim in it, too."

The lake in question was no doubt Lyman Lake, where my mother spent a large part of her childhood. Situated near South Range, Wisconsin, about twenty-five miles southeast of Duluth, the lake was the weekend retreat for any number of first and second generation Swedish immigrants. Henry's sister Esther and her husband, Charlie Tallakson, built one of the first cabins on Lyman Lake, a simple structure to be sure but perfectly suited to thrifty Scandinavians. Uncle Charlie, as we all called him, owned the general store in South Range, located right across the road from the railroad tracks and next door to his and Esther's home. He was a tall, stately gentleman with white hair and a flannel shirt perpetually buttoned to his chin, winter or summer. He never failed to treat the children of visiting relatives to a small gift upon their arrival—a paper bag filled to overflowing with root beer barrels,

Tootsie Rolls, jawbreakers, and licorice whips, each child given his or her own bag. On the wall above the store's meat counter hung Charlie's trophy muskie, rumored to be the largest fish ever taken from Lyman Lake, its gaping mouth wide enough, in my childhood estimation, to swallow me whole.

My mother would tell us stories of her own visits to Uncle Charlie's cabin dating as far back as the 1920s: of the Gypsy caravans camped beneath the ore docks in Superior and Allouez; of the "five-mile hikes" she and her cousins would take to Bird's Point, located around the bay from Charlie's cabin; of the little bait store beside the slough that now stood abandoned and mysterious; of afternoons spent visiting Cousin Ida, who wore men's clothing and had lost a thumb in a farming accident; and also trips to see Cousin George who had served as General Black Jack Pershing's personal horse groomsman in World War I.

When Grandpa retired in 1959, he and Grandma bought a cabin a few hundred yards down the shore from Uncle Charlie's, a place they would move to permanently in 1964 and where I would spend many of my own childhood summers. Lyman Lake is where I learned to swim, row a boat, operate an outboard motor, shoot a rifle, and fish, all of it in strict compliance to Grandpa's incessant warnings. "*Wear a lifejacket!*" he would call to anyone who even approached the rowboat tied to his dock. "*Walk out and swim in!*" was his standing order for anyone venturing into the water.

(Years later, when I was a Coast Guard Search and Rescue coxswain in Boston, I was once dispatched in a fierce winter gale to assist a ship that had broken in half off Cape Ann. The story made the national news, and when I stopped off to visit my grandparents on my way home the next summer, the first words out of Grandpa's mouth were, "I hope you were wearing a lifejacket!")

Her questionable grades notwithstanding, Mom managed to graduate from high school in June of 1943 at the tender age of seventeen. Commencement ceremonies were held on Friday, June 11, and one week later she and her best friend, also named Lois, moved to Minneapolis. She had finally fulfilled her life-long wish of escaping Duluth, and she never lived there again. In Minneapolis, the labor shortage created by the war made finding a job relatively easy. Within a week she landed an entry-level mail clerk position with Employer's Mutual Insurance Company, located in the Rand Tower on Marquette Avenue downtown. Her starting salary was $80 a month, of which $25 a month went for the upper half of a duplex the two girls rented on 31st and Oakland Avenue South. The duplex lay a block south of Lake Street, where a main streetcar line ensured easy transportation to all the entertainment venues in the area, including Fort Snelling with its wealth of servicemen. In one of her first letters home she reported that she had gone roller skating the night before, where there were "plenty of sailors, but no luck. Still trying." She was a vivacious redhead with an outgoing personality and an eye for fun. But she had inherited her mother's wide hips and thick legs, and she began making a conscious effort to slim down, presumably to increase her chances. To judge from her photo album from the period, she began to have much better luck in the ensuing months, dating both sailors and soldiers of all rank and description. Most of her suitors look as young and untested as she was—an entire generation of teenagers and young adults thrown into a war that would permanently alter their lives.

In the spring of 1946, now twenty years old, Mom and Lois attended a dance at the Fort Snelling NCO club, where she caught the eye of an older chief petty officer. He was tall and rail-thin with a dark countenance that hinted at some of the weariness he still carried from his wartime experience. His uniform held an impressive array of service ribbons, from which she could tell he'd seen a lot of action. She didn't wait for him to make the first move, telling Lois, "I'm going to ask that nice-looking Jewish fella if he wants to dance." Apparently the nice-looking Jewish fella, my father, did indeed want to dance, so much so that afterwards the two adjourned to a quiet booth where they could talk. One thing led to another and a few weeks later, in March, she asked him to join her on a trip home to Duluth to meet her family. There's no record of the impression he made on my future grandparents, so I can only guess. He was nearly ten years older than their daughter, a heavy smoker, and Catholic—a religion often looked down upon in those days by the Scandinavian Lutherans of my mother's society. Still, they thought enough of him to invite him back in late May. And the romance blossomed.

First date at the NCO Club, 1946

It's not hard to see why my father found her so attractive. She was young and beautiful, but she was also a woman who'd seen enough of the world to know what she wanted. And she wasn't afraid to make the decisions that would affect both their lives, at times almost motherly in her instincts. He might have found this last quality especially endearing given his motherless childhood. And it probably didn't hurt that she was a girl from the North Country, a land of forests and lakes which were such a verdant respite from the dustbowl existence of his South Dakota childhood. I don't know if he visited Lyman Lake on those initial visits, but he would certainly spend many summers there in the years to come.

He proposed to her on Memorial Day, 1946, giving her an engagement ring she showed off to everyone in Duluth. She had returned home that June to go on a week-long vacation with her family, the four of them traveling by car on a circular route through eastern North Dakota, Winnipeg, Lake Kabetogama on the Minnesota border, and finally back home to Duluth. She wrote her fiancé every day, sometimes twice, beginning every letter with "Darling" or "Dearest" and filling it with pre-nuptial eu-

phoria. Reunited in Minneapolis, they spent all their free time together and began making plans for their future. Somewhere along
the way their passion for each other got careless, and he managed
to get her "knocked up," in the parlance of the day. A wedding
date was set for August 24, barely six months after their first date.

None of this could be considered unusual in the aftermath
of the war.

While it's possible my father's lineage (as my mother suspected) included some Jewish blood, he was born and raised a
Catholic and continued to be a devout practitioner for the rest of
his life. The Pleasant Avenue neighborhood of South Minneapolis where we grew up was overwhelmingly Catholic, anchored by
the Church of the Incarnation, one of the larger parishes in the
Archdiocese of Minneapolis/St Paul. Every Sunday morning my
father would rouse us from our beds, making sure we washed our
faces, brushed our teeth, and combed our hair, before loading us
into my mother's old Plymouth for the three-block drive down
Pleasant Avenue to attend Mass. To accommodate the enormous
population of the parish, the church offered two Masses simulta-
neously—upstairs and down—at 5:30, 6:30, 7:45, 9:15, 10:30
and 11:45—a total of *twelve* Masses every Sunday morning. For
reasons my father never explained, he insisted on attending the
9:15 Mass *downstairs,* where services were conducted in a drab,
low-ceilinged room lit by fluorescent lighting with all the ambi-
ance of a prison cafeteria.

By comparison, the upstairs church was a soaring cathedral
of colorful domes, ornate stained-glass windows, marble statuary,
hand-carved woodwork, and rich brocaded tapestries. The choir
sang from an enormous loft to the accompaniment of a grand,
bellowing organ whose deepest notes sent a shiver down my spine
every time I heard it. In the eighth grade, I was elected president
of the altar boys and was given free rein of the premises, which
included the sacristy, the priest's quarters, and the bell-tower
where, before every service, I pulled the rope to ring the heavy
bronze bell. The momentum of its oscillating weight was enough

to lift me ten feet off the floor—so high that my fingers gripping the rope sometimes got pinched in the hole through the ceiling. Other times I would invite my friend Tim to take a break from his job selling religious magazines and the *Catholic Bulletin* at the entrance of the church to join me in a climb up the bell-tower. Picking our way through the dried pigeon shit and lethal bat guano on the wooden stairway, we would finally reach the bell-tower roof, where through a hatch we could see all the way to the Foshay Tower in downtown Minneapolis.

At the basement services there was no music at all, unless you want to call music the tepid refrains from a cheap console organ played by a novice parishioner. As much as he would try to sing, my father's voice was so weak and off-key I used to cringe at the sound of it. He would quietly scold us for fidgeting or talking, and every once in a while he would have to revive me or my brother Jim when we fainted from hunger or boredom, whichever came first. We were never allowed to eat beforehand, in accordance with the church's required practice of fasting three hours before Mass. The only thing that sustained us was the promise of the huge breakfast waiting for us at home, prepared by our mother. For you see, Mom rarely if ever went to church, as she had never converted to Catholicism. It was one of the great mysteries of my childhood. We were told that she was Lutheran, and because she had never converted, it would be inappropriate or even a sin for her to attend Catholic services. Or at least that was the excuse we were given. In any event, she always stayed home.

Her apparent agnosticism confused me. Every other mother in the parish went to Mass, yet many of these same women became lifelong friends of my mother. So it wasn't like she was hiding her faith, or lack thereof, from anyone, or even that she stayed away for any philosophical differences. Indeed, for many years she was president of the parish Women's Club, played cards once a month with the parish bridge club, made cookies and cakes for the parish bake sale, sewed costumes for the school plays, volunteered for the annual Octoberfest fundraiser, and knew every one of the nuns and priests by name. Sometimes a priest might even stop by our house on Christmas Eve to say hello and sample a piece of Mom's superb pumpkin pie. But never once did anyone make an issue of the fact that she never went to church, at least to me. Mark claims that one of the priests once took him aside in the school hallway and insisted they were going to work on our mother to get her to come to Mass. But either they didn't follow through or they failed to convince her, because she continued to be a non-attendant. Certainly my father must have *suggested* to my mother that she convert to Catholicism. The fact that she never did suggests she could be just as stubborn as he was.

Mom made up for her religious recalcitrance by taking us on what she liked to call "culture tours" throughout the Twin Cities. These included visits to the American-Swedish Institute on Park Avenue, the Ford Assembly Plant in Highland Park, the Sibley and Faribault houses in Historic Mendota, and the Planetarium at the Minneapolis Public Library; all this in addition to our regular weekly visits to the Hosmer Branch of the public library on East 36th Street where we were encouraged to check out as many books as our library cards would allow. On one such visit to the library she discovered me amidst the stacks talking to an African-American boy whom I'd recently competed against in a Saturday morning basketball game at nearby Bryant Junior High. She nearly hauled me by my ear out to the car where she sat me in the front seat and issued a stern warning:

"I don't ever want to see you talking to one of those ... *jigaboos* again!"

"*Mom!*" I shouted. This sudden exposure to her dark side both angered and confused me. Had she always felt this way? "We were only talking about the game last Saturday!" I told her, still shouting.

My response must have surprised her for in the next moment her expression changed and her words became conciliatory, almost apologetic. "I just don't want to see you get hurt, honey, that's all."

She once thought enough of a colored-pencil rendition I made of Woody Woodpecker at age seven to enroll me in Saturday morning classes at the Art Institute. While Jim and Betsey got to stay home and watch cartoons, I had to wear a silly smock and learn how to make paper mache likenesses of some elephant character named Babar who seemed to be well known by the other students—kids who were remarkably different from my Pleasant Avenue gang. I hated it, but when I told Mom I wanted to quit she informed me she'd already paid the twenty-dollar enrollment fee up-front and it was non-refundable. I kept going for her sake, not mine, and I doubt I ever drew another picture for her.

With Dad gone three or four nights a week on his sales job, Mom was tasked with raising all five of her children practically alone. She was absolutely fearless when it came to navigating the city she had adopted as her own, and would think nothing of loading all five of us in the back of her second-hand DeSoto, Plymouth, or Mercury to drive to Hopkins or wherever to redeem a coupon good for three cents off on a jar of peanut butter or a ten-pack of toilet paper. With her savings she might stop at a White Castle on the way home and treat us to a sack of seven-cent hamburgers, and maybe a small Coke if we behaved. She took in sewing on the side, and every weekday night you could find her in the TV room seated at her Singer sewing machine, stitching wedding dresses, prom dresses, or even the pajamas we got every year for Christmas. Late at night she'd relax on the couch with a cup of coffee and the evening paper, humming along to the stereo before finally turning in.

I'll never forget the surprise we got one morning when we awoke to find Dad at the breakfast table, an unexpected arrival from the night before. For some reason he had come home a day early from a sales trip, and when he found the house locked and everyone asleep, he got a ladder out of the garage and came in through the porch door on the second floor balcony. Apparently his unexpected arrival had startled Mom. At breakfast that morning she described the alarm she felt when she awoke and realized someone was breaking into the house. She looked Dad squarely in the eye and said, "If I'd had a gun, you'd be dead right now." We all paused over our soggy cornflakes and stared at her in disbelief: would Mom really have shot Dad for climbing in through the back porch?

But that's the least of the questions I have about her.

27

Who's Smiling Now?

"How come Mom never went to church?" I ask him now as we approach the outskirts of Wichita. Interstate-35 has become a toll road, running all the way to Kansas City, and I'm not sure there will be adequate rest stops ahead. Before he can answer my first question, I pose another: "Do you have to pee?"

"No," he says abruptly. "As for the question about your mother, you'd have to ask her that yourself. She could certainly be stubborn when she wanted to be. And careless." I detect a hint of frustration in his voice.

Careless indeed. There is written proof from a letter to her mother that Mom once failed to properly latch the back door of the family sedan. As the car pulled away from the curb, one- year-old Kathy fell out onto the street—thank God she wasn't hurt! Oops. According to family legend, I was once plopped down in my diaper along the sandy shore of Lake Harriet while Dad and my older siblings waded out into deeper water. Mom, who was supposed to be keeping an eye on me, looked up from her magazine and discovered me missing. "*Russ!*" she screamed, "*The baby!*" to which my father came bounding to shore. He discovered me just beneath the surface of the water on my back, my blue eyes wide open with a happy grin on my otherwise toothless face.

(It's entirely possible this was my baptism into the maritime world in which I would spend most of my career. I like to think my mother was indirectly responsible for it.)

In grade school I contracted measles and was sequestered in my bedroom with a vaporizer and a steady dose of sulfa administered by Dr. Mom. One morning she came in to inform me that

Dad's sore back was acting up and he'd taken the day off to stay home and recuperate in bed. On one of her medication rounds she poured a tablespoon of something into my mouth that didn't taste like the same stuff she had given me before. When I pointed at the label on the bottle, she immediately realized her mistake. *"Russ!"* she shouted in panic. *"I just gave Johnny a spoonful of your back ointment!"* And then she ran from the room. A moment later I saw my father in his wrinkled boxer shorts heading down the stairs, groaning as he clutched his back, at the same time cursing my mother for her carelessness. In the meantime, Mom hurried me into the bathroom where she initiated gag procedures, forcing her finger down my throat as I knelt before the toilet; it didn't work. Dad returned with a tumbler of raw eggs, the yolks undulating in a sea of viscous-looking snot. Just the sight of it was enough to make me puke. When Dad handed her the glass, Mom ordered, "Drink it," and as I did, my stomach began churning like an active volcano. Crisis avoided, Dad staggered back to bed.

Another time, I had a severe toothache and instead of taking me to the dentist Mom installed me on the couch in front of the TV. Her attendance was required that afternoon at a bridge club luncheon so she left me with pieces of a Hershey chocolate bar which I was to place on the sore tooth as needed for temporary relief. I was old enough to know that my rotten teeth were probably the result of too much candy in the first place, so her remedy seemed like throwing gasoline on the fire to me. But it sure tasted good.

In the eighth grade I suffered another dental setback during a pickup hockey game at Lyndale Farmstead when an errant puck found my front teeth. I remember the sudden taste of blood and how my tongue gingerly tested the wobbly locations of all those loose teeth in my mouth. A Minneapolis cop drove me home and escorted me into the front foyer of our house where I dropped my skates and called out, "Mom, I wrecked my teeth!" It was late Saturday afternoon and she was upstairs getting ready for an evening out. Dad was out tinkering in the garage. When Mom didn't immediately respond, the cop shouted, "Ma'am, you'd better get down here. Your son's going to need to see a dentist, probably sooner rather than later."

"I told that kid I didn't want him playing hockey in the first place!" came her angry reply from above. *"And why weren't you wearing a mouth guard?"* she added, directing her wrath at me. She was very upset. As I recall, Mr. Downham from across the street, himself the father of three hockey players, was enlisted to take me to the dentist. But I despairingly remember the repair work I had to have done later and how my mother, lacking family dental insurance, forked over most of her hard-earned sewing money— all of it in cash—to pay the endodontist.

Once all five of her children were safely established in school, Mom decided to better herself. She'd always had an eye for beauty, and even with her limited budget she managed to decorate our home tastefully and to the high approval of guests. Somewhere along the way she must have realized her skills were befitting of a career in interior decorating. So, in 1968, when I was still in grade school, she enrolled in the LaSalle Extension University, a nationally-accredited, at-home correspondence school with home offices in Chicago. Their ad campaign displayed recent graduates showing off their diplomas and proclaiming, *"Who's smiling now?"*

Mom mailed away more of her sewing money toward the considerable initial expense of textbooks and course materials, which included a small slide projector for in-depth visual instruction. I'd often come home from school to find her in a darkened bedroom studying an image of someone's living room or den projected on a bedsheet clothes-pinned to a curtain rod. Sometime later, and after X amount of dollars were mailed-away, she was awarded a diploma, on the strength of which she landed a job at Gabberts, an upscale furniture store in the wealthy Minneapolis suburb of Edina. She took her new career very seriously and eventually worked her way up to a senior design consultant with Montgomery Wards. On the wall behind the bar in the basement of the St Louis Park home, where Dad had moved all his World

War II memorabilia from the attic of our old house, Mom began hanging the awards and plaques she'd earned as "Salesman of the Month" or "Employee of the Year" with Montgomery Wards.

It's possible there may have been a bit of professional jealousy between two salespeople living beneath the same roof. On more than once occasion I heard her challenge him as he returned from one of his road trips with, "Well, did you sell any *Americans* this week?" (*Americans* were the large dragline cranes he sold—easily the most expensive pieces of equipment in his catalog.) The competition could get tense, and sometimes tempers boiled over. I remember more than once when Dad arrived home on a Friday night and didn't bother coming into the house, instead making himself busy weeding the garden or playing with the dog. That's when Betsey would quietly inform me that Dad and Mom weren't talking, the end result of a fight neither of us knew anything about. This could go on for days, even weeks, before one of them finally broke down and everything would return to normal. Neither of them was effusive in their public displays of affection. He called her "Ma" for as long as I can remember, and I don't ever recall him saying he loved her. Once, when we were all packed and ready to leave on our summer vacation to a cabin up north, we sat waiting in the car for Mom to finish up inside. Dad grew impatient.

I happened to be sitting beside him in the front seat. "Godammit," he said, "go in there and see what's taking her so long." I went in through the back door and stopped dead in my tracks at the bottom of the half-flight of stairs leading up to the kitchen. Mom stood at the sink crying, something I had never witnessed before. It made me want to cry seeing her so distressed. She must have sensed my presence because in the next moment she turned to me and wiped her eyes with the back of her wet hands. "Tell him I'll be out as soon as I finish the dishes," she said. I don't doubt for a minute her grief was from something he had said or done.

But they were a good team. Even though she never attended church, she got deeply involved with the social aspects of the parish. They were a welcome addition to bridge club gatherings and also at any sort of function requiring volunteers. Mom was always quick to enroll their services. And wherever they went, she was definitely the "life of the party" compared to Dad's shyer nature. She also supplied the "eye" for all the projects they completed in the succession of houses they owned, while Dad supplied the labor. She cooked and cleaned, chauffeured us to our endless activities, clothed us with her limited budget, and consoled us in our early disappointments.

Yes, she could be tender. Once, when my first girlfriend sent me a "Dear John" letter (e-mail and texting were still some forty years in the future) Mom assured me it was nothing to worry about. "Girlfriends are like busses," she said sagely. "You miss one and ten minutes later another comes along." How could she know?

Once, she even needed to console my father. He was out of town, as usual, and had called home to see how the plans for my brother Mark's upcoming wedding were progressing. Mark happened to overhear the phone conversation and was moved by our mother's empathy. Dad was worried he hadn't done enough. He was despondent that maybe he hadn't provided enough money for a decent reception, or that because he was gone all the time he hadn't helped with any of the planning. He got to feeling so bad he suddenly started to sob loud enough for Mark to hear from across the room. Mom quietly reassured him that everything was going to be alright and that all he needed to do was come home; she had taken care of everything. And I've no doubt she had. In my recollection, the wedding was perfect, with everyone, including my father, having a wonderful time.

She worked as long as my father did, until 1977 or '78 when they both retired and moved up north to the lake home. By then she had accumulated a nice little nest egg—something like twenty or twenty-five thousand dollars, a tidy sum in those days. But apparently not enough to satisfy her. She wanted more. Upon retiring, she made the bold decsion to invest her savings in the stock market, to make it a source of income that would be hers and hers alone to do with whatever she wanted. She shopped around and discovered an institution that advertised a return nearly double what all the others promised, but with a catch: investment funds were not insured. She didn't care. It was a risk, but she must have felt it was a risk worth taking.

The funds actually did well for a couple of years, and she would happily tell anyone who cared to listen about the returns she was realizing. I even remember her once suggesting that I cash-in the government bonds I'd accrued in my time with the Coast Guard to start a portfolio of my own. But I had bigger ideas. (I would eventually cash them in to buy a houseboat, which in retrospect, was a move as misguided as hers, considering its eventual outcome.) In any event, almost without warning, the investment company folded overnight, and in the course of a few short days she lost everything. She tried for awhile to hide the devastating news from those close to her, including my father, but he didn't have much trouble figuring it out.

"She spends all afternoon out on the goddamn deck," he told me in one of our Sunday night phone conversations. "She opens a bottle of wine and after awhile I hear her out there sobbing and carrying on as if she just lost her best friend."

Mom eventually got over the loss, focusing her energy and design talent on a neighbor's burgeoning craft and souvenir shop, as well as her growing number of grandchildren. But she would never talk about the failed investment scheme, and Dad advised all of us to avoid bringing it up in her presence. The story gets even worse, however. Mom spent her summer of despondency lounging in the sun. Fair-skinned and prone to burning, she contracted melanoma, the deadly skin cancer that would claim her life a few years later.

"*FUCKING SHYSTERS!*" MY father seethes now beside me. He mutters the name of the financial institution responsible for the loss of Mom's money, and goes into a diatribe about how they should all be in prison. Up until this sudden outburst it's been a wonderful morning, but he's angry now. We're approaching Kansas City and the traffic is beginning to tighten. I need to concentrate, both on the road and the time-bomb sitting next to me. I don't need any of the theatrics he pulled yesterday in Albuquerque.

Was that really only yesterday? Is this trip ever going to end?

28

THE BIRD IS THE WORD

As we approach Kansas City I stop for gas. Dad makes quick work of his visit to the restroom and emerges from the station zipped-up and dribble-free, swinging his cane like he's Charlie Chaplin. He looks to be at peace with the world.

"God, what a beautiful morning," he says as he settles into his seat. "It was so damn nice to see all those cows in green pastures this morning. I'd almost forgotten what a real spring looks like."

Amen.

The freeway through Kansas City, Kansas, is sliced up with road repairs. We careen through lane changes and detours, all the while dodging traffic that seems to converge from everywhere. The trailer chains occasionally scrape the surface of some of the steeper grade changes, and the GPS voice is on the verge of a nervous breakdown—"RECALCULATING RECALCULATING!" Dad takes it all in without too much concern, glancing over once when the roar of a tractor/trailer jake-braking beside us becomes deafening, another time slapping the dashboard when a punk in a pickup truck cuts in front of us heading for an exit ramp.

"*Christ almighty!*" he exclaims, "What the *hell's* the matter with that jackass?" I can't help but smile; this is the dad I remember from my youth, the expert driver, the road warrior who yielded to no one.

I manage to get us to the Missouri River in one piece, after which we're suddenly in Kansas City, Missouri, our sixth state in two days.

"Is that the Missouri River we just crossed?" he asks. When I tell him it is, he nods his head in agreement. "I thought so," he says. He's got an odd expression on his face.

"Why?" I ask.

He chuckles. "I shouldn't tell you this, but I think you're old enough now."

"I'm fifty-seven, Dad. For god sakes."

"Yes, I suppose that's old enough," he says. "But please don't tell your wife." He's playing with me, and I play along, enjoying all of it. Still, I remember a few times from my childhood when he would start a story with, "I shouldn't be telling you this," only to realize later that yes, he probably shouldn't have. One of those stories would haunt me for many years. He had driven Jimmy and me to South Dakota to spend a week at Aunt Grace and Uncle Lester's farm. He helped carry our luggage inside, and as we followed him upstairs to the spare bedroom, he stopped on the stairwell and pointed to the overhead banister in the hallway.

"I probably shouldn't be telling you this," he said, "but the farmer who once lived here hung himself from that banister, right about where you're standing." I felt the hair on the back of my neck rise and I quickly ran up a few steps to separate myself from the ghost I imagined to be on the premises. For the next week I ran up and down those stairs whenever I had to visit our bedroom, and that staircase continued to give me the creeps for as long as I can remember. The house sits abandoned now but the acreage is still owned by my cousin. I once took my own two sons to visit there but wasn't inclined to go inside.

The memory of the anxiety I experienced way back then gives me pause; why would he have told me that story in the first place? To frighten me? I turn now to look at him.

"Are you sure this is a story I want to hear?"

He smiles sheepishly. "Probably not."

"Can we skip it then?"

"Yes, I suppose so. But goddamn it, what are we doing for lunch? I'm hungry."

"*Hungry?*" I shout. "Really?"

He's already finished off the last of the banana bread and most of the cookies, and also a couple more fruit cups. But we've been on the road for nearly six hours so I suppose we could stop for lunch. In Liberty, Missouri, I exit into a suburban landscape of chain hotels and fast-food restaurants, but then spot something a little out of the ordinary, at least for Minnesotans.

"You ever eaten at a Waffle House?" I ask him.

"Can't say as I have."

"Then you're in for a real treat," I tell him.

"If you say so."

The parking lot is fairly full, and because of the U-Haul we have to park along the far perimeter of the lot, a long way from the door. Before we leave the car I ask to see if Dad has his teeth and he does his chimpanzee act again to prove that he does. And then, without a peep of refusal, he lets me take his arm, leaning on me as we shuffle our way across the parking lot. Inside, there's a good lunch-hour crowd but I spot an empty booth along the windows. As we make our way across the floor Dad turns to stare at someone sitting at the counter, a man in a Stetson hat.

"That guy looks familiar," he says.

"I don't think so," I reply and I nudge him along toward the booth. There's a small jukebox at the end of the table and the menus are large and garish, with pictures of just about every entree. The sun streaming through the glass is warm, and from here I can keep an eye on our rig out at the end of the parking lot. The waitress, a friendly young Black woman, comes over to take our orders. Predictably, Dad wants a hamburger, fries, and a Coke. The waitress asks, "Would you like a waffle with that?"

Dad looks up her, confused. "Why the *hell* would I want a waffle with my hamburger?"

I reach across and grab his hand. "It's okay," I tell him. "That's their specialty here and they ask everyone the same question. I'm going to have one, but you don't have to. You can have part of mine." I give the waitress an apologetic look. "No waffle for him." She departs with our order but Dad is still agitated.

"What the hell's the matter with her asking me if I want a goddamn waffle with my hamburger?"

Uh oh. It's much too early for Sundown Syndrome to be kicking in.

"Do you need to use the bathroom?" I ask.

"No."

"Are you too warm sitting here? Do you want to move to the shade?"

"No." I fish a few quarters out of my pocket and feed the jukebox. After the sudden outburst about the waffle I fear I'm on the verge of losing him again. I flip through the selections hoping to find something he might like, anything to distract him. And then bang, like magic, that something appears. I push the keys.

"Remember this one?" I ask quietly. Before he can respond the speaker erupts with a growling voice, announcing:

"Ah wella everybody's heard about The Bird,
ah wella bird, bird, bird, the bird is the word…"

His face melts into a knowing smile and suddenly he's laughing, the song bringing back not only fond memories of family nights at home, but also of something else.

As FRUGAL AS he may have been, my father knew a "sure thing" when he saw it. In the 1960s, now securely established in his career as a salesman, he invested some money in a recording studio owned by a fellow Incarnation parishioner. Kay-Bank Recording Studios had known a few smaller successes with tunes like "Muleskinner Blues" and "Six Days On the Road," but it struck gold in 1963 when it released "Surfin' Bird" by a Minneapolis rock and roll band called The Trashmen. The song rose to number four on the national charts and my father realized a nice dividend on his investment. With this unexpected windfall burning a hole in his pocket, he bought a boat.

I can't recall any family discussion about a boat or even any sort of conversation he and Mom might have had about boating in general. But one cold Saturday afternoon in mid-November he told me to get in the car and go with him to look at something. I had no idea what he had in mind. As we headed north through downtown Minneapolis there were heavy gray clouds in the sky and the unmistakable smell of snow in the air. Maybe he was looking at buying a snowmobile, I mused. The winter before he had rented one at Meadowbrook Golf Course and we took turns sitting behind him as he cruised up and down the fairway hills. Even though the thing kept breaking down, he had seemed somewhat interested; but enough to buy one? Now, as we crossed the river and headed up Central Avenue into Northeast Minneapolis, he suddenly pulled to the curb in front of Hannay's, one of the largest boat dealers in the Upper Midwest. I felt a knot in my stomach as I began to realize what this might entail.

The salesman greeted Dad like an old friend and led the two of us out back to the service bays, where a shiny new *Starcraft* runabout sat beneath an overhead shop light. It had a glistening gold and white paintjob, chrome deck fittings, and a tinted wraparound windshield. I'd never seen anything so beautiful.

"*You're buying this?*" I asked incredulously. He smiled and replied, "I'm thinking about it." The salesman suggested I climb in, and then showed me where to put my foot on the trailer fender so as not to bend it. Once aboard, I stood transfixed, as if I'd just been granted access to the Gemini space capsule. The salesman motioned me forward and patted the seat behind the wheel, urging me to sit. The mustard-colored carpeting felt stiff beneath my tennis shoes and the leatherette seat sighed when I eased myself down onto the cushion. The chrome gauges and knobs stared at me from the painted dash and the control lever of the 50 HP outboard clicked easily back and forth when I tried it. The knot in my stomach grew tighter; I began imagining the lakes and rivers I might someday explore in this, my first command. The salesman, eager to finalize the deal, said, "Shall we take her for a test drive?"

I glanced over at Dad. "Isn't it going to snow?" I asked.

The salesman laughed. "Hells bells. If the water ain't froze, the boat don't care." So Dad went out to retrieve our car and then he and the salesman wrestled the trailer onto the hitch. We headed south, to Bryant Lake, a body of water nestled between what were then the pastures and cornfields of Eden Prairie. We were the only boat on the water, the entire lake our private ocean. When Dad accelerated and the boat climbed up on plane, the breeze was so frigid my eyes felt frozen in their sockets, my teeth cold enough to crack. But that was only because I couldn't stop smiling; my dad was actually buying a boat!

We raced up and down the lake until my father finally shouted, "We'll take it!" and we headed for shore. The paperwork was completed on the front seat of the salesman's car as I shivered in the back seat, uncertain if it was the cold or the sheer excitement of the moment that had me feeling so.

The snow had begun falling by the time we started for home, my new command in tow. On Pleasant Avenue, Dad backed it up the driveway and straight into the garage, pausing only to brush the snow off before covering it with a tarp. He warned me to "stay the hell off it" until spring arrived, or at least until the first day nice enough that we could take it out for a cruise. But as soon as he left on his next sales trip I began giving tours to my friends, instructing my closest confidantes, Kenny and Kevin McDevitt, how to climb aboard without denting the fenders. I offered each of them the co-pilot seat while I sat in the captain's chair and steered for ports unknown in our garage. And it was Kenny and Kevin who got to come along on our very first excursion the following spring, joining Jimmy and me as Dad launched the *Star-craft* on the scenic and popular Saint Croix River. Boats came whizzing by from every direction, Dad's head cranking side to side as he tried to steer out of harm's way. No aircraft carrier in all of World War II had to employ such evasive maneuvering as he did that day. The real scare came when he misjudged the wake of an enormous cabin cruiser and the cresting combers tossed our little aluminum boat around like an empty beer can.

"That's enough of this shit!" he cursed through grimaced lips. And we headed for dry land.

Eventually, Dad got the hang of handling the little boat, but he refused to relinquish command to me, his most eager and willing deckhand. It was a matter of trust, and he simply didn't think an eleven-year-old boy capable enough to safely navigate a boat on something as unpredictable as water. When summer came and we headed north for our annual vacation at a lake resort, he finally gave me my first real chance behind the wheel. With the whole family aboard to watch, I squeezed in beside him at the helm and fought his big meat-hooks for control of the boat. "Turn right!" he ordered. "Now left! More left! Goddammit, you're coming in too fast! You're going to hit the dock!" He was an impatient teacher at best; a trait I've come to believe was passed down from his own father.

Fishing was the worst, the only time we actually tried it. One fall he and Mom took Jimmy and me north to Trout Lake, a place where he'd once caught his limit of lunker lake trout with a contractor who knew a lot more about fishing than he did. For our trip he bought all the expensive lures and downriggers, a depth finder and a detailed chart of the wilderness lake. The day was beautiful, with the fall colors in full bloom and the sun warming us in the quiet bays. But we didn't catch any fish. And this infuriated my father. After five minutes of frustration in one bay, he would loudly curse and order us to "reel-in, we're moving!" Around the lake we went all afternoon, Dad's anger building with every fishless bay. After awhile it got so bad that Mom suggested he put me and Jimmy ashore to explore a deserted island nearby, and when we arrived we both leapt from the boat, happy to be free. Fishing with Dad was pure torture.

I should have learned my lesson, but I didn't. Flash forward twenty-five years. Dad had now been married to Eunice for three years and her alcohol abuse was beginning to create problems. In our Sunday night phone conversations I could hear a tinge of despondency in his voice, and it gave me concern. It finally reached a point where I thought I needed to do something to cheer him up, and one Sunday night I broached the idea of a fishing trip—nothing extravagant, just an afternoon on the lake in the company of me and my two sons, Sam and Nick. I'd bring everything we'd need—my boat, the fishing gear, the bait—and we'd go to the lake where he and Mom had lived before she died. His only responsibility would be pointing us to the fishing holes where he'd had all his luck in the past. This was of course a joke; he'd never really been much of a fisherman. But catching fish wasn't my intention; I merely wanted him to enjoy some time away from Eunice, and also spend some time with his two grandsons, whom he barely knew, nor they him.

I wasn't surprised when he came up with a litany of excuses as to why he couldn't go, but I cut him off early. "C'mon, Dad," I said. "Just say 'yes'."

Silence, and then, "Well, okay. But goddammit—"

"Great!" I shouted, interrupting him again. "We'll be up next Saturday afternoon. I have to work in the morning but we should be there by three."

We arrived on schedule because with him, if you said three, by God it had better be three and not 3:01 or even 3:10. Eunice had put together a small cooler of sandwiches and chips, along with some cans of soda pop for the boys and beer for Dad and me. And because I had towed the boat up behind my pickup, she drove Dad down to the landing in their car. So far, so good; Dad seemed to have a new attitude about the outing and had started kidding the boys about who was going to catch the biggest fish. He even offered a nickel to the one who caught the first fish, himself included. My sons looked at me uncertainly; a nickel? Was Grampa serious? I assured them he was.

Saturday afternoon traffic at the public landing was heavy, and after dropping the boys off to go skip stones, I took my place at the end of the launch line. Dad and Eunice parked their car, then took a seat at a picnic table to wait. When it was finally my turn I summoned Dad to come help me, handing him the bowline with instructions to tie the boat to the dock once it floated free of the trailer. He understood his instructions and seemed only too happy about the prospect of being useful again. When the boat floated free, he tied it securely to the dock while I went to park the trailer. When I returned, we all climbed aboard, except Eunice, who remained at the picnic table to watch us get underway.

My boat was a rugged tri-hull built of welded aluminum, formerly a part of the Forest Service fleet in Voyageurs National Park. It had been a project boat that I'd spent long hours over two winters restoring in my garage. In fact, just recently I'd installed a new (to me) outboard motor on the transom, and I had revved it up in the driveway before we headed north to make sure it was working properly. Now, as I turned the key to start the motor, nothing happened—no ignition, no tilt, no trim, nothing. I ran back to check the connections, tested the manual bilge pump (good), the running lights (good), the horn (loud), and then tried starting it again. Nothing.

"Jesus Christ ..." Dad muttered. "What the hell's the matter with the goddamned thing?" The boys, who were sitting in the bow playing with the pint of leeches I'd brought along, looked up at the sound of Dad's swearing. Then Eunice came strolling down the dock with her tumbler of "ice water."

"How come your boat don't start?" she shouted. She was smiling, as if she found this amusing. Behind her on the ramp, other boaters were waiting patiently to launch, though one of them shouted, "Let's go, pal! You're holding up the process!"

Dad's eyes flashed on me in anger. "Jesus Christ," he muttered again.

"Not a problem!" I cried cheerfully, and I jumped to the stern again, this time to lower the trolling motor, a ten-horse Evinrude, which started on the first pull. "Sam," I shouted, "turn us loose!" A minute later we were putt-putting away from the landing at a nice clip, the trolling motor more than adequate to the task of pushing the boat along. I sat down on the padded transom to steer and headed for the middle of the lake. "Okay, Dad," I said. "Point us to the fish."

"Kiss my ass," he replied angrily.

"What?" I said.

He was seething, his eyes full of the terrible wrath I remembered from my youth. He shouted, "You haul this goddamn piece of shit up here and expect me to fish without a working motor?"

In the bow the boys had turned again at the sound of my father's fury and were watching me now with stunned expressions. I felt Dad's sour omnipresence filling the boat as surely as lake water, threatening to sink our afternoon of fishing. I brought the trolling motor to an idle and then killed it. We were now a good half-mile from the hubbub and noise of the landing. The lake was calm, and except for the call of a gull circling overhead, it was suddenly very quiet aboard the boat.

"What's wrong with *this* motor?" I asked patiently.

"Shit!" he hissed again. And I had to turn my face toward the lake. I couldn't believe how worked up he'd let himself get over something so innocuous. At that moment I realized I'd better control my own temper before I made things worse. I turned back to him.

"You know, Dad, I'm really sorry the big motor won't start. I mean, I ran it in the driveway last night and it was perfect—tilt, trim, idle, shifting, everything. It ran so well, in fact, I didn't even think to bring my tools along, which I realize now was a huge mistake. But really, Dad, why let that spoil our day? This trolling motor will be fine for what we're doing, don't you think?"

He wasn't buying it. "Bullshit!" he cursed again, albeit in a quieter tone than before. But the damage was done. I got up and walked forward to where the fishing rods were stored, reached for the leeches and then baited the hooks for the boys. I'd put Lindy-rigs on the night before so I then announced we would be trolling for walleye, even though we were in sixty feet of water. I really didn't care. What I *wanted* to do was tie the fifteen-pound anchor around my father's neck and push him over the side.

But instead I said, "Sam, you want to run the motor?"

"Yes!" he shouted.

"Okay, you got her, Skipper," I said. "Come sit here beside Grampa and give him your rod. You'll be too busy steering to fish."

As Sam made his way to the stern I took his rod and held it out to my father, sitting in the rear seat facing backward. He glanced up at me with a look of disgust.

"*Take it,*" I said through clenched teeth. Which he did, reluctantly, perhaps sensing that he'd managed to make me as angry as he was. Which I was. He had ruined the day.

We fished for a half-hour, no one catching anything, no one really even trying. We barely talked. The boys were obviously perplexed by the appearance of their grandfather sitting stone-faced in the stern staring out at the tip of his rod. Just before calling it a day I asked that he please turn around so that I might take a photo of him, proof that he had in fact been in a boat fishing with his grandsons. But he was so determined to be angry at me for ruining *his* day that he refused even that.

Back at the landing I was surprised to find Eunice still sitting at the picnic table. She wobbled down the dock to greet us, loudly imploring us to "*hold up yer stringer of fish!*" But there weren't any fish, a fact that seemed to amuse her even more. "We'll have fish for supper anyway!" she announced. "I'll go buy some."

"We won't be staying for dinner," I informed her. 'We're heading home."

My father looked at me. "You said you were spending the night. Jesus Christ, she put clean sheets on the hide-a-bed."

"Nope, sorry. We'll be heading home as soon as I'm loaded up."

"God dammit to hell!"

"Yeah, no kidding, Dad. *God dammit to hell.* I guess we'll have to talk about it when I call you next Sunday."

The problem with the outboard, I later discovered, was a burned-out fuse buried deep within the wiring harness. Once I'd replaced it, it never failed again. There were times when I had to wonder if a karmic influence was at work in our troubled relationship.

29

TWISTING THE NIGHT AWAY

Before we leave the Waffle House Dad tells me he'd better go pee again. I finish up the last of my waffle as I watch him shuffle off to the men's room. I pay the bill and ask the waitress for another refill on my coffee. As tired as I am, I could easily lie down in the booth and take a nap, but I'm afraid I'd never wake up. I sip my coffee and keep an eye out for Dad. A little while later he emerges from the restroom, zipped-up and dribble-free, to my relief. As he shuffles down the aisle he studies the patrons at the counter. I watch as he spots the guy in the Stetson he noticed on the way in. Stetson's sitting next to a guy wearing a red ball-cap, the two of them sucking on toothpicks near the cash register. They appear to be about my age, wind-burned and a bit rough-looking. The guy in the Stetson looks over his shoulder when he notices Dad scrutinizing him.

"What's up, Pops?" he says. He's not smiling.

Dad leans on his cane and I can hear him from where I'm sitting as he replies, "I know you from somewhere."

"Don't think so," Stetson says coldly. "I don't go nowheres." Now both men have turned in their swivel chairs to stare at Dad. I jump up from the booth and hurry over. They size me up as I turn Dad toward the door. But he resists, struggling to see past me as he insists he has something to say.

"That's Cliff!" he suddenly blurts.

"Cliff?"

"My neighbor!" he says, and he turns again to the Stetson, grinning. "I thought you'd be back up in the Palouse country by now, Cliff!" Stetson looks at his pal and they both begin chuck-ling. The pal's got a tattoo of a snake on his neck and letters spelling something across the knuckles of his left hand, which I don't bother trying to read.

"Dad, that's not Cliff," I say quietly.

He gives me a confused look. "Sure it is."

Stetson holds out his hand. "Name's Raymond, young fella. What's yours?"

But before Dad can answer I've got my forearm under his armpit to turn him toward the door. He doesn't need this confusion. "That's not Cliff," I tell him again. "Let's go."

"Hey!" the Stetson shouts after me. "It ain't like I'm gonna bite him!"

It's warm in the car and as I help Dad into his seat, he yawns.

"You tired?" I ask.

"I think so," he says. "I think I could take a nap." Now here's a news flash! Without waiting for an affirmation I grab his seat release and lower him into a prone position.

"How's that?"

He responds with a slight nod, then folds his hands across his waist, yawns again, and closes his eyes. I can't believe it. He's actually going to take a nap! Now I'm not tired at all, and I hurry around and climb into my side of the car, as jubilant as a young father with a newborn baby. We head down the frontage road to the ramp for I-35 and slide in behind traffic headed north. After setting the cruise control I look over to check on him and find that he's sound asleep, his breathing deep and at times accentuated with a gentle snoring.

It dawns on me that this is the first moment in the last three days he hasn't been awake beside me, watching my every move, questioning every road sign or exit ramp. For the first time in three days I won't have to wonder about what I'm going to ask him next, how I'm going to occupy his mind. I feel giddy. I reach for the radio but then decide against it, worried it might wake him up. I fiddle with the GPS, pan ahead on the route and the exits, check our ETA to La Crosse: we're now on schedule for an 8:45 p.m. arrival. I decide I should call Mark to confirm our itinerary, tell him I'm going to sleep for three days once we get there, and inform him I won't be much help unloading the trailer.

Mark answers after the first ring. I clutch the phone to my ear and turn toward the window. Mark assures me he's got it all covered, that my job will be over once the old man is safely delivered. When I hang up I feel rejuvenated, feel like we've already arrived, trip over. And I know I shouldn't.

Dad doesn't sleep long—forty-five minutes, maybe an hour. All of a sudden I hear a voice below me saying, "How long do I have to stay like this?" Apparently he's been watching me for awhile; his eyes are alert.

I smile. "What, you're done with your nap?"

"I didn't take a nap."

"Yes, you did. You slept for almost an hour."

"No, I don't think so."

"Well, you did. You fell asleep as soon as we got in the car."

He scowls, indicating he still doesn't believe me.

"Okay, you didn't take a nap. You were checking your eyelids for cracks. Here, let me help you up." And with this I help him struggle to an upright position. Suddenly he's happy again. He turns toward the window and begins humming some tuneless melody that I suddenly recognize as "Surfin' Bird."

Out of the blue he says, "Seems like we used to have an autographed copy of that album around the house somewhere. I wonder what ever happened to it?"

"You mean *The Trashmen* album?"

"Yes. Probably worth some money now, wouldn't you think?"

"I've got it," I tell him. "You gave it to me with the Motorola about ten years ago."

"I gave you the Motorola?"

"Yes, you did." I'm afraid to tell him what I did with it. But I do anyway.

I DON'T KNOW WHAT motivated him to buy a stereo set in the first place, but my mother's love of music probably had a lot to do with it. One day when I was still in kindergarten, a delivery truck backed up our driveway and two men unloaded a Motorola console stereo unit. It was bigger than our Philco TV set and heavier, its mahogany cabinet featuring a pair of gold, fabric-covered speakers along with a cushion-mounted turntable powerful enough to throw clay pottery. Mom had to move a few chairs around in the living room to make room for it, and one of the delivery men gave her a brief tutorial in its operation. But she waited until Dad and my brothers and sisters arrived home before she dared play it. Dad was the last to arrive, and we all gathered around him in the living room as he queued up the demonstration LP that came with it: *The Twist*, a compilation of the latest dance craze hits.

I don't mind telling you I've had some thrilling experiences in my life. I've seen the face of God in the fury of a North Atlantic gale, cut the umbilical cords of two newborn babies, even shaken the hand of Lawrence Welk. But nothing will ever compare to the sound of those swinging saxophones filling every corner of our living room that night. We all began dancing in our own interpretation of the music, each of us gyrating and jumping around, *"twisting"* as Chubby Checker implored us, our inhibitions set free. Mom and Dad loved to dance—we all knew that—but this was something else, something new; this was rock and roll! They both laughed hysterically as they chicken-strutted with their arms, twisting their stocking feet into the carpet, and swaying to and fro into each other like the cool cats we saw on *American Bandstand*. I couldn't help thinking they looked just as cool as Rock Hudson and Doris Day in *Pillow Talk,* from the movie trailers we saw every night on TV. Dad about wore the grooves off the vinyl that night playing the same album—our only album!—over and over again. As far as I was concerned it was the only album we needed to own.

The Motorola became our prized possession, more valuable than Dad's car and certainly more entertaining than the TV. Within days Mom took control, holding the vinyl discs by their edges and giving them a quick wipe across her thigh before setting them onto the turntable. Every time she turned it on, a small indicator light glowed brilliantly amber in the lower right corner of the cabinet, which to me was pure magic. I stared into the glow, imagining the presence of a small orchestra performing the music, with the ability to change styles according to the genre. Mom started buying more LPs and within a year the storage compartment inside the console began filling up. Her taste in music was eclectic and in my opinion superb. She liked the crooners for sure—The Ink Spots, The Ames Brothers, Andy Williams, Perry Como, Dean Martin, (she *swooned* over Dean Martin), though for some reason not Sinatra. She branched out into folk music—The Kingston Trio, The New Christy Minstrels, Glenn Yarborough, and Burl Ives. I'd listen to Burl sing "Little Bitty Tear," and wonder aloud about the "grip" that Burl carried as he left through the door. "What's a *grip*, Mom, and why doesn't he use a suitcase like everyone else?" She bought compilation albums, and I was introduced to the music of Harry Belafonte, Trini Lopez, and Rosemary Clooney. When Gogi Grant sang "Wayward Wind" I imagined myself living someday "in a lonely shack by the railroad tracks." After hearing Eddie Arnold yodel "Cattle Call," I stood in front of the bathroom mirror trying to train my Adam's apple to yodel like Eddie's.

Mom liked to put a stack of LPs on in the morning before she began working around the house, humming along in harmony with the tunes, her voice clear and pitch perfect. Later, when we were old enough to buy our own albums, she liked to listen to those, too—Elvis, The Mamas and the Papas, Simon and Garfunkel, The Beatles. She kept her tastes open to everything. When she discovered "outlaw" country with Kris Kristofferson, Waylon Jennings, and Willie Nelson, she believed "Blue Eyes Crying in The Rain" was one of the most beautiful songs ever written. In high school, when I worked nights at Dayton's, she'd stay up until 11, when I got home, and feed me the dinner she'd saved in the oven. She might put a Sons of the Pioneers album on the stereo and we'd sit and talk, just the two of us. It was a small comfort in those frightening years of the Vietnam War, when I was sure I was going to get drafted. When I wound up enlisting anyway, I arrived home one spring from an overseas tour to find *Breezin* by George Benson in Mom's record collection.

"Since when did you start listening to *George Benson*?" I asked, incredulous.

"You should listen to him, too, honey!" she insisted. But I already had, overseas, and I loved it.

I loved her, too. In spite of her occasional lapses in judgment, I always felt that I'd inherited her soul, good or bad, and shared in her affinity for fun, her spirit of adventure. She had a silly side, sometimes embarrassingly so. When my sisters were young she made up names for them—"The Queen of Poops" and "Katie Cuke," which she was never shy about using in public, much to their mortification. At a wedding reception once she sat down at a table to visit with Betsey and some of her college-age girl-friends. A handsome groomsman kept passing their table, and on one such approach Mom leaned in conspiratorially. "You girls get ready," she whispered. "I'm going to trip him next time he comes by and one of you better catch him." Betsey's friends thought her hilarious but Betsey wanted to die. Why couldn't her mother be as dignified and graceful as other mothers?

There were times when I used to wonder if she regretted her choice in a husband, wondering if my father's moodiness and irrita-bility didn't sometimes drag her down. But she didn't live long enough for me to ask. Or I should say, I hadn't yet reached the age where such a question might be taken seriously; I was twenty-nine and just start-ing a family of my own when she died. My kids would never know the brighter side of a trip to visit Grandma and Grandpa, or the fun she injected into every social situation. It's not hard to imagine my father might have been a much happier man had the two of them grown old together, and my question would have become moot.

In any event, she liked the music of Tom Jones so much that Dad selected "Green Green Grass of Home"—one of her favorites—to be played at her funeral. The mortician balked but Dad insisted. "None of that morbid shit," he said. "This is what she would have wanted."

The Motorola would survive many moves. Years after Mom's death it finally found its way to the corner of the garage up north, in the home where Dad and Eunice lived. One summer he held a rummage sale and hung a sign on it: $25 or Best Offer. No one offered anything.

"I don't understand it," he told me over the phone. "I had the thing playing during the sale and it sounded as good as the day I bought it. No one even bothered to look. I hate like hell to junk it."

"I'll take it," I finally told him, more as a tribute to my mother than anything else. One of my sons helped me carry it down to the basement where I would listen to it occasionally while working on a project. I'd gotten all of Mom's old record albums in the deal, too. Then one winter I decided to remodel the basement and the old console got in the way. One morning I hauled it to the dump, pushing it off the tailgate onto a bigger pile of scrapped appliances. Not a very fitting burial for something that had given our family so much happiness; in a way I felt like I was burying my mother with it, too. I'll never forget the look on her face the first time we danced along to Chubby Checker, "twisting the night away."

"You took it to the *dump?*" my father shouts. He's incredulous. "Jesus Christ!"

"Saved you a trip," I tell him. He's got a sour look on his face and I can tell I need to change the subject.

"Where did you buy that stereo anyway?" I ask him. "It certainly wasn't a cheap model." We're approaching the Iowa border and it's nearly seventy degrees. I crack the rear windows to let in some fresh air. Dad's got his sweater buttoned to his neck but I don't care.

"I got it at Sears," he says. "It was top of the line. Paid a lot of money for it."

Sears. Of course; it was his favorite place in the world.

30

LOST AND FOUND

Back in the sixties my father liked nothing better on a Friday night than to walk the aisles of the giant Sears store on Lake Street, just to look at things. The building was enormous, a towering art-deco skyscraper that served as the company's regional mail-order headquarters, but at the same time offered two floors of retail space. On this particular Friday night he had brought along Jimmy and me, the two of us no more than five or six at the time. We had come, of course, in Mom's old Plymouth, which Dad parked half a block away on Elliot Avenue before taking our hands and crossing busy Lake Street to the store. Once inside, it was no less majestic than the Grand Bazaar of Old Constantinople, the aisles crammed with shoppers, the counter folks busy pushing their merchandise, the air filled with intoxicating smells of caramel-corn, roasted peanuts, and popcorn.

Our first stop was always the candy counter, where Dad purchased two boxes of buttered popcorn—one for himself and one for Jimmy and me to share. We stayed close behind as he led us through the maze of sensual delights—the sparkling glass cases of the Jewelry Department, the hushed silkiness of Women's Fashions, the smell of new leather in Shoes, the whir of domestic machinery in Home Appliances. Beneath the escalators to the second floor the exhaust-tube of a noisy Hoover vacuum cleaner spun a giant beachball on an invisible column of air, a sight that never failed to mesmerize me. One time when I was there with Mom I tried walking up the "down" escalator to get a better look at the suspended beachball. The agent who sold life insurance in the Allstate kiosk below spotted me and shouted, "Hey kid! Get offa there!"

On this particular night Dad must have had something specific in mind—a new tool for his workshop perhaps, or even a gift for Mark's or Betsey's June birthday, something he didn't want Jimmy or me to see. Whatever the reason, he decided to ditch us. Not ditch us exactly, but leave us to our own resources for a few minutes while he went off to conduct his business. He led us to the rear of the store, where we climbed the two steps to the raised mezzanine of the Toy Department. Here, the endless aisles overflowed with more than enough treasure to occupy the imaginations of two small boys for as long as he needed. Or so he thought. He parked us in front of the Tonka Toy display and issued a stern order. "You boys wait here. I'll be right back."

Jimmy seemed only too content to finger the bright finishes of the toy trucks and tractors, testing the movable doors, cranking the tiny steering wheels. But as I stared down the aisle of toys and watched my father descend the two steps back into the main part of the store, his familiar head slowly melting into the mass of humanity, I began to panic. Why is he abandoning us? I grabbed my brother's arm. "Come on," I said. "We need to find Dad."

Without a word of protest (I was his big brother, after all) Jimmy fell in behind me as I began my search pattern. We passed all the known landmarks from our earlier route in, but the once familiar counters now seemed foreign in this sea of strangers. The spinning beach ball was my lone beacon of hope, and I paused before it, thinking that surely Dad must be somewhere nearby. But he wasn't, and after a while we moved on, searching down one aisle and up another.

When I felt like we had searched the entire store I did what any other six-year-old would do in the same situation: I stood with my brother's hand in mine and looked bewildered. Within moments, a matronly woman bent to console us, her brow raised in concern. "Are you two boys lost?" she asked. I nodded in the affirmative, my chin too quivery to speak. To my relief she took my hand and pulled the two of us in the direction of the main door, where a Minneapolis cop stood talking to an agitated customer. We waited. The woman looked down at me and smiled. "He'll know what to do," she said, and we continued waiting while the conversation between the cop and the customer only seemed to intensify. I pulled on the woman's arm.

"I know where our car is," I informed her.

She raised an eyebrow. "You do?"

"Yes," I replied, and I motioned toward the door. "It's not very far."

She led us out onto Lake Street and west down the sidewalk toward the intersection with Elliot Avenue. As we waited for the light to turn, the sun was just then disappearing at the far end of Lake Street, dipping into the distant waters of Lake Calhoun. We crossed the street and walked a half-block south down Elliot until I saw Mom's lime-green Plymouth slouched at the curb. The doors were unlocked, as most doors were in those days, and the woman ushered us into the back seat.

"Now you boys stay right here until your daddy shows up," she said. "I'm sure he'll be along any minute." And then she turned and headed back to the store.

Jimmy and I sat in the rear seat of the car eating what was left of the popcorn, staring at the faces of other shoppers as they streamed past, the evening light growing dimmer and dimmer. It was nearly dark by the time I spotted Dad coming along the sidewalk, his silhouette crouched low as he approached the car, his eyes frantically searching the shadows of the back seat. Suddenly the door flew open and his strained face was inches from mine, his voice breaking with emotion.

"Godammit, here you are!" he shouted. I couldn't tell if he was laughing or crying, so peculiar did his voice seem. Then I realized that he was upset and it frightened me that he was so upset, and I began to understand that I had done something terribly, terribly wrong. We should have stayed in the toy department as he'd ordered. Now totally ashamed, I began to cry, but quietly so he wouldn't hear me; I didn't want to make him any more upset than he already was. Jimmy, meanwhile, picked through the last few kernels in the popcorn box, his own innocence assured. Dad finally slammed the door shut and stomped around to the front, cursing a blue streak as he climbed in behind the wheel. He started the car and drove recklessly down the side streets, muttering to himself, his eyes menacing in the rear view mirror. All of his anger seemed focused on me and I knew I was in big trouble.

But by the time we made it over to Blaisdell, the one-way heading south, his driving had become more focused and I could tell he'd calmed down a bit. He'd even turned on the radio, tuning it to the Twins game on 'CCO. Halsey Hall's familiar gravelly voice filled the car with a needed degree of comfort. When a Hamm's Beer commercial came on and Dad began humming along—*From the land of sky-blue waters*—I could tell he'd calmed down even more, and I began to wonder if maybe my punishment might not be so bad. At 38th Street, where he should have continued south, he turned right instead, passing Incarnation Church on our left and then on to Grand Avenue where suddenly things seemed to get a lot better. Across the intersection glowed the welcoming lights of the Dairy Queen and I sat a little higher in the rear seat. He pulled the car up to the curb and got out. I watched as he approached the take-out window, the moths and mosquitoes flitting about his head beneath the yellow lights. He bent and gave his order through the screen, and a few moments later he returned to the car with a couple of nickel cones, each of them dipped in chocolate. He leaned in through the window of the back seat

"Here," he said, his voice now much more conciliatory, and he reached across me to offer the first cone to Jimmy. Jimmy took it without comment, but smiled at this unexpected treat. Dad paused before offering the second one to me, his face inches from mine. "We won't tell Ma about any of this, will we," he said, his words more an order than a request. I nodded silently in the affirmative. "Good," he said. Then he handed me my prize and walked around to the front to get in. Jimmy bit into the chocolate crust of his cone and a string of ice milk ran down his chin. Dad passed a handful of napkins over the seat. Then he started the car and we continued on our way home. When he started singing the Hamms beer song again I knew for certain that everything was going to be alright. I bit into my cone, the chocolate still warm and melting on my tongue. This had turned out even better than I could have imagined.

"Did Mom ever find out?" I ask him, "About us getting lost at Sears?"

"I think so. Somebody must have told her, you or Jim. She thought it was funny. She said it taught me a lesson."

"It wasn't me!" I assure him.

"Jim then," he says. He starts humming the Hamms beer song again as we approach Des Moines, too early for the afternoon rush hour, so of no real concern. He stops mid—tune and turns to me with a question, one I've been anticipating since this trip began. I'm frankly surprised it's taken this long to come up.

"Say, do you ever see Jim?" he asks.

I don't even look at him, fearful it might encourage him. "Nope," I say.

And I pray that's the end of it.

But I know it won't be.

31

JIM

Jim might have been the brightest of us, certainly brighter than me. He was only a year behind me in school yet our paths remained divergent; we were never close, even as youngsters. We shared a bedroom on Pleasant Avenue with our brother Mark, who was some six years older than me. Jim and I slept in bunk beds built by our father—me on top, Jim on the bottom—while Mark enjoyed the room's lone single bed, located in front of the window where it was not quite as hot on warm summer nights. Dad also remodeled a corner of the room into an L-shaped study carrel which featured a wrap-around desk with bookshelves above. Unfortunately, the desk was only large enough to accommodate two scholars, which in reality became one after Mark permanently claimed the longest side for himself. What with my shorter attention span and predilection toward sports, the remaining half of the desk naturally became Jim's.

We all three attended De La Salle High School, located downtown on Nicollet Island, which in those days was the epicenter of Minneapolis' Skid Row. The school was steeped in history, but by the time I started there in 1969 it was in decline and struggling to stay afloat. In an attempt to attract a more progressive type of student, the school administration had recently adopted a "modular scheduling" format which featured an open campus, allowing teenage boys to choose their own curriculum, combining classroom study with the resources of downtown Minneapolis. I didn't do well in the open campus environment; the temptation of the downtown "resources" were too much for my wandering attention span. Jim, on the other hand, excelled under the format. He built a curriculum heavy on science and math, scheduled time at the downtown library, even attended labs at the nearby University of Minnesota. He easily made the National Honor Society and was a member in good standing of Key Club International. Sometimes as I was heading out to explore the urban jungle beyond Nicollet Island, I'd pass by the glass wall of the school library and spot Jim at a table, a pile of reference books beside him, his calculator poised, his pencil busy scribbling notes—the very picture of scholarship. He was dark and brooding, with Dad's olive complexion and wavy hair. Some of the girls in our old neighborhood thought he was cute but also painfully shy. He may have been interested in girls but they were never as high a priority as his studies.

It goes without saying he chose Option One of our father's "Post-High School Career Directive." He went to the U and majored in aeronautical engineering, took Russian as an elective, and carried a Texas Instruments on his belt wherever he went.

When I joined the service in 1973 the number of siblings still at home had dwindled to two: Jim and Betsey. They were quite the pair. Home on my first Christmas leave I discovered the two of them communicating entirely in Vulcan, the fictional language from the *Star Trek* TV show. "Pass the me-lok," Jim might say at breakfast. "Itaren" meant thanks. They greeted each other with the Vulcan hand signal: *Live long and prosper.* I shook my head in amusement but at the same time felt a bit like an outsider in my own home.

Upon my discharge from the service I started winter quarter at the U, majoring in English. I wanted to become a writer like John Updike, Phillip Roth, or John D. MacDonald, writers I'd read and admired while standing long watches overseas. Jim was just then finishing up his engineering degree, already fielding job offers from some of the big aerospace companies. By then, Mom and Dad had moved up north, requiring Jim to find his own housing. He moved into a hovel above the Bridgeman's ice-cream parlor on Washington Avenue, well within walking distance of everything on campus. I was living with friends in South Min-

Me, Jimmy, Mark

neapolis but suggested to Jim that we try getting together once a
week for dinner at a campus dive. I figured we were both adults
now and it was time to forge a new relationship.

One Friday night when we'd agreed to meet for dinner at
Stub and Herb's, a campus fixture, Jim didn't show up. After
waiting an hour, I finally left and climbed the fire escape on the
back of his building to see if there was something wrong. When I
peered through the dingy window of his bedroom I spotted him
at his desk punching numbers into his calculator, scribbling figures on a sheet of paper. It was 6:30 in the evening and he was
still in his underwear, his hair a tangled mess. I suddenly had an
image of him as a young Albert Einstein, brilliant but a bit drifty.
When I banged on the window he looked up startled, but finally
came around to let me in.

"Holy crap!" he cried. "I started this physics problem last night and I guess I lost track of the time!"

"You *guess?*" I said. "C'mon, let's go drink some beer."

And he willingly agreed; we were making progress. Over spring break we drove his car to California, then down the Baja Peninsula in Mexico to go fishing. We had a great time.

His first job out of college was with a defense contractor in California, designing nuclear missiles. Not so much designing them, actually, as refining them, improving their accuracy. He explained this to me one winter when he came for a visit. By then I had scrapped my plans of becoming a writer to focus on my new career, that of a Mississippi riverboat pilot. I'm afraid I'd let the river get in my blood and was now using my GI Bill to attend diesel school, learning skills more apropos to a life on the water. And even though I was living summers on the houseboat I'd recently purchased, I was spending that particular winter as caretaker of a spacious yacht in the downtown harbor, with plenty of room for overnight guests. One afternoon I returned to the boat from my shop classes to find Jim still in bed, awake but staring at the ceiling. "You okay?" I inquired.

He cast me a vacant look. "You ever noticed the sound the ice makes as it grinds against the side of the hull?" he asked.

I eyed him suspiciously. "Did you find my bag of pot?"

"You smoke pot?"

"You don't?" I replied. And it was later that night he began sharing with me the peculiarities of his job.

I'd like to say the vacancy I noticed in him that winter was an aberration. But in reality it was most likely the beginning of his long decline. The next winter, on a Hawaiian vacation, he nearly choked to death on a poisonous root he'd eaten while trying to emulate his idol Euell Gibbons. The summer after, he started a major forest fire in California when he over-filled his Coleman stove, setting the meadow on fire in his campsite. A forest-service fire truck spotted his license plate as Jim fled the mountain. He was caught and heavily fined. He switched jobs and moved to

St. Louis, again finding work in the defense industry. For his new job he listed Kath as his next of kin and it wasn't long before she started getting calls from his new supervisor, concerned about Jim's mental health. More and more often he'd been discovered in his cubicle staring vacantly at the ceiling, his work going undone. We found out later that he'd refused to see a company psychiatrist, and was summarily let go.

In August of that same year he showed up in St Paul, asking if he might stay for awhile on my houseboat. I didn't know yet that he'd been fired so I told him he was welcome, but also that the boat sat high and dry in a corner of the marina boatyard, out of the water. In the past year I'd gotten married and was living in an apartment on Crocus Hill. The houseboat was for sale. Jim didn't mind. In fact, he seemed to welcome the isolation of the boat's location.

He'd been living there for a couple of weeks and when I didn't hear from him I decided to stop by to see how he was faring. He wasn't home when I arrived, the parking space beneath the cradled boat empty. I climbed the stepladder to the front deck and couldn't believe what I found. My little boat—my simple, Walden-esque floating cabin—was a mess, an absolute shit-hole. Brown grocery bags stood heaped with garbage everywhere inside the cabin. The countertops were covered with dried food, the sink filled with mold-covered dishes, and flies buzzing everywhere. I opened the windows to let the cabin air out, and began cleaning. As I cleared dishes from the cluttered table I discovered something interesting amidst the filth: a small tape-recorder with a cassette tape loaded inside. Curious, I decided to turn it on in an attempt to discern my brother's taste in music. But there was no music. Instead, the recording was nothing but the sound of someone's breathing, slow and rhythmic, in and out, in and out. I fast-forwarded it through various intervals and heard the same breathing all the way through, sixty minutes a side, 120 minutes total, an endless recording of someone's breathing, presumably my brother's.

Just then a car pulled up on the gravel below: Jim, home from wherever. I went out on the deck to meet him at the top of the ladder, to give him the good tongue-lashing he deserved for the condition of my boat. He didn't seem too concerned and in fact smiled benignly as he pushed past me into the cabin. But once inside he looked around at how I'd begun cleaning and I could see that it upset him. He acted as if he'd been violated, as if I'd somehow invaded *his* space, as if this was even his space to begin with. But it was when I ejected the cassette tape and held it aloft, asking him what the hell this was about, that he finally exploded.

"You had no business listening to that tape!" he shouted, his face turning red as he snatched the cassette out of my hand. He was seething, and I have to admit his anger was a bit unnerving. I backed away but kept my cool, calmly reminding him that it was *he* who had no business trashing *my* houseboat. I warned him that if it continued he would have to leave.

He turned away. "Fine," he said to the wall. End of conversation. I departed.

I called Kath immediately. Ever since Jim's supervisor had alerted her to his condition, she'd been poring through resource materials on mental health, trying to put two and two together. When I told her about the cassette tape and Jim's outburst, she groaned. "I knew it," she said. "I think he's schizophrenic. He may have been trying to record the voices he's hearing in his head, to see if they're real."

We tried repeatedly to get him to see a doctor but he refused. He insisted there was nothing wrong with him and would disappear if he thought we were getting too close. One time, though, we nearly tricked him into seeing a psychiatrist, fooling him into thinking it was an optometrist's office and that we wanted to get him new glasses for Christmas. He figured it out at the last minute and literally ran out the door to escape, me in hot pursuit. It was frustrating but also agonizing to watch our once brilliant brother slowly deteriorate. He found work washing dishes, sweeping aisles after Metrodome sporting events, shoveling snow. Summers he lived in his car, winters in a cheap room in the worst parts of town. One morning he called me from the Hennepin County courthouse in downtown Minneapolis. He'd been arrested for shooting pigeons with a pellet gun downtown along the river. I went to bail him out. On the ride back to his flop I asked him why he'd been shooting pigeons in the first place.

"I gotta eat," was all he said.

His room was just off Franklin Avenue, and I followed him up three flights of stairs to check his arrangements. When he opened the door the stench inside was so bad I nearly gagged. And then I saw the source of the odor: in the middle of the squalid room sat the remains of an enormous snapping turtle, the open voids of its shell strung with bits of dried flesh.

"I found him along the riverbank," Jim said proudly. "I strapped him upside down on the back of my bike and brought him home. He kept clawing at my back most of the way."

He went on to explain how it had taken over two-hundred shots to the head with the pellet gun before the turtle finally succumbed, right there on the living room floor. He planned to varnish the shell and make some sort of table out of it. The rest of it he'd eaten, he said, except for what was now soup in the refrigerator. I didn't stay for lunch.

He made me so angry at times I once even threatened to kill him, afterwards feeling deeply ashamed by my ignorance. He had come to spend Christmas with us, as he often did, usually staying long after the holidays if the weather turned cold, which it sometimes did. He made himself welcome by always arriving with presents for my two little boys, usually some sort of intricate puzzle or game, with which he would spend hours on the floor in their company explaining how it worked. But he would refuse to bathe during his visit and after awhile the house would begin to smell like him—a combination of body odor and the rancid grease from his dishwashing clothes, which he also refused to launder. We got into a heated argument over it, me losing my temper and in the end throwing him out with the threat I wanted to kill him. He disappeared for a long time after that and I feared I'd never see him again. But I did, a number of years later, in a surrealistic encounter along the Mississippi River, of all places.

It was the end of October—one of those four-day Teacher's Convention weekends. The weather was glorious and I loaded the boys into our runabout for one last day-trip on the river. On Pike Island, below Fort Snelling, we pulled ashore to roast wieners and drink grape soda for lunch. I sent the boys into the woods to gather more kindling while I started a small fire on the shore. A few minutes later they raced from the forest with excited expressions on their faces.

"Uncle Jim's back there!" they shouted. "He's taking a nap under a tree!"

"*What?* I replied, too dumbfounded to say anything else. What strange twist of fate had brought us ashore in the exact same spot as my long-lost, slumbering brother? A few moments later Jim emerged from the woods looking like an escaped political prisoner from a Russian gulag. He was quite heavy, no doubt the result of dumpster-diving from his dishwashing days at the greasy spoon. His long woolen overcoat was buttoned to the chin and looked grossly out of place on a day when my boys and I were dressed in tee shirts and shorts. He wore the same busted eyeglasses and his matted hair held twigs and bits of dried leaves. But it was his beard that gave me pause: it had grown so wild and unruly I estimated it must have been years since he last trimmed it. Without so much as a "Hi" or "How you doin?" he lumbered over and sat down in the sand beside the fire. A steady breeze carried embers from the flame into his beard, igniting it in little puffs of white smoke. With my luck, I thought, he'll catch fire so I said, "Jim, why don't you move around to this side of the fire?" He gave me a stern look but obliged.

He didn't say much but finally responded when I got around to asking him how he happened to be on Pike Island on such a beautiful fall day. He pulled a handful of rocks from one of the deep pockets of the overcoat and a small powerful magnet from another. He touched the magnet to the rocks and immediately they clung to it like metal. My boys' eyes grew wide at such an amazing phenomena and Jim held the magnet out for them to try. Then he got to his feet and suggested they go look for more. I watched as the three of them wandered down the shoreline, stopping here and there to lift a stone and test its magnetism, keeping some, skipping the others over the water. My boys had always admired and loved their Uncle Jim, even though he was a bit strange.

Of the two packs of wieners I roasted, we ate a total of four and Jim ate the rest. He ate most of the potato chips, too and drank a couple cans of the Grape Crush. He never said anything about where he was living or, for that matter, working, but I suspect he'd been camped out on the island for awhile. After eating, he opened up a bit and at one point described in great detail a story about a towboat he'd seen on fire one night, just downriver along the bluff below Lilydale. The firefighters, he said, had rappelled down the bluffs to put out the fire. The story had been on all the news channels but from the way Jim described it I could tell he'd been right here, watching it from the vantage point of his camp in the woods. For all I knew he may have been living on the island that summer. But I didn't ask.

When it was time to go, we loaded up our things and climbed back aboard the boat. Jim followed us down to the shoreline and helped push the bow free of the sand. I started the motor and backed out into the current, the three of us waving and shouting our goodbyes over the sputtering noise of the outboard. Jim nodded in response. The current began to carry us on our way and he continued watching, his face expressionless. I pointed the bow downriver and just before I opened her up I turned back for one last look. Jim hadn't moved, but his blank eyes still followed our every movement, his brooding figure growing smaller and smaller in the distance as I opened the throttle and steered for the next bend.

It would be nearly twenty-five years before I or anyone would see him again, tragically when Betsey was diagnosed with terminal cancer. I sent Jim a note, care of the post office box he sometimes checked:

Your Vulcan sister is dying. A mind-meld from you might be a welcome respite.

He arrived unannounced and got to spend a few final moments alone with her. He hadn't changed much since our last encounter.

ᴄʌ

I ʟᴏᴏᴋ ᴀᴄʀᴏss at my father. We've been talking about Jim for over an hour, and even though he's heard the stories dozens of times, he always wants to hear them again, like picking at a scab. Years ago, during one of our Sunday night phone conversations, I accused him of hypocrisy—of how he always wanted to *hear* of Jim's plight but never offered *to do* anything about it.

"*He's your son!*" I shouted. "Why won't you help him?"

An outburst like this might get him backpedalling and he'd offer some sort of excuse about how he wouldn't know where to begin, the same excuse he'd use when confronted with Eunice's alcoholism, or even his dog's lack of house training. Specialized care or treatment cost money and he wasn't about to part with any of his without a guarantee of tangible results. In fact, he was still upset that Jim had never repaid him for the money he'd loaned him years ago to buy a car. If Jim needed psychiatric help, he could damn well cough up his own money to pay for it.

For many years Dad was convinced it wasn't schizophrenia that afflicted Jim but something else, like alcohol or even drug abuse. "Why the *hell* would you ever give him marijuana?" he shouted at me over the phone one night. He'd somehow gotten wind of our pot-smoking evening aboard the yacht and was convinced that was the true source of Jim's problem. "He's probably a drug addict, thanks to you."

"No," I replied flatly. "Drugs or alcohol have nothing to do with Jim's problem. It's more complex. Ask Kath."

"I wouldn't be so goddamn sure of that if I were you," he replied.

His response didn't surprise me. He once held the notion that I was a low-life drug addict myself, or at least that's what he wanted me to think. I blame myself for that. Years ago—after I was out of the service—I was hired-on as navigator/engineer for the delivery of a fifty-foot sailboat from Detroit to West Palm Beach. Near the end of the trip, about a hundred miles off the coast of Florida, we happened upon seven bales of Colombian marijuana floating in the Gulf Stream. I've since come to learn that this was a fairly common occurrence in those drug-running days of the late seventies, so much so that Florida locals dubbed the contraband bales "Square Groupers" as they were hauled aboard like fish. For us it was an amazing discovery but also a weighted one. We now had a decision to make; should we grab all seven bales and become rich, or run the risk getting caught with all seven and spend the remainder of our lives in prison.

Cast your votes, everyone: Rich man, poor man, beggar man, thief!

In the end we did the prudent thing and kept just one bale, dividing it equally amongst the crew for our personal use. Back home, I shared a house with four high school buddies where we threw some outrageous parties and had a high old time. The story of the bale discovery became one I enjoyed telling, in much the same way my father enjoyed telling of his exploits at sea. So I genuinely thought he might like to hear it.

He and Mom had moved north by then but he still made occasional visits to the city. On one such visit we met for dinner at the Rainbow Café in Uptown, and I decided it was time to finally share the story of my amazing discovery. He seemed completely enthralled at first, smiling at my descriptions of dolphins racing alongside the boat, of how we dined on lobsters thrown from passing fishing boats, of the incredible stars at night and also the phosphorescent glow of our wake. He smiled as he remembered some of these same experiences from his years in the Navy. But when I told him about the discovery of the bale and how I'd brought home my share of it for me and my friends to enjoy, it was like someone drew a curtain across his face. He immediately summoned the waiter, paid the bill, then walked out of the restaurant, leaving half a drink on the table.

Two days later I received a four-page letter in the mail. In it, he wrote of the deep disappointment he felt for me, more or less disowning me, implying no son of his would ever show such a complete lack of character, and such a selfish disregard of the family name. He sprinkled the letter with words like *junkie, pusher,* and *low-life,* terms I presume he'd gleaned from the mafia and gangster movies of the era, taken in during his lonely nights on the road. I was warned that I was never to mention any of this to our relatives in South Dakota or Duluth, and certainly not to my mother. Of this he was quite adamant: My mother was never hear a word of my drug-related criminal behavior. *Never!*

I honored his demands. But in retrospect I've come to I believe Mom, with her spirit of adventure, would have enjoyed the story a hell of a lot more than he ever did. In any event, I had ruined the family name and my father was completely disgusted, writing in closing that he never wanted to see me again. But then he must have had second thoughts because, before mailing it, he added a post script: It would be a long time before he ever got over his disappointment in me, but he hoped that he might.

I never mentioned the bale again in his presence, but in all honestly, I had hoped my transparency in telling him the story would somehow bond us in a way we never had before – a mutual feeling of trust that only comes through shared experiences, both good and bad. When it didn't, I vowed never to tell him anything so deeply personal again, for as long as either of us lived. But the subject of my brother's mental illness would never go away and would become such a point of contention that I found myself judging him more severely than he had ever judged me. Which is not fair. He was never equipped intellectually or emotionally to deal with a problem like Jim's. But I could never see that at the time, perhaps because I was also lacking.

THE TRAFFIC IS SLOWING and up ahead and I detect an obstruction, some sort of construction project, a new river bridge, perhaps. The Interstate is reduced to a single lane in each direction. Over the roofs of cars in front of us I spot the mast of a construction crane, then another. As we slow to a crawl I am able to count a total of five crane masts in all. Except for the slowdown, this is good. I'm done talking about Jim. It's time to change subjects. I point out the distant masts to my father, a former salesman of construction cranes.

"What kind are they?" he asks with real interest. "Can you see the names?"

As we inch nearer I can. All five are *Americans*, the same crane company he once represented; *American Hoist and Derrick,* of Saint Paul, Minnesota.

"You're not going to believe this …" I tell him. And already I can see the excitement building in his eyes.

32

TODAY WAS A GOOD DAY ...

In the summer of my mother's decline and death, she was moved to a hospice care facility in Alexandria, Minnesota. I drove up as often as I could to be with her. The cancer had metastasized into her brain, and the chemotherapy was wreaking havoc with both her mind and her physical appearance. During the last conversation we had, she kept interrupting me to point up at the NASCAR race on TV, telling me to "Be quiet now! I need to see this."

She had about as much interest in stock car racing as I do in badminton. It's not the way I care to remember her.

Dad took her illness very hard, never once imagining that his much younger wife would be the first to go. He spent most of every day by her side in the nursing home, Mom unconscious or delirious as her situation worsened. When any of us would come to visit, it allowed him a few precious hours to go home and cut the grass or weed his garden—a couple of simple chores to take his mind off his dying wife. During one such visit, I stopped by his place after visiting Mom and offered to take him to dinner. His diet over that summer of forced bachelorhood had consisted largely of canned soup and baloney sandwiches, so you can imagine how readily he agreed. We headed to the municipal bar in the small town near his lake home, where the menu offered a nightly dinner special—hot roast beef sandwich with mashed potatoes and gravy. We placed our orders and the manager, who knew of my father's circumstance, treated us to a complimentary drink—Seven and Sevens all around. The alcohol worked to release some of the pent-up emotion Dad had been holding inside, and we began talking, bringing up all kinds of things that had been bothering him. After dinner, a few of the men from Dad's horseshoe league stopped by the table to offer their condolences, and to buy us more drinks. By the time it had grown dark outside, we were both quite intoxicated, a situation I'd never before experienced with my father. In our mutual inebriation I saw an opportunity to bring up some things that had long bothered *me*. For one, I asked him why our relationship during my high school years—and even afterward—had soured, why everything I said or did seemed to displease him. We sat bleary-eyed staring at each other before he finally admitted, "I was under a lot of pressure in those days."

"Pressure from what?" I demanded.

"My job," he said. "I hated it."

"Really? You were certainly successful enough. You must have been good at it."

He turned to me with a doleful expression, his weary eyes studying me for a moment before he muttered "Shit ..." Then he pushed his chair back and tried standing, but began wobbling to the point where I had to grab his arm to steady him. "I need to go home," he finally muttered, barely audible. "Need to lie down."

When the war ended, he was on thirty-days leave back home in South Dakota, having survived his long ordeal in the Pacific as well as the cruelties of Captain Shit-head. He would later lament the fact that he hadn't been aboard ship when the war ended, where the rejoicing would have been significant and well-deserved. The sudden dropping of the atomic bomb and the subsequent Japanese surrender changed things in a hurry. His orders to report to a minesweeper on the West Coast were cancelled and he was instead assigned to the Naval Air Station in Minneapolis to finish out his enlistment. He spent his last year of active duty processing discharge papers for the thousands of Midwestern sailors returning home from the war. He missed a chance for a permanent billet at the air station when a chief petty officer with more seniority edged him out of it. In retrospect, he claimed he was glad he didn't get the assignment, believing a full-time Navy career would have put him in a rut from which he would never have escaped. He did, however, join the Naval Reserve and eventually logged a total of some twenty years service.

Over the course of his life Dad could be guilty of procrastination, putting things off until it was too late, which forced other people to make decisions for him When he met my mother in the spring of 1946 and they began dating, the idea of marriage never fully took hold. I've come to believe it was my mother who proposed to him and not the other way around. (She did, after all, ask *him* to dance on the night they met at the NCO Club.) Whatever the case may be, it was probably after my mother became pregnant that my father realized he'd better start taking things more seriously. He'd spent nearly all of the past ten years either serving in the military or working in a defense plant—"feeding from the government trough," as he used to say. They got married in Duluth in August of 1946, barely a week after his discharge from the Navy. He was thirty years old and he needed to find a real job.

Desperate for work, he pumped gas for awhile at a Hiawatha Avenue service station—certainly not a career opportunity, though it paid the bills. Next, he took a temporary job shuffling paper with the Veteran's Administration, a position more in line with his skill set. The job was not permanent but it did expose him to other opportunities within the government hierarchy, and it was during this period that he sat for the Civil Service exam in hopes of getting in at the post office. Unfortunately, he was in competition with thousands of other returning GIs, and he didn't place high enough on the list.

In March of 1947, a month before his first child arrived, he expanded his search along Hiawatha Avenue and finally succeeded in landing an office-manager's job with Gopher Equipment, a fledgling construction-equipment company. For the next seven years he put all his chief yeoman's skills to work, doing everything the small business demanded: he answered phones, processed paperwork, wrote service orders, took inventory, figured payroll, and typed, typed, typed. He gained enough confidence in himself to purchase a small home within walking distance of the company, and then a larger home a few blocks away where my brother Mark was born in 1948. It's interesting to note that the boundaries of his world during this three-year period centered on an area a few blocks either side of Hiawatha Avenue from about East 40th Street south to the Naval Air Station at Fort Snelling.

By 1950, he had realized enough success in his newfound career to move again, this time a few miles west to the two-story Craftsman-style house on Pleasant Avenue which he would call home for the next twenty years. He needed the extra space; by 1956, the number of children had grown to five. Whether or not he was happy with the career path he had chosen might be better explained by his employment record between the years 1947-57; he changed jobs no fewer than six times, albeit within the realm of the construction-equipment industry, but with different bosses nonetheless. What exactly was he looking for?

The question might have been answered in 1957 when he joined the Hayden-Murphy Equipment Company at 4501

Dad at the Dale Carnegie Institute, 1959

Hiawatha, as office manager again but this time with the understanding that he get a chance in sales, a move he believed would advance his career and provide the income his middle-class lifestyle required. In 1959, the company kept its promise and sent him to the world-famous Dale Carnegie Institute in Chicago. (As far as anyone knows, the plane trip to Chicago would be the last time he would fly commercially.) The intensive course of study was called How to Win Friends and Influence People, from which my father gleaned a nugget of inspiration he would recite (often with a bit of sarcasm) for the next thirty years:

"Today was a *good* day, but *tomorrow* will be even better."

My own memories of this transitional period in his life are vague, but if, indeed, he was beginning to feel inordinate pressure, I never saw it. What I do remember from this period would lead me to believe he was content if not happy: all of *my* memories are good. He loved little children, and would do anything to entertain them. I've often wondered if the abandonment and loneliness he experienced in his own early childhood didn't somehow instill in him a vow that his own children would never experience the same neglect. What a wonderful childhood he gave each of us!

Books were an ever-present source of entertainment and enlightenment in our home. Reading was the key, and our imaginations were stimulated early and often. Somewhere along the way an entire fifteen-volume set of *Childcraft Books* wound up on the shelves of our living room, and Dad wore out the pages of the *Poetry* and *Folk Tale* volumes reading to us every night.

Music was another. Before the arrival of the Motorola, he bought an old upright piano which he painted the same lime-green as the radiator covers he built in the front room, where the piano sat. Ostensibly purchased for my mother's pleasure, it is my father whom I remember most at the keyboard, belting out an old standby he taught himself to play:

> *Doctor, doctor can you tell*
> *What will make poor Kathy well?*
> *She is sick and she will die,*
> *That will make poor Marky cry.*

The song went on for five verses and by the time he got down toward the bottom of the pecking order, where my name came, he was really hammering the keys and singing with an almost falsetto pitch to his voice, enjoying himself immensely. Years later he confessed he'd once had a shipmate in the Navy who could sit down behind a piano in a wharf-side bar and within minutes have the whole crowd singing along. No doubt it was an ability he hoped to match with the acquisition of the piano, but I think singing "Doctor, Doctor" to his kids was about as far as he ever dared go. Nevertheless, the song became one of our favorites, especially in his interpretation.

He liked to play a game in which he ordered all five of us to lie down in front of the fireplace. Then, he would pretend to walk away. At the sound of our stealthy (and expected) movements behind him, he would suddenly spin on his heel and shout, "*You lie down in 'dem oats!*" and chase us around the living room like we were escaped slaves. At the time we didn't quite grasp the historic context of the game; if we had, I'm sure we wouldn't have loved it so much.

As we grew older he liked nothing better on a Saturday night than to play charades. Even more fun was when he and Mom sat on the couch and acted as judges of the impromptu speeches we were asked to deliver on any variety of subjects. "Mark," he might say, "I'd like you to talk for three minutes on the subject of... 'Cutting the Grass.'" Or, "Jimmy, gives us two minutes on the correct way to make a peanut-butter sandwich." Once, while waiting our turn, Betsey and I snuck upstairs and dressed in Mom and Dad's clothes, then came back down and danced the "Charleston" to a record Betsey had secretly put on the Motorola. Dad thought it the funniest thing he'd ever seen, especially since we'd devised it ourselves.

I can now confess it was all Betsey's idea, that she was the Gilda Radner of our childhood household. And while we were certainly no Glass Family from a J.D. Salinger short story, we were clever enough in our own right, our imaginations stimulated early by the books we were encouraged to read and also by our parents' commitment—especially Dad's—to make it all seem like fun.

In winter he flooded a backyard skating rink which required no small amount of labor. Dressed in his old Navy khakis and with a red-checked lumberjack coat buttoned to the chin, he re-

Jimmy, Betsey, Mark, me, Kath with our parents in Duluth, 1957

ligiously dragged a garden hose up and down the basement stairs for his nightly floodings, the ice sheet growing thicker and thicker until he finally pronounced it ready for skating. He liked to push smaller kids around the rink on the paint-splattered chair he used for everything, happily puffing on a pipe while wearing skates he bought second-hand at the hardware store. But even this wasn't enough. One night he arrived home with an empty shipping barrel made of heavy cardboard, the top of which had been removed. "Hang on!" he ordered as he deposited someone inside, and then sent the barrel spinning across the ice until the occupant became so dizzy he could barely stand up.

One summer Dad screwed a basketball hoop to the garage and for years our driveway was the scene of countless neighborhood games. He loved competition. Sometimes he'd line up a dozen kids along our backyard fence and challenge each of them to catch a tennis ball he had thrown as high as he could. Those who successfully fielded their chance moved on to the next level until there were only two fielders remaining. The eventual winner was awarded the grand prize of a nickel from my father's pocket. He gave away a lot of nickels.

Too frugal to pay for barbershop haircuts, Dad nonetheless bought a 1920s vintage barber chair from the Goodwill and got Mr. Westlin to help him carry it down our basement stairs. Until I was fifteen I had to endure monthly sessions in his basement barber shop. He cut hair the only way he knew how: long on top and nearly shaved on the sides, so that his victims bore a strong resemblance to a John Dillinger mug shot. Besides me and my brothers other customers included the McDevitt twins, Kenny and Kevin, who were each given a nickel at the end of their appointments. That infuriated me. They were already the recipients of a regular ten cent per week allowance from their father. In our family we got nothing—no allowance and certainly not five cents for suffering through Dad's hideous haircuts. In fact, my only source of income in those days was the empty pop bottles I found in the neighborhood, which netted three cents apiece at Marty's Kwik Shop.

From this pittance, along with a generous donation from my Aunt Grace, I saved enough money to buy a hamster, my first pet, which I named Grace after my benefactor. Betsey was jealous and lobbied Mom for money to buy her own hamster, which she named Lois. We kept Grace and Lois in a small cage in the basement rec-room, recently remodeled by our father. They were curious and wily little creatures, and on more than one occasion they escaped our nervous hands to explore the inside of the basement's plasterboard walls. For days on end we could hear them gnawing their way through my father's handiwork, a sound only slightly more excruciating than his cursing as he tried to scare them to daylight by pounding along the walls with his fists. But they would only emerge when they were hungry, we discovered, and in Lois's case it would be too late. We discovered her dehydrated corpse one morning lying in her food dish, which reduced Betsey to tears. To my father's credit he didn't flush the dead rodent down the toilet but instead fashioned a small coffin which he lined with satin and fitted with a pillow. At the funeral—the deceased reposing in an open casket on the altar of the fireplace hearth with a crucifix displayed overhead—we all bowed our heads in prayer. When the dead hamster suddenly sat up in its coffin, its body contorted by rigor mortis, Betsey screamed. I glanced up at Dad; he was grinning sideways at Mom. He couldn't have planned it any better.

He loved practical jokes: the match that burned twice, the observation of stars through the sleeve of his coat (better have a towel ready!), or even his offer of a dollar to anyone brave (or stupid) enough to swallow a small teaspoonful of horseradish. I often fell for that one—anything for a buck—and tears would stream down my face as my sinuses caught on fire. "*Russ!*" Mom would shout as she ran for a glass of water. And a month or two later he would dare me to try it again.

If feeding horseradish to a gullible ten-year-old might seem a bit sadistic, I can assure you his antics knew no bounds. On a scheduled Saturday every spring and fall he spent a tedious day switching the storm windows to screens or vice versa, as the seasons required. He would send either Jim or me to the top of the extension ladder to wash the glass in the second-story fixed sashes. As soon as we reached the top rung he would pull the ladder away from the house and begin tipping it back and forth as we hung on, screaming for our lives. When, after a few years of such treatment, I flatly refused to climb the ladder and become part of his deranged amusement, he feigned sorrow that I no longer trusted him.

For many years I was reluctant to bring friends home, worried about what kind of stunt he might pull at their expense. This especially applied to any girl I might have been dating, who would have been easy prey for his twisted sense of humor.

I eventually came to realize that Dad had developed his twisted sense of fun in the course of a childhood filled with boredom and isolation, but that didn't make it any easier to swallow at the time.

33

Got Milk?

The bridge construction slows us down considerably, at times bringing us to a complete halt. And with it, our conversation. "What the hell's taking so long?" Dad complains, and he begins fidgeting. I work to keep him talking.

"Do you remember taking us to your office Saturday mornings?" I ask. "The one at Hayden-Murphy? My god, that was so much fun! It was an old firehouse, right? Even had a bell on the roof!"

After becoming a salesman he made a habit of going in Saturday mornings to process his paperwork, often taking Betsey, Jim, and me along for the experience. While he sat at his desk we'd glide around the office on roll-away chairs, colliding with each other like bumper cars, raising all kinds of hell. Mechanics working overtime shifts would come in from the yard to clean up, squirting Go-Jo waterless hand cleaner into their greasy mitts, which miraculously got rid of the deepest grime. This of course precipitated Dad's having to squirt Go-Jo into *our* hands, wasting both it and the reams of paper towels it took to wipe it off. Then up on the roof we'd go to ring the massive old fire bell, followed by a daring slide down the brass fire pole, still intact in the middle of the office. Like everything else in those early days of his sales career, Dad made all of it fun for his children. Unfortunately, that would soon begin to fade.

What I remember most about Dad's new life as a salesman was the abrupt change it made in his physical appearance. He gained weight—a lot of it. Food became his crutch. Out on the road three or four nights a week, always alone, no doubt bored and lonely, he must have taken comfort in food. Food, that is, over alcohol.

Years ago, in one of our Sunday-night phone conversations, he reminisced about his early years on the road, and how he'd come to the conclusion that alcohol posed a definite problem in the life a traveling salesman. He didn't quit the booze altogether but instead made a conscious decision to limit it, to imbibe only enough to seal a deal or, at the very least, to convince a client he was a "regular Joe." As far as I know, he stuck to this plan, as I don't recall any traumatic scenes from my childhood where he ever stumbled home drunk or was in any way incoherent. But it may be that he replaced one compulsive urge with another—food. He began to enjoy a bowl of ice-cream after dinner, never without a generous dollop of Hershey's chocolate syrup. On weekends, he perfected the art of making fudge, a skill at which he became so proficient it became a regular and expected treat, and no one enjoyed the end result more than he did. And of course popcorn. To watch wrestling on a Saturday night, followed by the *Lawrence Welk Show*, or the televised football games on Sunday afternoon, he had to have a bowl of popcorn in his lap. He made the popcorn on the stove in a cast-iron skillet and then melted a stick of butter in the same pan to pour over it. He usually made two batches, one for Mom and us kids, the other for himself. He would shovel the greasy popcorn by the handful into his mouth, the errant kernels bouncing down the plateaus of his ever-expanding gut to stain his Saturday khakis. His stomach eventually grew so large that by the time he'd reached fifty, his navel had become herniated and had to be surgically removed. But even this didn't curb his voracious appetite.

The weight gain, coupled to the long hours he spent behind the wheel of his car, led to other problems. His lower back began to bother him, the pain at times paralyzing. He claimed his bad back was the result of a childhood fall in the barn while playing hide-and-seek, but I had my doubts. I remember watching him as he got out of his car Friday nights after a week on the road. I wanted him to play with me or at least race me across the yard to the back door of the house. But he could barely walk, hunched over and holding his back, his stomach bulging from lack of exercise, his lungs clogged with nicotine. The small, cylindrical green tins of Doan's Pills seemed to be everywhere around our house, and I came to believe he was addicted to them, psychologically if not physically.

He smoked heavily, and his daily purchase of Salem menthols provided me with a small but regular source of income. He would send me to Marty's Kwik Shop every day to buy a pack, which cost twenty-one cents, with a quarter and a handwritten note: *Please sell my son John one pack of Salem cigarettes to be smoked by me. He has permission to spend the change. FR Halter, Ta5-7531*

Marty, the store-owner, always crumpled the note in his hand before disposing of it, never to be used again by an enterprising eight-year-old. Four cents bought a nice little sack of candy in those days: two-for-one cent root beer barrels, Lik-M-Aid sticks for a penny apiece, Fizzies, jawbreakers, and Tootsie Rolls for the same price. If, on my five-minute walk to the store, I happened upon an empty pop bottle tossed onto the boulevard by one of the neighborhood Greasers, I was able to add the three-cent deposit to my fortune. Many candy bars cost a nickel, as did a packet of the popular Fleer Baseball Cards which also contained a powdery slab of grape gum. I came to expect that the smiling faces of obscure rookies would be among the cards I'd just bought, but occasionally a Carl Yastrzemski or a Don Drysdale would appear and you had something of value, something worth trading. Better yet was when a local player emerged, a Lenny Green, a Bob Allison or a Harmon Killebrew, which meant a mad dash to the McDevitt's to share my good fortune with Kenny and Kevin. Dad's cigarettes would then be a little late in their time of arrival.

Dad quit smoking when he turned eighty, hoping that Eunice might follow, but she didn't. After a chest x-ray that same year, his doctors informed him he had the lungs of a nineteen year-old, or so he claimed. He was never shy about sharing the details of his health—his ailing back, his diabetes, his failing teeth. In his early nineties Dad began complaining about constipation, and eventually it became almost *all* he wanted to talk about.

His sales trips took him all over southern Minnesota, and judging from the matchbook covers deposited on his dresser, I know he got into the routine of staying in the same hotels and eating in the same restaurants. He could tell you the prospects for the upcoming pheasant–hunting season from the number of birds he counted picking gravel along the highway, also the snow depth and subsequent flood forecast from what he saw in the stubble fields. He kept his eye on the inventories of every small-town car lot, always looking for Mom's next jalopy. And he always claimed he got his best deals on a new car from dealers in rural areas.

By the time he got home Friday night the radiator of his car would often be cluttered with an array of dead butterflies and moths that the neighborhood kids were eager to inspect. Some of the moths were so big they resembled birds, and sometimes they *were* birds. The trick came in peeling the delicate, heat-dried wings from the fins of the radiator in one piece. Dad usually paid scant attention to our specimen-gathering, too busy brushing peanut shells off the seat of his car or checking on his tomatoes. But if, in passing, he noticed someone approaching the radiator with a butter-knife or a screwdriver—he might issue a warning: "You nick one of those goddamn fins, buster, and I'll give you one right in the nose!"

By his own admission, Dad wasn't a "super salesman," lacking, as he put it, the "charisma" to be truly successful at it. By charisma, I'm fairly certain he meant the ability to socialize with his customers, to wine and dine them in an attempt to make a deal. I'm sure his forced abstinence had something to do with it, admirable in that he realized drinking could be a problem, but at the same time deterring him from the huge successes he knew other salesmen enjoyed. Decades later, in the course of my own career, I was once wined and dined by one of his former contemporaries, a man known far and wide in the industry for his charm and expensive tastes. We were riding to lunch in the leather-appointed interior of his Lincoln Navigator when I told him, in passing, that my father once worked as he did, as a salesman of heavy construction equipment.

"For who?" the super salesman inquired, truly intrigued. He muted the volume of the quadraphonic wraparound stereo system and turned to me with a look of wonder. When I revealed the name of my father's employer, he said, "Well, I guess we all need to make a living somehow."

My South Dakota cousins informed me years later that Dad was a frequent visitor at their farms when they were growing up. His sales area lay just across the border, and I suspect that on those days when the beat-down of his job got the better of him he enjoyed escaping to the scenes of his childhood adventures. My cousins loved the stories he would tell, not only of the war but also the stories of their parents and the childhood they shared with Dad on the farm. Of course they were the same stories he told us, but to my cousins they had an added dimension. None of their parents had served in the war, so my father's experience might have seemed enticing, at times even providing them an exit strategy for their own escape. Indeed, more than one of my cousins would go on to enlist in the armed forces.

There were certainly some good days in his sales life, too. Who can forget the Friday night he arrived home and summoned all of us into the dining room where he pulled a fat envelope from his sports coat. He opened it on the buffet and counted out seven thousand dollars in cash, a down payment on the Cadillac of his equipment line—a brand new *American* dragline. I'd never seen him so exited.

"Now goddamnit," he warned us. "Don't you kids go running all over the neighborhood telling your friends about this!" The money would be hidden in our house overnight before he brought it to the office Saturday morning; loose lips sink ships. I, of course, headed straight to the McDevitts, two houses away, as excited as Dad had been. Kenny and Kevin were like brothers to me, my confidantes in everything I did. Why shouldn't they be allowed to see Dad's haul? Dad could never tell them apart and always referred to them as "KennyKevin"—all one word. As I recall, he was only too happy to show KennyKevin the loot.

The good days notwithstanding, from my angle his life in sales looked tepid at best. He was never happy. In fact, in my high school years he seemed so perpetually pissed-off at the world that I couldn't help but think it was all because of me. Everything I did, from the acne on my face to the bell-bottom jeans I wore, to the summers I spent working with the Teen Corps (the hippies) at the St. Peter State Hospital—it all seemed to disgust him. And in my own anger, I extracted revenge. He would show up at one of my high school basketball games and I'd spot him during warm-ups sitting high in the bleachers in a business suit, a clear indication he'd come straight from work. His presence might have been some sort of attempt at reconciliation, but for me it was going to take a lot more than that. I'd scowl at him as I ran to the back of the lay-up line, my expression implying, "I don't want you here."

In my senior year I made all-conference in football and received letters of interest from colleges around the country. He started mentioning the son of a client who'd made starting tight-end at a college out west, and wouldn't it be something if the same fate awaited me? That ain't happening, I assured him, and to prove it I enlisted in the Coast Guard for four years. "I'll show you," I thought. Could I have known I was only repeating the escape he had made from his own father forty years earlier?

Four years later, as I approached the end of my Coast Guard enlistment, he must have perceived a change in me, perhaps even believing that in my maturity all our troubles now lay behind us. He saw an opportunity. He was in the final phase of his career, the senior sales rep at Olson Equipment, the company with which he'd spent the last ten years. He and Mom had recently sold the house in Saint Louis Park and were then in the process of moving north to the new lake home near Alexandria. At the end of May, about a month before my enlistment was up, Dad mailed to me in Boston the plans for a two-and-a-half stall garage he wanted to build at the new lake home. He thought it was something I might like to help him with over the course of the summer, just the two of us working side-by-side until September when I would most likely begin college. College? Me? In reality, I'd been spending my free weekends of the past year driving up to a wilderness lake in Maine to canoe and camp. I'd come to know the canoe outfitter well enough that he'd offered me a job working for him once my enlistment was up. And although it was only a temporary job, I thought it might be a fun way to spend the summer in a part of the country I'd come to love. After that? Who knew?

On the other hand, I'd never done much carpentry work so I thought my father's proposal presented a great opportunity to learn, and with it an opportunity to begin a new relationship with him. I agreed to help him with the garage, reluctantly informing the outfitter I would be going home. At the end of June I loaded up my VW Bug and headed straight to my parents' new lake place in Minnesota.

I arrived late at night after driving all the way from Michigan. The address on the mailbox out on the road was the same one Mom had sent me, but as I continued up the driveway I began to have my doubts. In the glow of the yard light I couldn't help but notice a garage that looked disturbingly identical to the one in the plans Dad had mailed me a month earlier. Was I in the right place? Just then the screen door of the house opened and Mom and Dad emerged grinning. "You found it!" Mom shouted.

"I did," I replied tiredly. I'd been on the road since 6 a.m. They came down off the landing to greet me, Mom giving me a big hug and Dad shaking my hand. I wasted little time in pointing out the garage.

"What's that?" I asked.

Dad dismissed me with a quick wave. "Oh, hell, I guess I should have told you. I hired a couple of local guys to build it. We'd have just screwed it up, you and me."

I stared at him in disbelief; this from the guy who complained of his own father never telling him anything. Tired and frustrated, I had half a mind to turn around and head straight back to the canoe outfitter in Maine. But I didn't. Mom pulled me inside and fed me, then asked if I'd be available to help with some wallpaper removal and painting around the new place. I reluctantly agreed; what else was I going to do?

A few days later I was back down in Saint Louis Park selecting things from among my mostly unwanted possessions to add to a garage sale my parents were having. I got to sleep one last time in my old bed before it went up for sale. I looked up old friends, went out for a few drinks, wandered around town feeling "cast adrift" by the upheaval in my plans. I really wished I'd taken the job in Maine for the summer.

Dad was then working part-time in his few remaining weeks before retirement, finalizing sales and hauling furniture up north in the old pickup. One morning in the nearly vacant St Louis Park house he invited me to join him for lunch that afternoon. He suggested we meet at his office and from there ride together to the "5-8 Club" on Cedar Avenue. He wanted to introduce me to his boss, Roy Olson, who was the proud owner of a yacht up on Lake Superior. He claimed Mr. Olson had wanted to meet me after learning of the dramatic rescue I'd been involved with last winter off Cape Ann, Massachusetts. A ship had broken in half during a gale. A life had been lost, a ship went to the bottom, and I'd gotten a medal. Apparently Dad had been talking about me around the office.

His final place of employment was of course on Hiawatha Avenue, a mere block north of the old firehouse where'd he'd started nearly twenty years ago. I arrived at the appointed hour and was ushered into Mr. Olson's office, taking a seat in a chair across his desk. Dad sat beside me. Mr. Olson was a spare, white-haired gentleman with blue eyes and a friendly smile. Mounted fish and stuffed animal heads adorned the dark paneling of his office walls, and the glass-block windows behind him muted the light coming in off the avenue. Roy wanted details of the big rescue. By then I'd told the story so many times I had it down to the climactic details—the blizzard conditions, the forty-foot seas, the man who died and those who didn't, including me, thankfully. I smiled and told him it felt good to be back amidst the cornfields and calm water of Minnesota.

"What are you going to do now?" Roy asked, an inquisitive smile on his face.

"I really don't know," I replied, and I honestly didn't. I had a free college education awaiting me in the form of the GI Bill, but I wasn't sure I was ready for that. There were some wild oats I needed to sow, some places I wanted to see, maybe even a trip back to the East Coast and an opportunity up in Maine. I looked over at Dad to see how this registered with him. But he seemed more interested in the floor, his hands clenched nervously in his lap.

"Well," Mr. Olson said calmly, and he leaned a little over his desk. "I can carry you for two years against a $1000 a month draw, but after that you'll be on your own, straight commission, twenty percent of the gross profit."

I smiled at him, confused. "Huh?"

"He's offering you a job," my father said quietly. He glanced over at me nervously, then at Mr. Olson.

"A *job?*" I said loudly, and I heard my voice break with an unexpected jab of ridicule, a snub. *Me?* I thought, in *sales?* after what I'd witnessed my father endure for most of his working life? *Are you kidding me?*

But then I saw the pained expression on Dad's face—his embarrassment at my outburst—and I realized they were serious, the two of them, and that this was no laughing matter. Worse, I could now see that my outburst had offended them, especially my father.

"It's way too soon to think about a job," I added quickly, trying to sound more reasonable, now in full damage-control mode. It was never my intention to offend anyone.

Mr. Olson stood up and said, "Of course. You take some time to think about it." But I could tell he already knew my answer, no doubt insulted by my brashness. We politely shook hands and I followed Dad outside, where he paused to size me up over the hood of the pickup.

"Well, you sure managed to make me look like a goddamn fool," he said.

I felt my anger rising. "Why didn't you tell me this was a job interview?" I said, trying not to shout. I felt like he'd blind-sided me again, twice in one week.

"It was supposed to be a surprise," he replied just as angrily. "I thought you'd jump at the chance. Nobody your age gets asked to go straight into sales. *Nobody.* He obviously saw something in you. But you're too goddamn ..."

"Too goddamn *what?*" I shouted. I stared at him, waiting for an answer. I couldn't believe he actually wanted me to follow in his footsteps, to be as miserable as he was, or appeared to be, for the rest of my life.

I continued staring at him until he finally said, "Get in. Let's go eat."

I shook my head. "I'm not hungry," I said. And then I got in my own car and left.

His true emotions about the embarrassing scene emerged a week later at the new lake home. As I'd promised my mother, I returned to strip wallpaper and do some painting before she and Dad moved in permanently. While they tied up loose ends in the city, I moved into the lake home's attic and went straight to work with the stripping, a tedious job at best but one I didn't mind as long as it kept me busy. I worked a regular schedule, played the radio loudly, went swimming or fishing at the end of each day, cooked for myself whenever I felt like it.

One day Dad showed up unannounced just as I was breaking for lunch. I was surprised to see him in a business suit, but he claimed he was working, making a final call on a customer in the area. He said he'd been near enough that he thought he'd just stop in to check on my progress, maybe see if I needed anything. I offered him one of the grilled-cheese sandwiches I was making for lunch, along with a glass of milk, and he accepted. There was no place to sit so we stood at the kitchen counter eating the sandwiches, the radio volume turned low. That's when he took a drink of the milk I'd poured for him. It just happened to be the last of the powdered milk I'd used on my canoe trips up in Maine. I'd only mixed it up now because I didn't want to throw it out. I'd been drinking it all week and was used to it, never once considering its taste, which wasn't exactly the same as regular milk. My mistake came in not warning my father; I'd completely forgotten he only drank whole milk. He nearly gagged as he spit his mouthful into the sink.

"*What is this shit?*" he roared. I apologized and explained what it was, at which point he began cursing me in ways he'd never cursed me before. His outburst startled me, the source of it obviously something more than the powdered milk. He called me a horse's ass, an arrogant prick, and, finally, a *big fucking hero,* this last delivered with such fury that I now definitely knew it was about something more than the milk. But he wasn't finished.

"I'm sick of your bullshit!" he shouted. "You want to go back to Maine? Go! And as far as I'm concerned you can leave *right now!*" And with this he stormed out, slamming the door behind him.

Since that day our relationship has ebbed and flowed for forty years, and now we find ourselves side by side on the seat of a car, my father's journey nearing its end.

Maybe it's time for some real answers.

34

America The Beautiful

Driving east on I-90 about fifteen miles past Austin, Minnesota, and like Don Quixote my father is tilting at the windmills along the highway. Not windmills exactly, but their modern counterparts—the giant wind generators charging the electrical grid. He seems mesmerized by them, but not frightened. It's going on 7:30 and the sun is setting behind us, once again casting the long shadow of the trailer out ahead. If this were last night or even the night before, I'd be looking for the first signs of sundown syndrome. But not tonight. Tonight I feel fairly certain he's in a better place, or at any rate he feels comfortable sitting here beside me, safe in the knowledge that nothing in the world can touch him. He's been like this since we stopped to admire the cows along the highway in Oklahoma ten hours ago. He's been in a much happier state of mind all day long, and I'm beginning to wonder if his separation from Eunice might be the reason.

"We need gas," I tell him. "It's possible we could make it on this tank, but why risk it now that we're almost there."

"Tell me where we're going again," he says. "I can't seem to remember."

"We're headed to Mark's farm in La Crosse."

"Mark's farm in La Crosse," he repeats. "Why can't I remember that?"

"It's okay," I tell him. "You're doing great. You need anything at the gas station? Peanuts? Popcorn? How's your Poly Grip holding out?"

He backhands me again, laughing. He's been backhanding me all day and I couldn't be happier. "Knock it off about my Poly Grip!" he shouts. "You're gonna be needing it yourself someday!"

And he's right about that; my boyhood hockey misadventures, along with Mom's questionable toothache remedies, have left me with more bridges than Madison County. Someday years from now I might very well be making a trip like this with one of my own sons, me riding toothless in the shotgun seat, slurping jello and making a mess of a muffin. Will I be as ornery as he was when we started this trip? Will I try to jump out at the first opportunity? Will my son have to distract me with pictures of my forgotten life?

And do I really believe I'm going to make it to ninety-six?

There's nary a town or strip mall in sight at the next exit, but as we glide up the ramp a blue signpost informs me there's a gas station some three miles to the south. I probably should have kept going but what's three more miles (six actually) at this point?

The station sits out in the middle of nowhere amid fields of freshly-turned earth. I ask Dad if he needs to use the bathroom and he replies that he doesn't, but he would like to get out and stretch. So I pull up to a distant island of pumps where the view is unobstructed and serene. He unbuckles himself and goes about the arduous process of climbing out, shunning my help. I get out to begin pumping our needed gas but discover my credit card doesn't work. What the hell? First time in three days this has happened. After a few more failed attempts a digital message finally says, "See attendant." Dad is walking toward the front of the car, and then to the edge of the pavement, presumably to admire the landscape.

"Now don't go chasing after any rabbits." I shout as I head for the station. "I'll be right back!" And he lifts his cane in response.

The attendant is a large man with mutton-chop sideburns wearing a short-sleeve shirt that hangs like a muumuu over his expansive gut. The TV above his head is tuned to some sort of crime-stoppers show and he barely takes his eyes off it as I enter.

"My card doesn't seem to work." I tell him. "First time in 1800 miles."

"Hmm," he replies.

"Is there something wrong with the pump?"

"Nope. I seen the U-Haul. Just makin' sure."

I stare at him. "Making sure? You actually thought I was going to pump-and-run with a U-Haul trailer and my ninety-six-year-old father?" I chuckle. "That's a good one,"

"Hmm," he replies again. He seems more interested in the TV than in my response. I hand him the card.

"How much you want?" he asks.

"I'd like to fill it."

"How much then?"

"I guess I won't know that until I fill it," I tell him. I hear my voice rising. He doesn't seem to care, just keeps looking at the TV. I get a whiff of Pine-Sol, or is it his after-shave?

"Give me thirty bucks worth," I finally tell him. He runs the card, hands me my receipt, returns his attention to the TV. Have a nice day.

As I head back out to the pumps I notice Dad is leaning against the front of the car, his hands at rest atop the cane. Beyond him, the last rays of the sun strike the budding branches of an elm tree, and a tractor far off in the distance is disking a field of stubble. The meadowlarks twir and tweet in their darting flights, and the scene is suddenly so peaceful and pastoral that even the distant drone of the tractor sounds as soothing as a growling puppy. I pause and study him for a moment. I should get a picture of him standing there, so at peace with the world, but my phone's still in the car.

He sees me coming and lifts the cane, pointing. "See there? Right on schedule," he announces. I assume he's talking about the farmer. "We always disked right around my birthday." He continues to watch the tractor while I pump the gas, all thirty dollars worth. Then, while I'm cleaning the windshield, he climbs back in the car without a word of complaint.

Returning to the interstate I merge into traffic, bring us up to cruising speed, and then settle in. We're almost there, our last leg; we've made up a bit of time and are now looking good for a 9 o'clock arrival. I chance a peek over at Dad. He's quiet, enjoying the scenery out his side of the car, and seems more relaxed and content than I've seen him in three days, maybe in my entire life.

"You're not talking," I say quietly. "You're not mad at me, are you?"

He lifts an eyebrow. "Why would I be mad at you?"

"Well, you've been stuck in this car with me for three days. I'll bet you're sick of it."

"Has it been three days? I'll be go to hell."

I'll be go to hell. Another of his phrases I've never quite understood. I glance down at the Styrofoam cooler and lift the cover off. "There's one last fruit cup in here," I tell him. "You want it?"

"Won't we be stopping for dinner?"

"Dinner will be at Mark's. Remember?"

He looks puzzled; clearly he doesn't remember, but I let it pass. I don't want to break the serenity of the moment. It's also true he may be "talked out," that we've reached the bottom of his well of stories.Maybe there's simply nothing left to say. It's feasible we could make it all the way to Mark's without talking, riding along in perfect silence. But there's one last subject on my mind, something I've wanted to ask him for a long time. And this might be my last chance.

"Tell me about 'America the Beautiful,'" I say.

Now both eyebrows lift. "The song?" he asks. Then he starts singing: "*Oh beautiful, for spa—*"

"Not the song. The story you wrote. The story you wrote about *me.*"

"Oh, Christ … Why would you bring that up? I hope you burned it."

"I didn't burn it."-

"Well, you should have. I don't know what got into me." He turns toward the window, embarrassed.

"No, I'm serious," I tell him. "I can still remember the first time I read it. You wouldn't believe how it lifted my spirits, how it arrived at just the right time."

"Now you're bullshitting me," he says. "I wish you wouldn't do that."

"Stop it," I say. "I mean it. You've never told me why you wrote it."

He grimaces. "*You* told me to write it."

"No. That's not entirely true," I reply. "I had encouraged you to *keep* writing, to write something else about your life, something in addition to the war memoir."

This had been during one of our Sunday night phone conversations, in which he'd begun yet another sermon about his digestive system or maybe a political headline of the day—Bill Clinton's sexual impropriety perhaps. The real problem was that he wasn't getting any intellectual stimulation from Eunice and found himself filled with a need to further express himself. In 1988 he'd written the ten-thousand-word memoir about his time in the Navy and World War II, had written it so well that Kath got it accepted into the archives of both the South Dakota Historical Society and the Minnesota Military Museum. The South Dakota folks even thought enough of the story to adapt it into a play which they then performed on stage in front of a live audience. Dad had been flabergasted that something he'd written could be so admired.

"You should write another memoir," I had told him.

"About what?" he said flatly.

"How about your childhood on the farm?"

"Too goddamn boring. Who'd want to read something like that?"

"The same people who read your Navy memoir," I told him. "And besides, when did you ever tell a boring story?"

So in 1999 he did write a memoir about his childhood on the farm, this one nearly twice as long as the military piece. But in between writing those two memoirs, for some reason still unexplained, he decided to try his hand at fiction. He never told a soul what he was doing, not even Eunice, as he worked on it over the winter of 1996-97. My copy of the finished piece arrived unannounced in the mail in April of 1997. It was titled, "America the Beautiful," and it was dedicated to me. The story's theme requires some explanation, a back-story if you will:

❦

IN THE SUMMER of 1977—the same summer I came home from the service to help my father build the garage that had already been built—I ran away. The decision had been spontaneous, a reaction, I'm now certain, to his unexpected outburst over the milk. At the time my only intention was to get as far away from Dad as I could.

I headed west in search of assurances. My first stop was at Uncle Bill's farm in South Dakota where I was happily installed on a tractor to do some field work on the back forty. Uncle Bill looked a lot like my father, but he had always struck me as infinitely more patient and understanding, and he also had a way of lifting my spirits. By the time I left there a week later, Bill had made me feel better about things, but I wasn't ready to return home. I continued west and took a job baling hay on a ranch in Montana; I camped in the national parks of Wyoming and Idaho; I toured museums and Indian battlefields; and I mixed with locals in small town restaurants and taverns all along the way. I eventually made it as far as Spokane, Washington, where I landed a full time job as an assistant ladleman in a large steel foundry. It was hot, miserable work, and every night I returned to a rented room overlooking the Spokane River where I rubbed salve on my burns and drank quarts of water to rehydrate. On weekends I drove to Seattle to visit my brother Mark and his burgeoning family. His wife, Sue, was then in the process of completing her medical school residency.

While in Seattle one weekend I looked up an old Coast Guard buddy who had been assigned to the icebreaker *Polar Star*, which was then getting ready to depart for Antarctica. I'd only been out of the service for four months and touring the ship felt a bit like a homecoming. Back in Spokane I got so melancholy for my former life that I called the local Coast Guard recruiter and told him I wanted to reenlist, preferably in time to make the *Polar Star's* impending voyage to Antarctica. Now, any other recruiter at that moment might have snatched me up like low-hanging fruit and added another tally to his monthly quota. But this one sensed that I was a little lost, perhaps even homesick, and suggested I return to Minnesota to try college. "You've got the GI Bill at your disposal," he reminded me. "Use it. You've earned it!" And so I did, returning home and enrolling at the University for winter quarter 1978.

I actually did well in my first semester of school, choosing English as a major, getting positive feedback for some of the early compositions I turned in (the Halter family predilection for bullshit has its useful aspects, I discovered). Over the summer break I took a deckhand/bartender job aboard a paddlewheel excursion boat in downtown Saint Paul and, what with my Coast Guard experience, quickly worked my way up to captain. I bought a houseboat and lived on the river year-round. My newfound friends were towboat pilots, river deckhands, and engineers. I got so immersed in the lifestyle I decided to quit college (and my English aspirations) to study diesel mechanics at the local vo-tech. At the time I believed it would enhance my future employment opportunities. My father thought I'd lost my mind.

"You've done a lot of stupid things in your life," he told me, "but this one takes the cake." From his own experience selling heavy construction equipment, he described to me in searing detail the kind of life I could expect in the trade I had so foolishly chosen. First off, he explained, I would be dirty for as long as I worked in this filthy profession, with grease and oil permanently embedded beneath my fingernails, my knuckles scraped raw, my hair and skin forever fouled with the acrid stench of spent petroleum products. Forget about any sort of home life, he added, because mechanics are the "poor sunzabitches" called out when everybody else is headed home, arriving after-hours to crawl down inside some greasy piece of broken equipment, usually at night and often in the rain or snow depending on the season. I could look forward to a life in which bosses and foremen would continually bitch at me about breakdowns that were not my fault, angry that I was taking too long to repair them. Salesmen would be the worst, he assured me, always bitching about the work not getting completed as they had promised, or completed incorrectly. He saved the best (or worst) for last: I'd have a wife forever frustrated that I was never home, or only home long enough to ruin her plans when I got called back for yet another emergency repair.

"Boy, that sounds like an awful lot of misery," I replied facetiously, "You seem to be implying I won't be happy."

"Goddamnit! Why the *hell* didn't you talk to me before you got this lame-brained idea?" From his anger I began to realize that he might have thought I was capable of better things, even though he'd never expressed as much. If I told him the truth, that I had chosen this career more or less in spite of him, I doubt he would have understood. In any event, he was correct in just about everything he warned me about, except one. He'd forgotten about children. He never mentioned that the kids I would eventually have would complain too, and also become disappointed every time I wasn't around to take part in some important aspect of their lives. In the end, I realized I probably should have listened to him. Just this once.

Over the next thirty years I would work on lots of boats for lots of different employers, some good, some bad, and one who even turned out to be as bad as Dad's nemesis on the *Langley*, Old Shit-head. Like Dad, I changed companies repeatedly, nearly equaling his record of nine different employers over the course of my career. Once, after I quit a job I'd grown frustrated with, I wrote him a letter in which I asked him to explain why *he'd* changed jobs so many times. I asked him to take his time and really give it some thought, hoping he'd have some real insights into the restlessness and impatience I often felt in my professional life. I wanted to know the *why*.

His response was pretty much what I expected. He said he grew tired of dealing with the same people every day, tired of their complaints and idiosyncrasies, tired of the same old bullshit. He said he'd always been in search of the "greener grass over the hill," when in fact he should have been looking for a different hill entirely—a career that would have satisfied him more than that of a salesman. I found this last part of his response particularly compelling. It was the one thing I could truly relate to, the feeling that, like him, I hadn't found my true calling. In his letter he confessed he hadn't been aware he'd changed jobs so often, and he found the fact embarrassing. He also felt bad that I was so similarly disposed. If only he had known.

My two sons like to remind me that my father and I are nearly identical in our personalities, and this too has always given me pause.

In any event, I forged ahead in my carelessly-chosen career, and by 1996 I had risen to the managerial ranks, responsible for the river operations of a large construction aggregate company. My boats and barges ran day and night supplying millions of tons of crushed rock and washed sand for the concrete industry, crushed limestone for roadbeds, ag-lime for the agricultural market, boulders for landscaping projects, pulverized grit for toothpaste. *"Crushed rock is the foundation of America,"* read the bumper-sticker on my company truck. I wore a white hardhat and smoked two packs of cigarettes a day, just like Dad. My weight ballooned and I managed to eat so much that my navel herniated, too. Like father, like son.

In the spring of 1997, a near-record flood on the Upper Mississippi created havoc in my world of river transportation. As the river rose it became "all hands on deck" in moving our stockpiles of valuable material to higher ground. We built dikes and pulled machinery, rafted barges and secured towboats to trees, crossed our fingers and prayed for sunshine. On the Saturday night of the river's projected crest, I staggered home feeling wet and defeated, wanting nothing more than to crawl off to bed and sleep. But as

I walked through the door my wife handed me a fat envelope and said, "This came today from your father. It's addressed to you."

From its shape and bulk I guessed it was some sort of written material, so I took it up to bed thinking I'd have a look at it before falling asleep. I tore open the envelope to discover a manuscript of some thirty-two pages carrying the title "America the Beautiful,"handwritten in my father's perfect calligraphy. Above the title was a photograph of a large river steamboat, a likeness of the *Delta Queen* perhaps, or something similarly-sized. The inside page held a dedication to my wife and me, in honor of our fiftieth wedding anniversary in the year 2031. *What the fuck?* The author, (obviously my father, but fictionalizing himself for the sake of the story) had long since passed away but was sending this missive from the afterlife, which seemed to be Hell, judging from his mention of a fallen angel named Lucifer.

My fiftieth wedding anniversary? Jan and I had just celebrated fifteen years that fall. What the hell was this about? And then I began to read.

I read it twice that night, robbing myself of the sleep I craved and needed. I read it straight through the first time, turning the pages as quickly as I could, eager to read what lay beyond. Then I went through it again, this time more slowly, wondering what on earth had possessed my father to write such a thing. The central theme of the story concerned my life on the river, beginning with the early stages when I piloted the sternwheel excursion boats in downtown Saint Paul. Then it took a bizarre turn as my character improved his stature within the company and eventually went on to own it, the holdings including an enormous overnight passenger steamer named *America the Beautiful*. Through hard work and self-sacrifice I had become famous and wealthy, in the end selling the business for a preposterous amount of money and retiring to a lake home up north. Within the main body of the story there were plenty of digressions and vignettes taken directly from my life— the sports and classroom activities my kids were involved with, summer canoe trips we'd taken, people I had met in my career, even the cadre of self-styled hoboes with whom I had once ridden boxcars on the rails. Some of the vignettes digressed into absurdity, my father's imagination running wild. But as I went through it a second time I began to realize that everything he'd written was based upon an actual event or anecdote I had once shared with him in our Sunday night conversations over the phone. Obviously he'd been paying attention, but to judge from the details of the manuscript, he must have been taking notes.

The story ended with Jan and me in our seventies, retired to our lake home where every fall the extended Halter family gathered for a huge festival, with kinfolk arriving from all over the country. Over the course of the three-day event, leaf forts and mazes are constructed by the various families; a mass is said by a local priest; songs are sung, stories told, and there's even a segment in which Mark and his family showcase their penchant for "cattle-bawling" at the nightly talent show, a skill passed down from their long-deceased grandfather (that is to say, my dad).

He sent copies of the story to all his children, and I remember some conversations between my brother and sisters in which we all wondered if the old man had gone off the deep end. I told him how amazed and impressed I was with his literary effort, but when I pressed him for details about the story-line he wouldn't offer much. And he didn't enjoy talking about the story in person either, obviously embarrassed and perhaps feeling a little overexposed. A while later he got busy writing the wonderful memoir of his childhood on the farm.

In the years since I first read "America the Beautiful" I've come to speculate that what he'd actually written was the dream of how he'd wished his own life might have turned out.

But his life had turned out vastly differently, and now here we were, the two of us, heading east, at sunset, in the final hours of his fading freedom.

35

La Crosse

It's dusk, and the highway is about to begin a long descent through what's called "the driftless area" of southeastern Minnesota, an area known for its deep ravines and lush hardwood forests. It will carry us all the way down to the Mississippi River, but by the time we get there the sun will have set and we won't be seeing much of. My father has deflected the question I asked about why he wrote *America the Beautiful.* He seems to be more interested in the changing scenery, and just now remarks that his ears are popping.

"Do you have any chewing gum?" he asks.

"'Afraid not."-

"Damn. My ears are completely plugged."

"Too bad. So, what about the story?"

"The story?"

"America the Beautiful!" I shout. "Why'd you make me the main character of that story?"

He gives me a suspicious look. "Why do you need to know that?"

I smile, trying to put him at ease. "What's the big secret?" I ask. "Why don't you just tell me?"

A long pause as he watches a car in the left-hand lane coast slowly past us. He swears quietly. "Jesus Christ…" Then, finally, he surrenders: "Okay, I will."

Another long pause, at the end of which he says, "I always thought you didn't like me."

So there it is. He thinks I didn't like him. I guess I'm not surprised. Perhaps he thinks I *still* don't like me. But he continues:

"All those times in grade school when they were looking for

drivers to take you kids to basketball games in Saint Paul? You never once asked me to do it."

He's got me there. I was always afraid to ask him, fearful he'd somehow embarrass me in a carload of my teammates. But I tell him, "There were plenty of other dads who volunteered. Jack knew you were on the road all week." Also true enough. Jack Marton was our basketball coach, a legend at Incarnation.

"Oh, bullshit," he replies.

"How many times did Mark or Jim ever ask you to drive?" I say in my defense. My brothers had also played basketball in grade school, and I don't remember either of them ever asking him to drive.

"I don't remember. *You* were the athlete in the family, anybody could see that."

I've got my foot off the gas now and the weight of the trailer is pushing us down the long grade, deeper into the darkness. It's now dark enough inside the car that his face is disappearing beside me. His voice in the darkness says, "I'd go to those games at De La Salle and you'd spot me sitting up there in the bleachers and give me the meanest goddamned look."

There it is, his memory of my shunning him as vivid as anything he remembers of the war or his childhood on the farm. And I don't deny it. I've never denied it. I didn't want him coming to my basketball games or, for that matter, to get involved in any aspect of my life; it was as simple as that. He had lost my trust and with it my respect. It's true I didn't like him, and now I've come to find out he suspected it all along.

His revelation sits like a wet turd on the console between us. We ride along in silence. Above us, the first star of the evening is visible through an opening in the canopy of trees. It's a cloudless night, and I might easily drop the whole subject of my youthful animosity toward him. But I can't. I've been living with this for too many years.

"Was it really so traumatic?" I ask him. "I mean, didn't you start it? How many times did you ever tell Mark or Jim they looked like a whore?"

"No idea what you're talking about."

"The summer after we moved. You were pissed off because I'd quit going to church. One morning at breakfast you told me I looked like a Philadelphia whore."

"We needed to move from Pleasant Avenue," he counters. "I was worried you kids were getting wild."

"What kids? Me?"

"Yes you! Christ, you were never home, out running around every goddamn night when you should have been home studying. Didn't you pretty much flunk out of freshman year at De? Christ, I built those nice desks in your bedroom and I'll bet in your whole life you never spent ten minutes up there studying."

"Oh, come on!" I shout. "You're avoiding the point."

But he's just getting started. Now he's shouting, too. "And then, years later, you come home from some goddamn sailboat trip telling me about the *heroin* or whatever that shit was you found floating around in the ocean. Jesus Christ! Doesn't that pretty much prove I was right? I'd have to say, moving to Saint Louis Park was probably one the smartest things I ever did."

He's got his story wrong. "It was *pot*," I remind him, "already legal in about ten states. And anyway, how does me finding me a bale of marijuana differ from you finding a wad of drug money outside the wall at Casa del Calor? Huh?"

"Oh for chrissakes," he mutters.

We ride along in silence again, neither of us, I'm sure, wanting this to escalate any further. It's been a great day; a perfect day. Still, I might never get another moment like this, the two of us alone, him so lucid, me so … reckless. There's one last thing I need to know, if not for me then at least for my mother's sake.

"Do you know that in my entire life I've never once heard you say 'I love you?'" I blurt. "Not to mom, not to me, not to anyone?"

I hear him turn toward the window and groan. It comes out more like a sigh, but it's enough that I can tell I've hurt him, though that wasn't my intent. I could pose this same question to the fathers of any number of my childhood friends, and probably get the same reaction. The Greatest Generation is not necessarily predisposed to expressing their feelings.

But he does respond. "It's not something I ever heard around the farm when I was a kid," he says. "In case you've forgotten, my mother died when I was four and my dad wouldn't say shit if he had a mouthful." There's a bit of an edge in his voice. And then he adds, "You wonder why I wrote that story about you? I guess that's my answer."

I stare ahead into the darkness, temporarily blinded. Is he trying to tell me that "America the Beautiful" was an expression of love?

Well?

It takes a few minutes but in the end I decide it is.

And for me, it's enough.

☙

AT THE BOTTOM of our long descent the coulee opens up into a wide clearing bathed in overhead sodium-arc lighting as I-90 merges for a few miles with Highway 61 coming down the Mississippi from the north. We follow the river some ten or so miles. On our right, the luminescent peaks of the limestone bluffs stand out against the starry sky. Ahead on our left I spot the distant lights of Lock and Dam Number Seven, a river landmark from my former life. I suddenly feel like I'm home.

"We're almost there," I announce. But Dad is fixated on the road ahead as we've entered yet another construction zone, our route again reduced to a single lane. Orange cones illuminated by our headlights mark a winding path back and forth in the darkness. Dad, who has been silent since his admission about the story, suddenly comes to life.

"Sonofabitch!" he says loudly, his voice panicked. "I sure as hell hope you know where you going because I am completely lost!"

I don't reply, focusing instead on the maze of traffic cones. Weary from the long day of driving, on top of three nights of less than adequate sleep, I'm running on fumes and euphoria as I weave in and out of the cones. We cross the river bridge into downtown La Crosse and I glance over at him as he reads the welcome sign.

"Tell me again where we're headed," he begs.

"We're in La Crosse, Dad," I say calmly. "We've still a few more miles until we get to Mark's."

"We're going to Mark's?

"Yep. That's been the plan all along."

"According to who? I sure as hell didn't plan this."

Uh oh. Is this the sundown syndrome I thought we were going to skip today? "Listen to me, " I plead. "We've had a great day. Don't ruin it now. We're almost there."

I simply can't let him lose it again, not now. I begin speeding up, ignoring the 30 m.p.h. speed limit and roaring south through town, past the used car lots, discount centers, motels. If a cop pulls me over now, I figure it will distract Dad long enough to carry us the rest of the way, giving him something to talk about. But we make it through town scot free and continue on into the darkness. We're on Wisconsin 35 now, following the east side of the river, heading toward the town of Stoddard. Traffic thins on the minor two-lane highway, with only an occasional car coming at us, though the headlights are troublesome to Dad. He's muttering, and I pray he's not on the verge of something stupid. I feel with my fingers for the electric lock button to make sure his door's secure. Up ahead, our headlights pick up the sign for County Road K, the turnoff to Mark's.

"*Now* where are we going?" he wails as I make the turn. The narrower county road winds along the bottom of a coulee, ascending gradually to the top of the bluff. Dad begins mumbling again, this time with more conviction. I hear my name mentioned, not in a loving way.

"Five more minutes," I tell him. I'm lying; it's more like fifteen.

I grab my phone and auto-dial my brother's number. When he answers, I turn away from Dad and speak softly.

"We're coming up K," I tell him. "Are the dogs out?"

"The *dogs*?" he says. "Why?"

"If they're not out in the yard, make sure they are before we get there. Just do it. You'll understand once we arrive." And then I hang up.

"Who are you talking to?" Dad shouts, his voice now taking on an edge of desperation. No doubt he fears the worst, and this dark, twisting route isn't making things any better. It must seem like we're headed straight off the end of the earth.

At the top of the bluff we turn right on the ridge road, another winding track. In daylight, all of this resembles a Grant Wood painting, with cornrows curving over hill and dale, red barns and brick farm houses standing atop the bluffs, and the Mississippi River shining like a jewel in the valley below. But now it's just darkness and confusion. "Where are you taking me?" Dad moans. It sounds like he's on the verge of crying.

But my own voice sounds desperate too as I yell, "We're almost there, Dad, almost there."

Then we turn right into Mark's driveway, and I slow, powering down the windows on both sides of the car. Dad leans forward in his seat and stares ahead at the farmhouse in the distance, a porch light glowing over the door. Mark's barn looms large and silent on our right, the air through the open windows carrying a familiar smell of livestock mixed with the fecund scent of spring. Now two figures emerge from the farmhouse and step into the glow of the porch light. Dad studies them intently.

"Do you recognize those people?" I ask.

"No."

"You will," I tell him.

"Goddammit," he mutters.

I ease the car to a stop in front of the farmhouse. My brother and his wife, Sue, stand arm-in-arm on the porch, smiling. It's the most welcome sight I've seen in three days. I kill the engine.

"Now do you recognize those people?" I ask.

"Am I supposed to?"

"That's Mark and Sue."

"Mark and Sue ... goddammit." He doesn't remember. He moans again.

And then I hear the dogs. They're whimpering, and I can see the tops of their heads and the tips of their tails whipping back and forth out Dad's side of the car. I reach across and push his door open. The dogs are on him at once, pawing at his legs and licking his hands, their gentle mouths playfully biting his thick fingers, wet tongues slobbering. In the glow of the dome light his face is jubilant, his smile one of sudden bliss.

"Well hello there!" he croons, and the dogs sneeze and snort in reply, their tails slapping the hollow door panels like bass drums. Then Mark and Sue are pulling at the dogs and unbuckling Dad's seatbelt, helping him to his feet. As he's pulled from the car he turns to me with a look of utter astonishment, surprised and perhaps elated that I've delivered him to such a wonderful place of slobbering dogs and friendly people. Then he's out of the car, ambling toward the house, his face filled with wonder as the three of them pass beneath the porch light.

I sit behind the wheel for a few minutes to let it sink in. We made it. We're here. My father is still alive, and I'm only slightly insane.

Inside the house it's warm and bright, and savory smells are coming from the kitchen. Dad seems relieved when he sees me coming through the door, but at the same time I can tell he's still confused.

Sue leads him to the bedroom where he'll sleep tonight. They're putting him in their own bedroom, I realize, on the main floor, just off the kitchen. Mark goes out and brings in Dad's suitcase. I collapse in a chair at the kitchen table, my mind still numb with the reality that we've arrived. After a trip to the bathroom Dad shuffles back into the kitchen, and again looks relieved to find me there. He shuffles into a chair beside me.

"We're going to eat here?" he asks.

I nod. "Unless you'd rather go somewhere else?"

"*No!*"

"Good. I don't either. I'm too tired."

In fact I'm suddenly so tired I feel like I'm going to fall asleep at the table. My mind goes blank. As far as I'm concerned, my job is finished; Mark can take the reins now.

Sue sets plates of steaming beef stroganoff in front of us, then returns with a plate of warm bread and a dish of butter. Dad sits beside me looking down at the food and then glances all around the room as if to make sure this is really happening. I get the feeling he's a little overwhelmed. But he returns his attention to the table, and the steam from the plate begins fogging his glasses. He takes his fork and lifts a helping of the stroganoff to his lips, but then stops mid-flight, the fork dripping with the warm gravy. Something is still bothering him and he turns to me with a worried expression.

"You did tell me we'll be staying here tonight, right?"

"I did, yes."

"Both of us?" he says, still uncertain.

I smile. "Both of us. Me and you."

He nods, the tension relaxing from his face. "I thought that's what you said. I just wanted to be sure."

And then he lifts the stroganoff to his mouth and begins eating, his jaw working quietly, his eyes vacant as his taste buds measure the quality of the food. After he swallows he nods again, this time with conviction, glancing up at Sue with a sly smile on his face.

"Gosh dot's goot!" he says, and then he reaches for the bread.

DAY 6

36

The End of the Road

Iawake to the sound of rain on the roof, with a cold gray light filling the window above my head. I have not slept well, my mind still restless with the events of the past week. I had hoped to sleep until noon, or even later, but when I check my phone I see it's just after 8 a.m. From downstairs comes the cheerful voice of my wife, newly arrived from Saint Paul to take me home. What time did she get on the road this morning to make it here this early? I decide I'd better get up.

Downstairs they're all sitting around the kitchen table with coffee and pastries. Jan gets up to give me a hug. "You made it!" she says.

"I did," I reply quietly. It still hasn't sunk in.

Dad watches us from across the table. "Is this your wife?" he asks. "Good-lookin' gal." He smiles at her. "Any chance you could move in with me for awhile?"

We all laugh. It's good to see the old humor returning.

"How'd you sleep?" I shout across the room. His hearing from this distance is bad. We've been so close to each other these past three days.

"Not too bad, actually," he replies. And then from out of the blue, he adds, "What time you think we'll be shoving off?"

Mark says quietly into my ear, "He thinks he's going home today."

I'm not ready for this. My role in this is supposed to be over.

"Let me think about it," I shout back across the table. "I

need to drink some coffee and wake up." This is going to be complicated.

After breakfast he starts pacing around and I can tell he's getting nervous. This isn't like the past few mornings, he's thinking; something different is happening here.

The rain lets up and we all go outside. On the front porch we pose for pictures, the first one just Dad and me, then all of us together. Jan tells me quietly, "I've got all your stuff packed and in the car."

Mark says just as quietly, "You should just leave now. We'll take it from here." Dad keeps looking at me, waiting for my signal that it's time to go. He regards everyone else as if they're strangers, like they're keeping us from leaving. He wants to go home now.

I duck back inside, not exactly sure how I'm going to handle this. I feel emotionally drained, like I can't tell him yet another lie like the ones I've been telling him all week. But I don't want to leave him like this, like I'm running out on him. I go back outside where everyone is still milling around, waiting. I decide I'd better get it over with, for everyone's sake. I grip his shoulder, smiling.

"Well Dad, I'm going to leave now," I say as steadily as I can.

"And I'm going with you, right?" he says. He's frightened; I can hear it in his voice.

"No, you're going to stay here on the farm," I tell him, "with Mark and Sue and the dogs."

"I'm going to stay here?"

"Yes."

He suddenly looks so bewildered I feel like I'm going to cry. A strained "Goodbye" is all I can manage, and then I turn and start for the car. But I can feel his eyes on my back and my feet are suddenly so heavy it feels as though I'm walking through wet concrete. I crawl in the passenger side of the car and fumble for the seatbelt with shaking hands. Jan starts the engine and puts the car in gear. It's started to rain again. The windshield wipers thump and squeak. As we ease ahead I chance a look back at the porch. Dad is just standing there with a terrified look on his face.

We've grown so close these past three days that it must feel like I'm deserting him, his best pal running out on him when he needs him most.

But that's not all. I feel as if I'm looking at myself. It has taken eighteen hundred miles across nine states to make me realize for the first time—to make me finally accept for the first time—that we're very much alike. And that this is not necessarily a bad thing. He's finally provided me some answers, and for the first time in my life I feel that I can love him, that I *do* love him.

Which makes leaving him like this especially hard.

I reach for the lever and lower my seat until I can't see him anymore. And he can't see me. Then the tears begin. I can't help it. And I can't stop.

I cry all the way down to the bottom of the coulee and I continue to cry all the way to Winona, an hour away, before I finally fall asleep.

Sometime, much later, Jan gives me a gentle nudge and says, "We're home."

I can barely open my eyes, but I can see that I'm in my own driveway. It's still raining. I have never felt so tired.

37

On the morning after we arrived, Mark drove the minivan and U-Haul down to the memory-care facility where he unpacked all of Dad's things. As I'd feared, I'd brought more furniture from Arizona than would comfortably fit inside the small apartment, and also a lot of unnecessary clothing. No harm done: much of it wound up going to the Goodwill. A month later Mark put the minivan up for sale and it sold quickly:

Arizona car, no salt, low miles and driven by Grandpa to church. Won't last long!

All the hoses and belts that the mechanic in Peoria had deemed questionable had proven sound. The overhauled transmission had performed flawlessly—so flawlessly in fact, that there were hours on end when I forgot I was pulling a trailer. I apologize for any disparaging remarks I may have made earlier about Mopar technology. I now drive a Chrysler Town and Country minivan myself. Is this an indication I may be getting old?

As for my father, the transition did not go so easily. He spent the first weekend of his new life in my brother's farmhouse dozing in a chair, no doubt catching up on his sleep, just as I had. One afternoon, in between naps, he told Mark, "I need a piece of paper." Mark handed him a yellow, legal-sized sheet along with a pen. Dad folded the sheet of paper into a manageable-sized square then asked Mark, "Now, how do I get back home to Arizona from here?" Mark gave him explicit instructions: left turn at the end of the driveway; followed by a left at the county road, and so on and so on, the directions eventually carrying him all the way back to Arizona. Dad wrote all this down on the piece of paper, after which he carefully slipped it into the pocket of his shirt. Then he announced, "I'll be shoving off first thing in the morning."

Mark reminded him he didn't have a driver's license, and that if something terrible happened—an accident, for example, where someone got hurt—Dad would be in big trouble. The next morning at breakfast when Mark asked him if he was still leaving for Arizona, Dad announced, "I'm not going; it wouldn't be safe." Later that day Mark brought him to his new home at the memory-care unit.

He didn't like it. He admitted that his new room was "a nice place" but then insisted he wanted to go home. For the first few weeks Mark parked the minivan outside his bedroom window where he could see it and be reassured his stay here was only temporary. Every morning he unloaded the contents of his dresser drawers into his suitcase, took down all his pictures and other memorabilia and loaded everything into a box. Then he informed the staff he would be leaving shortly. Mark asked the staff if behavior like his was common, and they assured him it was; his father would get over it in time. He did, but in Mark's words, "it wasn't a pleasant experience for anyone."

At mealtime, they tried seating him at a table with other men, but most of the other male residents were aphasic and uncommunicative. Those who were still capable of conversation tended to be combative, and then the bickering and swearing would begin. I've no doubt Dad held his own in the swearing department and was probably responsible for instigating a lion's share of the arguments. The staff began seating him at tables with women, and it was here that he finally settled. Throughout the home he became known as "The Charmer," from both the female residents and female staff. But he never lost his acerbic eye. Once while Mark was visiting, a full-figured aide entered the room to retrieve something, and upon her departure Dad remarked, "Look at the size of the ass on that one!" Such a charmer, indeed.

I returned a month later for my first visit. He was sleeping in his recliner when I arrived and I didn't bother him. When

he finally woke up he recognized me at once and expressed joy that I'd come to visit. He told me he didn't much care for his new surroundings, but he seemed to accept the fact that this was where he belonged. With the help of a walker, he took me on a guided tour of his new digs, shuffling down the wide hallways and stopping to peer in through the opened doors of his fellow residents. I averted my eyes as much as possible. In spite of the cheerful décor and friendly staff, it was everything I had feared it might be: people lying unconscious in bed or hunched over in their wheelchairs. We toured the activity room, the dining hall, the kitchen, the front desk. The woman on duty asked if we'd like to go outside and Dad assured her we would. She activated a buzzer on the door lock and I pushed it open. None of this seemed to particularly bother my father and we went out to sit on the front porch to talk for an hour or so. The conversation was cheerful and upbeat, so much so that I dared to ask, "How exactly did you get here? I know how you hate to fly."

I wasn't being cruel. I simply wanted to gauge how much he remembered of our three-day odyssey. His answer surprised me:

"Some sonofabitch out in Phoenix shanghaied me and drove me here," he said. "And in my own car, too. He was a big bastard, but if I ever find the sonofabitch I'm going to kick his ass!"

I couldn't help but laugh. This was my father as I like to remember him.

Eunice died a couple of months later. He'd now outlived two wives, both of them much younger. It was never supposed to be this way. Had we known Eunice would die so soon we might have waited, allowing him the comfort of being with her until the end. But the situation in the trailer park had become desperate, and with Eunice you could never be sure. When Dad was informed of her passing, he had to be reminded who she was, and even then he didn't say much. It's possible he'd forgotten her by then. His memory got worse and worse.

We celebrated his ninety-eighth birthday with a small party at the memory-care unit. A number of his children, grandchildren and great-grandchildren enjoyed cake and ice cream in his honor, and he received greeting cards from many who couldn't make it. He'd always enjoyed getting greeting cards. For the party he wore his most colorful cardigan and posed for pictures.

He started going downhill quickly after that. He became prone to falling, and the staff had to install trip alarms around his bed and recliner. Every time he got out of bed or tipped forward in his recliner, a staff-member came running. You can imagine how he liked that. I drove down to see him one afternoon and he never woke up the entire time I was there, even when I nudged him to say goodbye. It was just as well; more and more he was failing to recognize me as his son.

At the beginning of October, 2014, Mark called one morning to tell me Dad had been diagnosed with sepsis and that the end was near. It was possible he wouldn't make it through the night. Braced for the worst, Kath and I drove down that afternoon. When we arrived we were surprised to find him awake and alert, but also uncomfortable. The sepsis had given him hot flashes and the close proximity of clothing to his skin made him itch. As we entered his room we found him sitting upright on the edge of his bed wearing nothing more than a diaper.

"Well!" he said as we came through the door. He was genuinely happy to see us. But the sight of all that bare skin brought back memories of his bath night on our road trip. It was a bit unsettling.

"What brings you folks here?" he said merrily. And we hurried in to hug him.

Mark and Sue arrived a little while later. Mark told us of the hallucinations Dad had been having over the past few days. He believed his brothers and sisters had all stopped by to see him. In fact, Bill and Ann had been there the previous night, and had invited Dad to join them for dinner.

He was ready to go. The staff brought in folding chairs and we sat around his bed, talking and singing. We sang all his old favorites: "Go Tell Aunt Rhody," "On Top of Old Smokey," "America the Beautiful," and "Doctor Doctor Can You Tell." We finished with his all-time favorite, "Edelweiss," and then he insisted we sing it again. Before we left I gave him a hug and told him I loved him.

To which he replied, "Okay then."

He died the following night.

The funeral was held at Incarnation Church. The organist played "Anchors Aweigh" and some other spiritual numbers that Kath had selected. She gave the eulogy and did her usual good job. She's more or less become the family eulogist, chronicling the lives of all our dearly departed. She once told me there's nothing more disappointing than attending a funeral where the deceased is described as "totally awesome," or "a wonderful dad," without the telling details. As she was walking up to the podium I heard one of my South Dakota cousins behind me whisper, "This is going to be good!" She knew. And Kath didn't disappoint.

We buried him on a crisp fall day at Lakewood Cemetery, not far from our old home on Pleasant Avenue. He was not buried *next* to Mom but on top of her, in the same plot he bought for the two of them years ago. He used to lament the fact that because Ma died first, she'd have to lie beneath him for eternity, which was never what he'd intended, chivalrous to the end. A military color guard came from Fort Snelling to do the rifle salute, a fitting tribute for a twenty-year Navy man and a World War II veteran at that. They folded the Stars and Stripes into a precise triangle and presented it to me, his only child to also serve.

I stop by the gravesite from time to time to check on them, usually at Christmas but also on their birthdays—Mom's in December, Dad's in April. I often wonder how he's doing in the afterlife, if it's anything like he feared it might be. I'm reminded of a morning on our three-day adventure, the one in Oklahoma when we stopped to admire the blooming countryside. Dad thought there was something wrong with the car when we stopped, fearful that we'd hit something. But I merely rolled down the window on his side of the car and told him to look.

I hadn't noticed it until then, but somewhere in the past hundred or so miles we'd left the dusty browns and yellows of the arid Southwest and entered the green lushness of the Midwest prairie. It was glorious. We were in the middle of a panorama of brilliant green pastures beneath an intensely blue sky. In the distance, nestled between the hills, the surface of a small pond glittered in the morning sunshine, and the hilltops were crowned with scatterings of elm and ash trees, the foliage a shade darker than the surrounding pastures. A breeze carried the rich aroma of budding flora and newly turned earth, and meadowlarks sitting atop a barb-wire fence serenaded us with their warbling songs. But best of all—and the reason I stopped—was the presence of cattle grazing contentedly all over the countryside, spaced evenly as if by design, their rich black hides glistening in the morning dew. Dad sat speechless, his mouth slightly agape at the sight. A semi roared past, its wake buffeting the van and seeming to pull us along with it, but Dad hardly noticed. I turned on the emergency flashers and killed the engine.

"Boy oh boy," Dad finally exclaimed, almost in a whisper. "Have you ever seen anything so beautiful?"

"Is this what you were talking about?" I asked. "Would this be the proper place to be a cow?" He turned and looked at me, obviously confused. I reminded him, "You've been complaining this whole trip about the plight of the cows! Would this not be the place where a cow would enjoy spending its life?"

"Oh boy, is it ever!" he agreed. Now he couldn't seem to get enough of it.

It was quiet inside the car for awhile and then I asked, "Do you ever wonder if this is what heaven might be like?"

He turned to me with his teeth bared—his dentures, actually—grinding uppers to lowers like he used to do when he was thinking. Thus I could see he was giving my question serious consideration. But in the end he simply shook his head and muttered, "How the hell would I know?"

"But don't you ever wonder?"

"No."

"What do you think happens when you die?"

He averted his eyes. "I don't care to think about it."

"Why? Are you afraid to die?"

He glanced over at me. "I guess I am. I'm certainly in no hurry to die."

In my entire life I'd never heard him express such a notion. "What are you afraid of?" I asked.

He turned back to the window. "I'm pretty sure I'm going straight to hell."

"What? Now why would you say that?"

He gave me a furtive look. "I've done some things in my life I'm not proud of," he said, and then he turned back toward the window. "And that's all I'm going to say about it."

But I was not about to let this pass. I said, "If you're so convinced you're going to hell, what do you think *that* will be like?"

"I told you, I'm not going to talk about it!" he said angrily.

"Now wait a minute…" I began. But he kept his eyes fixed out the window, refusing to look at me.

So we sat there in silence for a few moments until I had another idea.

"In high school," I told him, "I read a book by John Steinbeck called *The Pastures of Heaven*. It was a collection of short stories, but the stories were not what you'd think they'd be. In fact, they were kind of sad. But the title stuck with me, and ever since then I've imagined heaven as a place full of pastures. Not that I'm religious or anything."

Now he glanced over at me, nodding. "I'm pretty sure nobody would ever accuse you of that," he said. Then he smiled, perhaps apologetically.

"Anyway," I continued, "there they are." And I gestured toward the horizon. "The pastures of heaven. Couldn't that be true?"

He turned and looked again, this time nodding in agreement. "I suppose it could."

"So, what if," I began again, hoping he was still with me. "So what if when you die, instead of going to heaven or hell, you come back to life as something else? Like another human being, for example, or even an animal."

"With my luck, it'd be a horse's ass," he said dourly.

"I'm serious," I said. "There are people—*religions*—that actually believe this, the Buddhists, for example. They call it 'reincarnation' and they swear it's true…"

He nodded. "I guess I've heard of that."

"So what if … what if instead of going to hell when you die, as you seem to think you are, you came back as one of those cows grazing up there, with all that green grass and not a worry in the world?"

This seemed to strike a chord in him and he turned back toward the pasture, staring intently into the distance as if to fully comprehend the gravity of this idea. He stared for what seemed an eternity before finally turning back to me, his face a picture of relief if not rapture.

"I guess I could accept that," he said. "Sure, that would be fine."

ɕɔ

IT BOTHERS ME THAT my best memories of him come so long after his death. Cruel as it may seem, I almost wish we'd been thrust together earlier in our lives, on an odyssey similar to the one we endured later. But he was always so intimidating, and I was so combative, that it would likely have had a different outcome, perhaps painfully so. I should be thankful we were able to come to the understanding we did, even so late in life. I'm now able to think of him in a better light.

Last summer, Jan and I were invited to spend the weekend at a friend's northern retreat. We took the interstate as far as we needed to, then escaped onto a two-lane road winding through the prairies and hardwood forests of Minnesota's central lake country. Farm houses and grain silos appeared around every bend, and it wasn't long before we happened upon a herd of cattle grazing along the fence line. I slowed the car and lowered the window. Jan looked up from her book, noticed the cows, and knew at once what I was up to.

"Really?" she said.

Without replying, I cupped my hands around my mouth and began *mooing* like some sort of distressed heifer. Jan merely smiled and returned to her book. I suspect that after forty-odd years, my bovine antics have become somewhat of a bore to her.

But I can't help myself; it's something I've been doing most of my life and I have no intention of quitting now. If I told you I think one of those cows might be my reincarnated father, you'd find it sappy, I'm sure. If my father were alive, I'm sure he'd scoff at such notions, shouting, "*What bullshit!*" And he'd be right.

The truth is I do it because it's something he taught me to do when I was a little boy, and every time I do it now it reminds me of him.

And the memory is a happy one.

About the Author

John Halter was born and raised in South Minneapolis and educated at De La Salle. The ins and outs of his professional life as a sailor, riverboat pilot, and marine mechanic are alluded to often in these pages.

Made in the USA
Monee, IL
15 November 2023

46588507R00194